DATE DUE

DEMCO, INC. 38-2931

Morri

Contemporary Film Directors

Edited by James Naremore

The Contemporary Film Directors series provides concise, well-written introductions to directors from around the world and from every level of the film industry. Its chief aims are to broaden our awareness of important artists, to give serious critical attention to their work, and to illustrate the variety and vitality of contemporary cinema. Contributors to the series include an array of internationally respected critics and academics. Each volume contains an incisive critical commentary, an informative interview with the director, and a detailed filmography.

A list of books in the series appears at the end of this book.

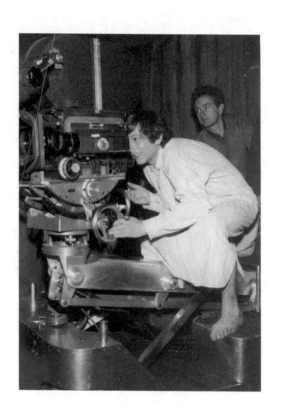

Roman Polanski

James Morrison

UNIVERSITY
OF
ILLINOIS
PRESS
URBANA
AND
CHICAGO

Library of Congress Cataloging-in-Publication Data
Morrison, James.
Roman Polanski / James Morrison.
p.   cm. — (Contemporary film directors)
Includes bibliographical references and index.
ISBN-13: 978-0-252-03205-9 (cloth : alk. paper)
ISBN-10: 0-252-03205-5 (cloth : alk. paper)
ISBN-13: 978-0-252-07446-2 (pbk. : alk. paper)
ISBN-10: 0-252-07446-7 (pbk. : alk. paper)
1. Polanski, Roman—Criticism and interpretation.
I. Title.
PN1998.3.P65M67   2007
791.4302'33092—dc22   2006100917

Dedicated to Joseph A. Gomez |

The author wishes to thank the Gould Center for Humanistic Studies and the Dean of the Faculty's Office at Claremont McKenna College for financial assistance toward the completion of this book. Thanks as well to Joan Catapano, Cynthia Erb, James Naremore, and Thomas Schur.

The first two phases of Polanski's career fall neatly in line with the consolidation of the European art film of the 1960s and the rise of the New Hollywood at the end of the 1960s and through the early 1970s. Polanski's reputation largely rests upon a sequence of films from this period—*Knife in the Water* (1963), *Repulsion* (1965), *Rosemary's Baby* (1968), and *Chinatown* (1974)—and his work continues to be viewed primarily in relation to these films. Yet his films of the 1980s and 1990s boast an elegant languor and a remote affect that pronounce a break with the attitudes of mainstream movies, a concerted departure that was preceded by perhaps his most sustained exercise in "prestige" filmmaking, *Tess* (1979), a version of Thomas Hardy's classic novel *Tess of the D'Urbervilles*.

The climate of Polanski's late films—especially *The Tenant* (1976), *Frantic* (1987), and *The Ninth Gate*—registers a definitive "post-Hollywood" sensibility, implying that certain homeostatic forces or stabilizing possibilities of the Hollywood model of filmmaking are lost to cinema, no longer available except as distant allusions or reconstructed fragments that can be understood only in their troubled, residual relations to an encroaching global order from which the Hollywood system had formerly sought, unsuccessfully, to insulate itself. In *The Tenant*, for example, such Hollywood elders as Shelley Winters and Melvyn Douglas hobnob with such sophisticates of the European neo–New Wave as Isabelle Adjani and Bernard Fresson. And despite the hammy bravado of Winters and Douglas and the more worldly mugging of Adjani and Fresson, all play second fiddle to the movie's overarching concern with Europe's splintered destinies, its terminal atmosphere of transience, for which the title character's literal condition of tenancy serves as a metaphor, embodied in his psychosexual confusion.

Polanski's films of the 1980s and 1990s pursue two main currents, psychosexual forays with political overtones (such as *Bitter Moon* [1992] and *Death and the Maiden* [1995]) or absurdist exercises in camp (*Pirates* [1986] and *The Ninth Gate*). Still, much of Polanski's work of this period falls into a distinctive genre of postwar cinema, the "international co-production": Luchino Visconti's *Conversation Piece* (1974), Bernardo Bertolucci's *Luna* (1979), and Nagisa Oshima's *Merry Christmas Mr. Lawrence* (1982) suggest the trajectory of the cycle over roughly this period, while Jean-Luc Godard's *Contempt* (1963) stands as perhaps the key precedent. The combination of slickness and coarseness that characterizes these films appears in their uneven production values, in the stark drone of flatly dubbed dialogue, and in the often illogical nationalities of the actors from a plot point of view. If the use of Hollywood stars in these films shows the effects of a rising internationalist commercialism, it also reflects the confusions of plot, theme, and style that seem to come with the territory.

The disorienting effects of these films—their sense of being curiously "foreign" to *every* place on earth—reveal a good deal about European cultures of this time, but Polanski's films are among the few examples (Godard's are among the few others) that really use these conventions to comment on the multiple identities and shifting forms of contemporary Europe, especially as its "imagined communities" are mediated through film. In *The Tenant*, the remnants of Polanski's most characteristic style—its free-floating anxiety and mordant comedy, its mercurial flashes of surrealist imagery and insinuating patterns of hyperrationalist logic—cohere lucidly with the more typical styles of the form, and the dubbing functions as a particularly creepy alienation effect. The more typical international co-productions thrive on nostalgia for old-world Europe, like the films of Claude Lelouch; or else they propose themselves, like those of Franco Zeffirelli, as paragons of international cooperation. But Polanski's are the kinds of movies one makes upon concluding that the condition of exile is irrevocable, that the idea of homeland is a sentimental fantasy, that there is no *place* to go back to.

The same set of conclusions informs the curiously impersonal textures of *The Pianist*. Based on the memoir by Wladyslaw Szpilman, the film follows the fate of Szpilman and his family from their "relocation" as Polish Jews to the Warsaw ghetto, and their subsequent transport to Treblinka. At that point, Wladyslaw is separated from his family, and the bulk of the film shows him hiding out from the Nazis, alone in attics, abandoned flats, and burnt-out buildings. One might expect that Polanski, during these scenes, would indulge the penchant for uncanny depictions of isolation familiar from *Repulsion, Rosemary's Baby*, or *The Tenant*. But aside from a single scene in which Szpilman's perspective edges over into hallucination, the treatment is doggedly unmannered, literalist, direct, and immediate. Though Polanski himself is a Pole who escaped the concentration camps—while members of his family died at Auschwitz—*The Pianist* is among his least personal films. It thus bears affinities with two earlier works, *Macbeth* (1971) and *Tess*. Well-tuned versions of classics, those films express the severe fatalism that is fundamental to Polanski's sensibility, but they have little of the trenchant grotesquerie or macabre, demonic wit. Nor does *The Pianist*, which recalls the blunt, matter-of-fact violence of *Macbeth* and the smooth, agile, impersonal technique of *Tess*. This impersonality is, by design, a means to approach the "unrepresentable" with some measure of humility. In much the same vein, Polanski refrains from showing the camps, preferring to portray the pervasiveness of Nazi horror in everyday life—in the streets or in the home.

This emphasis on the presence of horror in the everyday ties the film closely to Polanski's deepest concerns, and any account of the various consistencies, ruptures, or contradictions of Polanski's career must consider the precedents in his work for even his most seemingly anomalous films: *The Fearless Vampire Killers* (1967) as a precursor of *Pirates,* for instance, or *What?* (1973) of *Bitter Moon*. This study, however, is less concerned with recovering some underlying coherence or deep structure from Polanski's work than with considering the representative implications of the apparent anomalies. Through them, we can extrapolate an evocative account of the major trends, drifts, twists, and propensities in film over the last fifty years.

Aside from looking to Polanski's career as a guide to various crises in cultural value over this period, or to the consolidations of the art film, or the breakdown and putative recoveries of the Hollywood system, or the rising and ebbing internationalisms of film cultures, this study will also revise a received notion of the critical reception of Polanski's work. Typically, Polanski has been understood as a displaced surrealist obsessed with the theme of repression. One can see where this assumption derives from; Polanski typically deals with narratives of the occult in some literal sense, returning again and again to the domains of the secret, the hidden, the underground, of covert operations and submerged machinations. Yet far from complying with the traditional logics of the unconscious, or considering them in some sense as a key to human experience, Polanski's work is best understood in the context of contemporary theoretical thought—the work of Michel Foucault, Gilles Deleuze, and others—that seeks to unravel the sociopolitical knot of "repression" as a generalized, entrenched metaphor with often destructive social effects. By locating Polanski's work within the two main genres that his films straddle—comedy and melodrama—and by examining his special interest in figurative imagery, I show that, far from being compulsively drawn to the notion of repression and its subtending structures of paranoia as explanatory factors, Polanski's principal interest is in the visible, the material, and the concrete—in what is out in the open, and in why it so often is *not* seen.

When Roman Polanski's most recent project was announced, some expressed surprise that the director would follow up his long-awaited film on the Holocaust with a screen adaptation of *Oliver Twist*. For such commentators, the quirks and vagaries of Polanski's modern temperament seem at odds with the sensibility of Charles Dickens's Victorian classic. It is not the first time Polanski's career has taken an unpredictable turn, of course, and this one has the clear precedents of two previous adaptations of classic literary texts in the director's oeuvre, including a prior film version of a Victorian novel in *Tess*. Rather than pointing in new directions, Polanski's *Oliver Twist* culminates dominant themes of his work that have been given insufficient attention to date.

Throughout his career, Polanski has mounted a consistent critique of modern instrumental rationality, especially as it manifests itself in the institutionalization of post-Enlightenment utilitarian social structures. In that light, the choice of *Oliver Twist* is not jarringly anomalous but strikingly consistent, especially considered in relation to Polanski's earlier adaptation of *Tess of the D'Urbervilles*. The authors of both books wrote in explicit response to the widespread adoption of Jeremy Bentham's utilitarian social reforms. Though they shared Bentham's spirit of reform, Dickens and Hardy also saw utilitarianism as essentially degrading to humanity, subordinating real needs and desires to calculations of outcomes, inevitably victimizing the impoverished, the working-class, and the otherwise socially marginal. At the outset of a new wave of European Enlightenment, Bentham envisioned his programs as correctives to benighted fundamentalisms and arbitrary belief systems; his brand of utilitarianism promised a new meritocracy that would measure all individuals against the same standard, in assessment of the consequence of their actions, to which considerations of belief or intention would become largely irrelevant. To foster social recognition of individuals, Bentham promoted new practices and technologies of visibility, notoriously including the Panopticon, but also encompassing forms of testing, tabulation, census taking, and other bureaucratic accountings of citizenry, like the assignment of numbers to persons. In Bentham's model, utilitarianism imposed rationality on social order by objectifying people, abrogating belief, and evaluating actions according to their visible effect in maximizing the general well-being of the social sphere, a condition Bentham identified with individual happiness on the ground that, sooner or later, all occupants of that sphere could expect to benefit.

Dickens's best-known and most systematic attack on the utilitarian model of social structure appears in his novel *Hard Times* (1854), in which the fictional factory village of Coketown satirically anatomizes the dehumanizing potentialities of Benthamite reform. But nearly all of Dickens's work has something to say about the ascendancy of social utility, and *Oliver Twist* suggests that there is little choice between being subject to the disciplinary space of the workhouse and being exploited by vagrants who have temporarily escaped social surveillance, even if they are themselves products of the heightened social inequities of utilitarianism. The plot is set in motion by the title character's meek request for seconds at mealtime ("Please sir, I want some more?"), an event Dickens depicts to mock the utilitarian chastisement of desire and need as disruptive surplus. Even more bluntly, Dickens exposes the utilitarian bases of allegedly reformed Poor Laws, showing how the poor's wish to live above mere subsistence, the standard that utilitarianism imposed in practice, could only be understood as a form of greed. Written a century after Bentham's most influential texts, Hardy's novels, from *The Mayor of Casterbridge* (1886) through *Tess of the D'Urbervilles* (1891) to *Jude the Obscure* (1895), concern characters who fail to achieve social recognition even as they suffer greatly from the claim of utilitarianism to account objectively for all individuals. In these books, that pretext means only further marginalization or dire punishments, especially when its inclinations to count and discount are internalized—as in Little Father Time's murders and suicide in *Jude* because "we are too menny." Polanski's version of *Tess* is fervently responsive to this aspect of Hardy's novel; in Polanski's adaptation, Tess is constantly looked at but never really seen, even by the viewer of the film.

Bentham limited his programs to public institutions—penitentiary houses, prisons, houses of industry, workhouses, poorhouses, manufactories, madhouses, lazarettos, hospitals, and schools, in Bentham's own extensive inventory. The private spheres could still be considered reserves of whatever liberty might remain in the advent of disciplinary society, which was more humane than what preceded it, Bentham argued, because it was chiefly designed to be preventative. In Bentham's pragmatic utopia, all individuals would behave well, whatever their inner urgings, because they would know they were being watched, and society would be spared the indignity and expense of punishing large numbers because smaller numbers would offend. The exhaustiveness of Bentham's tally of the institutions in question indicates a totalitarian inclination of his platform, but his pointed exemption of the institutions of private life deserves further consideration. Critics of social utility, notably Michel Foucault, argue that Bentham's programs, once instituted, quickly penetrated the deepest recesses of private life to produce new intentions and compulsions, while simultaneously minimizing the significance of individual inner experiences.

Polanski's adaptation of *Oliver Twist* follows the logic of the director's other film versions of literary sources. Taking into account the inevitable compression of Dickens's sprawling narrative, Polanski's film is strictly, even relentlessly, literal, stripping away the literary trappings of authorial commentary, interior monologue, and antecedent exposition. Transposing Dickens's garrulous and eclectic verbal text into a singlemindedly visual one, Polanski realizes a key Dickensian theme, the supersession of visual surface over inner essence—a concern that famously made Dickens, for Sergei Eisenstein, a precursor of the cinema. In Dickens's novel, this theme is sounded in the first description of the title character:

> What an excellent example of the power of dress, young Oliver Twist was! Wrapped in the blanket which had hitherto formed his only covering, he might have been the child of a nobleman or a beggar; it would have been hard for the haughtiest stranger to assign him his proper station in society. But now that he was enveloped in the old calico robes which had grown yellow in the same service, he was badged and ticketed, and fell into his place at once—a parish child—the orphan of a workhouse—the humble, half-starved drudge. (Dickens 3)

The Benthamite flavor of this passage is unmistakable, even if its intent is to castigate a Bentham-like social accounting based on visible evidence. The novel is filled with examples of characters' suppositions, reliant on superficial, literal appearances, that are dramatically exposed as inadequate or false, and the novel is about the process by which Oliver is pitilessly made visible as a wretch while being rendered systematically invisible as the valuable human being Dickens would have us see behind this false surface.

Under the influence of Dickens, the classical nineteenth-century English novel exploits Benthamite programs of social visibility in its enterprise to objectify social reality, but it does so in the name of preserving a redemptive interiority that abides beneath the surface. Under the influence of the realist novel, the narrative film, in spite of its status as a photographic instrument of modern visuality, attempted to maintain this project through techniques of "inner speech," for instance, or other devices such as flashbacks, dream sequences, and voiceovers, all initially intended to correspond to dimensions of literary subjectivity. In his adaptations of literary materials, Polanski largely rejects such techniques, typically in a spirit of bleak irony infused with gravity and dejection, to lay bare ever greater endangerments to human subjectivity that Dickens's work already heralds at the outset of industrial modernity.

The best-known film adaptation of *Oliver Twist*, the 1948 version made in England by David Lean, begins with a sequence of great stylistic virtuosity that reveals the movie's ambition to preserve subjectivity against the objectifying forces of modernity. The scene shows Oliver's mother, in the throes of labor, making her way across a rain-swept moor. Crafted to emphasize the mother's torment, the sequence inventories the heady slate of expressionistic cinematic devices that characterize the film's style until the final scene: oblique camera angles, startling visual juxtapositions, lighting redolent of film noir, and a general emphasis on the imagistic or "poetic" above the merely semantic. The film's techniques amount to an extended exercise in the pathetic fallacy, recalling John Ruskin's famous critique of that tendency in modern culture.

Writing in 1856, Ruskin saw the pathetic fallacy as a reaction-formation against an emergent rationalism that would refuse a sentimental or distorted equation of objective reality with subjective impression or desire. By contrast, Lean reads Dickens to locate possibilities for social justice in a congruence of outer and inner worlds, as against Bentham-ite claims that the public sphere should concern itself only with the objectively perceptible, leaving the inner lives of persons to take care of themselves.[1] Lean marshals the heated rhetoric of a horror movie—a mode of brutalist lyricism—to infuse his images with a powerful strain of expressionist interiority. The exterior spaces of the film, from the moors to the workhouse to the courts to the streets to the humid environment of Fagin's lair, all have an ashen, dreamlike quality, awash in feelings that are given no real outlet there—as when the mother's suffering is correlated with the ravages of nature. The effect is to suggest a world out of joint, in which the disaccord between social structures and human needs gives rise to a fervid atmosphere shot through with a morbid subjectivity, the grotesque reflection of what has been forcibly excluded. This atmosphere lifts only in the final scene, showing Oliver's reunion with his bourgeois savior, Mr. Brownlow, a triumphal coda so crisply and brightly rendered that it could have been imported from another movie.

Polanski's treatment of Dickens's novel is similarly concerned with erasures of individual subjectivity by social programs of Benthamite utilitarianism. Unlike Lean, however, Polanski never implies that such conditions can be relieved by individual victories—which rarely occur in Polanski's work. The style of Polanski's adaptation is marked by an unforgiving exactitude; where Lean upholds expressionist subjectivity as an antidote to the objectifications of modernity, Polanski pursues a relentless objectivity to discover what remains, if anything, of the subjectivity that utilitarianism discounts. Polanski's *Oliver Twist* presents a shadowless world of unyielding surfaces, compositions wrought with rigid lines and sharp, unvarying textures—it is the least tactile of films—in which even what is most friable has been turned brittle and precise, fixed in a steely gray glaze. Early scenes evoke Hogarth, in images like blunt etchings in metalwork, to convey some of Dickens's mercurial whimsy, but once Oliver flees the workhouse, Polanski reverts to a studied, clinical neutrality, dourly invigorated by the intricate machinations of Dickens's plot.

Like most of his characters, Polanski's Oliver Twist is a creature of the present. Whereas Lean plays up aspects of the plot concerning Oliver's mother—including an insistent subplot revolving around her locket, implying that Brownlow is really a blood relative—Polanski admits no such redemptive genealogies. His film begins with Oliver's arrival at the workhouse and ends with a final encounter with Fagin on the eve of his execution. This strict bracketing sharply impacts the capaciousness of Dickens's plot, and Polanski's inclusion of this last scene—cut in every other film version—is especially crucial to his interpretation of the book. In the novel, the scene serves double duty as moral imperative, to assure the reader of Fagin's unhappy fate, and reformist zeal, to expose the wrongs of cruel and unusual punishment. Here again, Dickens colludes with the utilitarianism he otherwise condemns in assuming that if all were rendered truly visible, social justice would inevitably follow: "Those dreadful walls of Newgate, which had hidden so much misery and such unspeakable anguish, not only from the eyes, but too often, and too long, from the thoughts, of men, never held so dread a spectacle as that. The few who lingered as they passed, and wondered what the man was doing who was to be hanged tomorrow, would have slept but ill that night, if they could have seen him" (434).

Though advised that the crazed and anguished Fagin, cowering in prison, is "not a sight for children" (435), Brownlow insists that Oliver see, "even at the cost of some pain and fear" (435). In effect, Dickens proposes an ethic of sight, fully compatible with Bentham's regimes of visibility, even while it circumvents Bentham's imperative of minimizing pain. For Dickens, the problem with Bentham's ideas is that they fail to reveal everything to perceptibility, fail to see the realities of human suffering, and therefore promote or enable social inequities.

For Polanski, the problem is that they objectify all reaches of human experience and submit people to an all-encompassing instrumental rationality. In the book, Oliver realizes the model of moral understanding that Dickens's work as a whole promotes; in this wrenching final scene, the orphan convulsively extends to Fagin the pity that has been denied throughout to Oliver himself. Polanski would have us see such pity as a product and a casualty of social utility, framing it as an outcome of delusory self-interest. Earlier in the plot, when Oliver is injured, Fagin tends to him, at which Oliver ardently declares, "You've been kind to me—I'll always remember it!" In the film's final scene, Oliver greets Fagin in his dementia with the words, "You were kind to me." Neither of these lines occurs in the book, and they alter the texture of the scenes markedly. They introduce a piercing irony, since Fagin's "kindness" is nothing but an arm of his exploitation of the boy—if it exists at all, it occurs as he is colluding in the plot to kill Oliver. A spectacle of unknowing, Oliver's pity is the perfect illustration of the enervated naivete that led the society of industrial-era England to restrict or withhold compassion and charity as a matter of principle.

Dickens's *Oliver Twist* is, among other things, a reaction to the "reformed" Poor Law of 1834, or the Vagrancy Act of 1824. As the novel shows, Dickens found such legislations wanting in compassion. It would not be too much to suggest that these acts, under the influence of Bentham, virtually outlawed pity, seeing it as a manifestation of weakness that could only contribute to the indolence and sloth of the poor. In response, Dickens mobilized forms of pathos to revive empathy and pity as social virtues. He could do so only through the same ethic of visuality that had produced such opportunistic "reforms" in the first place. Bentham claimed that his own social programs were compassionate insofar as a generalized surveillance, by preventing crime, was said to lessen the need for punishment. Bentham's relatively high-tech workhouse at New Lanark, raised in advance of the Poor Law reforms and providing models for some of them, instituted panoptical facilities to encourage docile obedience and submission, while obscuring from its detainees any views of alternative ways of living that might foster unflattering comparisons with their own conditions and foment dissent. Even so, Bentham regarded himself as a philanthropist, and one can sometimes glean a progressive disposition in his writings, as in his calls for emancipation of colonies or his pleas for social measures to reduce infant mortality.

Polanski's *Oliver Twist* is a complex meditation on Betham's legacy. Alluding briskly to twentieth-century totalitarianism, retaining troubling residues of the novel's otherwise disavowed anti-Semitism, the film exposes a true dialectic of enlightenment. As Theodor W. Adorno and Max Horkheimer argue, "Pity has, in fact, a moment which conflicts with justice. . . . It confirms the rule of inhumanity by the exception it makes. By limiting the abolition of injustice to fortuitous love of one's neighbor, pity accepts as unalterable the law of universal estrangement it would like to alleviate" (Adorno and Horkheimer 80). Dickens's novel illustrates this axiom, while Polanski's film traces the process by which instrumental rationality—the phrase Adorno and Horkheimer employ to name a generalized form of modern social utilitarianism—makes kindness a sin and domination a virtue.

The extent to which utilitarian social structures pervade the modern world is perhaps best illustrated by how rarely their profound influence is noted. Bentham is seldom read, even as his intricate fancies, objectified in every quarter, confront us daily, fulfilling Foucault's observation that the inevitable internalization of these structures by individuals leads to their becoming increasingly less visible, and therefore more proliferous. The point at which Benthamite programs are no longer considered as reforms but rather perceived as given, deeply embedded social structures is the point at which it can be said that utilitarianism *is* modernity. (As one commentator puts it, "We are all utilitarians now" [Cottom 168].) This is exactly the point at which Polanski's work commences. The director's attentions to the oppressions of social utility could be called Foucauldian, if the filmmaker's art were theoretical and polemical instead of visual and dramatic, or if the tendency of these ubiquitous structures to elude perceptibility even while demanding total visibility of all they elect to acknowledge were not a basic condition of his interest in them. Polanski's work is chiefly concerned with the effect of utilitarianism on the "private" spheres of human life. Given the monolithic institutionalization of social utility in all its forms, and given that its proposal to maximize happiness has obviously failed, what happens, Polanski's films ask, to the realms of experience that utilitarianism claimed it would spare—the personal, the private, the nonsocial? What happens to consciousness, or rationality, once it has been defined to include only what is certified in a given order, a society that objectifies even its own power, through technologies of recognition and neglect?

Each of Polanski's most characteristic themes bears closely on these questions. By common consent his films are about isolation, paranoia, voyeurism, and the irrational, but it takes only another step to see how what is distinctive in his handling of these themes connects them directly to the larger issue of social utility. His treatment of isolation just as often concerns escapism—a conscious effort to remove oneself from the social sphere—as it does abjection, and the secluded settings of *Cul-de-Sac*, *What?*, *Bitter Moon*, and *Death and the Maiden* are idyllic to the extent that they stave off the imperatives of administered society, and successively more nightmarish to the extent that they ultimately fail to do so.

Polanski's work has little of the explicit imagery of bureaucracies, social engineering, and institutional space that characterizes, say, the films of Stanley Kubrick because what interests Polanski is how the preserves that are supposed to be outside the domain of social utility are inevitably permeated by it nonetheless.

Even movies like *The Fearless Vampire Killers* or *Pirates*, the most peripheral of his films in their relation to his central concerns, wryly illuminate the director's critique of utilitarian assumptions. In Polanski's spoof of the horror film, he mocks the idea that the tools of modern science and detection can conquer the forces of the supernatural, framing the confrontation between the vampire hunters and their fanged quarry as a clash of dueling irrationalities. The genre Polanski sends up, in its origins in works like Bram Stoker's *Dracula* (1897), conventionally approaches the matter quite differently under the direct influence of Bentham. In Stoker's novel, rational science must adapt itself to combat the vampire (whose villainy is connected explicitly to eluding social visibility, down to failing to cast reflections in mirrors), even if it means subsuming the irrational, because that is what it takes to get the job done—and because, once subsumed, the irrational has been automatically rationalized anyway. Even the pirate movie can be traced back to Benthamite roots if one looks to *Treasure Island* (or even to Bentham's *Introduction to the Principles of Morals and Legislation* in 1781, which takes an interest in the topic of piracy as a challenge to Bentham's own models). Robert Louis Stevenson—like Polanski, who told Orson Welles long before *Pirates* that he wanted to film Stevenson's novel (see Welles and Bogdanovich 269)—was less interested in utilitarianism itself than in what appeared to escape its reach, in what happened after it was so fully in place that it began to be taken for granted. Tales like *Dr. Jekyll and Mr. Hyde* (1886) or "The Bottle Imp" (1893) pursue these concerns explicitly. The former allegorizes the topic in its story of a respectable doctor and his ignominious alter ego, framed less in pre-Freudian terms as a conflict of id and superego than as a clash between the demands of social utility and what cannot be accounted for in these terms. Like Stevenson in *Treasure Island*, Polanski in *Pirates* depicts the pirates as loveable rogues who have rejected the networks of commerce and who place themselves outside the norms and constraints of society, which are seen in both cases as fictions serving a dominant class. Not surprisingly, Polanski favors the pirates—also like Stevenson, who was of the pirates' party without knowing it—even if he cannot resist portraying the melancholy isolation that is their irresistible fate.

In many of his other films, Polanski turns his attention to the question of how heterosexual relationships have been "modernized" by utilitarian assumptions. Formerly the quintessential refuge of privacy, marriage in these films is subjected to the usual forms of social scrutiny. In *Chinatown*, Jake Gittes is in the "matrimonial business," making a living by trailing unfaithful spouses, secretly photographing their infidelities, and displaying the pictures to the cuckolded partner. Every married couple in Polanski's work is either tempted to adultery or assaulted by other external threats to their sanctity (as in *Frantic* and *Death and the Maiden*), and both circumstances establish the objectification of desire: In films like *Knife in the Water, Cul-de-Sac,* and *Bitter Moon,* the private estate of marriage can no longer hold its own in a free market. As Frances Ferguson puts it in a discussion of how deeply utilitarianism influenced the modern novel, especially in its adoption of adultery as one of its principal themes, "[M]odern marriage . . . is simply not competitive with the efficiency of modern adultery" (116). In Polanski's movies, whenever a third person intrudes into the orbit of a couple, sexual tensions appear instantly. The theme of triangulated desire is so ubiquitous in these films as to realize exactly the paradigm of another theorist of the utilitarian stamp on modern culture, René Girard. In the modern world, Girard argues, desire is no longer inner-directed but externally produced; it attaches to objects or persons not because the desiring individual is driven to covet them by some intrinsic impulse but because someone else wants them (Girard 148). Desire becomes artifact, and sex itself, in Polanski's movies, is produced as action, rationalized by the mere fact of its exhibition.

The same can be said of any cinematic rendering of sex, from the pornographic to the genteel, if we view all such depictions as objectifications of private life intended to rationalize taboo by rendering it as visible action available for assessment, in relation to other such actions, according to its outcome—the level of satisfaction produced by the "money shot" in a porn film, for instance, or the degree of happiness promised by the climax of a conventional romance. Polanski's specialized participation in these general trends evinces awareness of cinema itself as an instrument of utilitarian objectification. That awareness attests to the director's effort to mount a critique of utilitarian rationalities by ironically adopting their own most characteristic attitudes. For example, behavior in Polanski's films is portrayed strictly as external action—motivation, intent, impulse, or any other inner incitement, while often in question, is seldom revealed and almost never visualized in the manner of traditions to which the director's work has been erroneously linked, like expressionism or surrealism. Rather, Polanski rigorously meets social utility on its own ground, training his camera remorselessly on surfaces, on exteriorized actions, on outer manifestations, refusing to broach inner causes. This strict logic does not mean acceding to the demands of rationalized modernity but rather showing by implication what is lost to human experience when interiority is so absented.

Despite Polanski's obvious awareness of film's role as a tool of the utilitarian social gaze, his work displays little of the overt self-consciousness of directors who turn the cinema against itself in an explicit critique of voyeurism, like Alfred Hitchcock or Michael Powell. Hitchcock demands complicity in voyeuristic processes by energizing the psychosexual impulses of the audience he fantasizes, often by insisting that the hypothetical viewer identify with the fictive voyeur. Powell does much the same thing with an emphasis on technologies of vision, like the camera obscura or the mechanized eye in *Stairway to Heaven* (1945), or the cameras and projectors in *Peeping Tom* (1960). In Polanski, though we sometimes find ourselves in the position of voyeur—as we often must when watching films—we are usually more conscious of characters on screen *being* watched than we are of their own intermittent acts of voyeurism, which are typically portrayed as pathetic or ineffectual efforts to defy an objectifying social gaze. Paranoia emerges in Polanski's films as a function of modern surveillance and objectified self-hatred, a reaction against imagined or real forms of contempt circulating through social spaces that once were private.

The critical obsession with Polanski's "private" life is especially problematic in light of this aspect of his work. Critics who approach the director's work through a biographical lens are quick to point out how readily the films lend themselves to such readings and how contemptuously Polanski greets such interpretations—a dismissal that, for many, only confirms the validity of the conclusions. Though this is not an avenue I have chosen to pursue, the temptation toward biographical criticism of this director's work may seem irresistible, considering that Polanski's life encompasses experiences that represent the full range of horrors that the twentieth century had to offer, from Nazism and the death camps to Stalinism and the thought-police, to the ravages of postwar countercultures and their woeful discontents, as manifest in the Manson family's murder of Polanski's pregnant wife, Sharon Tate, in 1969, or in Polanski's statutory rape of a thirteen-year-old girl in 1977—explicable in these terms if one views that event as an instance of the failures of a certain brand of sixties-style sexual liberationism.

Nearly every critic with biographical propensities has had to confront how indirectly Polanski's work treats such social, historical, or "personal" materials. To read Polanski's film of *Macbeth* as a reaction to the murder of his wife—as an astonishing number of reviewers did—is, at best, to discover an oblique relationship between reality and representation in his work. To solve the problem raised by this indirection, many commentators adopt a frankly allegorical model of interpretation that sees sociohistorical and cryptobiographical references everywhere. Lawrence Wechsler, for instance, cites the Polish film critic Maria Kornatowska to this effect in his critical profile of Polanski:

> [Kornatowska] made a particularly astute observation, it seemed to me, when she pointed out how, superficial appearances aside, *all* of Polanski's films, especially including *Knife in the Water,* have been about the war, and in particular about the simultaneous combination of claustrophobia and agoraphobia which so characterized that ghetto experience. "In *Knife in the Water,* for instance," she pointed out, "the water is only seemingly an open horizon; in fact, it encloses and entraps absolutely. And that's the quintessential Polanskian universe." (93)[2]

True enough, but what is most striking about Polanski's work is how powerfully the century's crises and malaises are conveyed through his films without being evoked directly. (*The Pianist* is the obvious exception, but the salient point is that it *is* such an obvious exception.) A more eloquent treatment of postwar alienation than any of its many competitors, *Knife in the Water* seemed nearly revolutionary in its context, even following the post-Stalinist thaw in Polish cinema after 1955, simply by abrogating explicit politics and calmly eschewing the still-dominant aesthetic of socialist realism. This abrogation—as well as this weird calmness, even amid a countervailing hysteria—is what, paradoxically, gives Polanski's films such a strong feeling for their particular cultural moments across decades.

To put this another way: Polanski's movies are about how these "superficial appearances" *contain* the world-historical terrors they never quite signify. His films do not present these appearances as the mask of an underlying crisis but as the embodiment of an omnipresent catastrophe. In Polanski's films, the worst has already happened—and the fact that causes are never adduced is very much to the point. To line up the disasters Polanski lived through as explanatory factors behind his work is to miss the point that these calamities are themselves products of an insidious logic of modernity that is everywhere. Even to give this logic the name of social utility, since Polanski never so designates it, is to attenuate the intransigent antinomianism that is perhaps this director's most distinctive feature. But if we understand modernity as the set of developments, ideas, and practices installed under the rubric of thinkers like Darwin, Marx, Nietzsche, and Freud, we cannot fail to note how each of these figures in some important sense developed his thought in reaction to, or against, utilitarian notions—Darwin in his promotion of a naturalized basis of utilitarian morality, Marx in his theory of labor and his concept of use-value, Nietzsche in his explicitly anti-utilitarian efforts to move beyond good and evil, and Freud in his ideas about the motivation of the pleasure-principle, echoing Bentham's homilies about the maximization of pleasure.

To call Polanski's aversion to modernity—an animosity that is crucial to his styles of modernism, and nothing new when considered in line with Marx, Nietzsche, and Freud—a revulsion against the utilitarian mindset not only has the benefit of accounting for the thematic indirections of his work. The avowed liberal rationalism of social utility is surely at odds with the overt irrationalism of fascism, but fascism still derives many of its brutal models of efficiency and its techniques of social engineering and bureaucratized mass-murder from social utility, and Nazism, like Stalinism, enacts its purges according to consequentialist and majoritarian dictates that would doubtless have horrified Bentham, but in which he might have recognized the terrible influence of his own thought. In *The*

Origins of Totalitarianism (1951), Hannah Arendt argued that Nazism and Stalinism were explicitly *anti*-utilitarian because their agendas were *in*efficient to the extent that they were undertaken at great cost, without regard for the economic well-being of the state or for other considerations of social stability. In making this argument, however, she went against the grain of Marxist dogma from the 1930s through the 1950s, which held, under the influence of the Frankfurt School, that these forms of totalitarianism were grotesque products of an instrumental pseudo-rationalism that had become completely generalized.[3]

Meanwhile, the original utilitarianism that remains where its architects hoped to place it—at the foundation of the modern liberal democracies—turns out, in Polanski's films, to be congruent with seemingly opposing versions that selectively borrowed from it to fashion their regimes of terror. In Polanski's vision of modernity, the obvious irrationalities that produced the millennial afflictions of our time are insulated not at all from the putative rationalities of liberal enlightenment. We should not lose sight of one of the clearest implications of this director's work, as derived from the evidence of his films: that Polanski, having survived so many of these afflictions, still found so little comfort in the supposedly enlightened states where, for the most part, he chose to set his films and to make them—the very places that were meant to be his refuge.

Comedy, Melodrama, and Genrification in Polanski's Films

The fact that horror is the cinematic genre with which Roman Polanski has been most closely identified is something of an accident of history. Of his fifteen features, only five are horror films: *Repulsion, The Fearless Vampire Killers, Rosemary's Baby, The Tenant,* and *The Ninth Gate. The Fearless Vampire Killers* and *The Ninth Gate* are actually horror burlesques, while *Repulsion,* for all its horrific imagery, has none of the supernatural trappings that purists of the form demand. Leaving *The Tenant* aside for the moment, Polanski's reputation as a director of horror rests almost entirely on *Rosemary's Baby.* Significantly, this is the same film that consolidated the filmmaker's international renown through his entry into the popular, mass-market cinema. This migration is the decisive moment of Polanski's career, prompting critics' revaluations of his earlier work and their reactions to his subsequent work in light of it. From that point on, the director was mainly seen as an exponent of an emergent, quasi-diasporic sensibility negotiating between a residual Euro-modernism and an ever-expanding, increasingly global mass culture. When critics note lingering elements of horror even in those of his films that seem most remote from the genre—such as *Tess*—they are often really remarking the persistence of popular forms amid seemingly esoteric or highbrow settings.

Because of such negotiations, Polanski's work has been a crucial vehicle for some of the key generic transformations brought about by contemporary cinema. His films are central, for instance, to Ivan Butler's effort in his influential study *Horror in the Cinema* (1970) to expand the parameters of that genre beyond the staples of vampires, monsters, and old dark houses to a broader, more philosophically inclined conception of horror, embracing films ranging from Carl Dreyer's austere studies in the limits of transcendence to Ingmar Bergman's neo-Kierkegaardian cinematic essays in fear and trembling. *Repulsion* gets a whole chapter of the book, while *Knife in the Water* and *Cul-de-Sac*, neither of which was discussed in terms of the horror genre on its first release, are duly conscripted for Butler's polemic as films that exemplify the pervasive powers of horror in everyday modern life. (Butler went on to write the first book-length study of Polanski in English in 1971, furthering the filmmaker's reputation as a director of horror films.) In parsing Polanski's relation to that genre, however, what is most noteworthy is how his work participates in fluid processes of "genrification" rather than locating itself stably within the realm of any particular genre.[4]

In that light, it is significant that Polanski has been drawn most persistently not to the formulae of horror but to the more free-floating ramifications of melodrama and comedy. The two forms typically work in tandem with one another in his films, despite their seeming incompatibility, to produce disquieting slippages and strange emotional juxtapositions. As genres, melodrama and comedy have been noted for their tendencies to vary and deviate, their resistance to ordinary classifications. Recent theorists have concluded that they are not genres at all but more open categories—unfixed practices or "modes." From the manner of Polanski's uses of these forms, it is clear that, for him, their transgeneric inclinations are their defining features, crucial to the generic modulations his films bring about. Similarly, melodrama and comedy, almost by definition, challenge traditional notions of cultural value, not least by virtue of their being typically relegated to the lower orders of the scales appointed to measure such worth. In Polanski's films, melodrama and comedy frequently combine to embrace disrepute and bad taste and to chastise, mock, or countermand the shibboleths, pretensions, and defensive posturings of high art.

Perhaps even more pertinent are the much-noted affinities of melodrama and comedy with modernity itself. According to most recent accounts, melodrama as a form is a product of modernity, its sensations and intensities arising in response to a rapid rise in urbanization, among other forces, and its proliferation aided by the consequent boom in mass communications and mass amusements. At the same time that it is linked to mass culture, many accounts take for granted the collusion of melodrama and modernism. In his influential study of melodrama as a post-Enlightenment genre, Peter Brooks associates it with a protomodernist existentialism—and conveys thereby the essence of Polanski's interest in it—when he says that it encapsulates a modern malaise, revealing a blank at the center of existence, indecipherable yet fraught with ultimate meanings concerning what is left of the "moral universe in a post-sacred era" (15). While comedy is among the oldest of forms, it is often said to undergo fundamental changes in the modern age, especially in reaction to a general diffusion of cultural forms and the growing instability of traditional hierarchies of value, such that "high comedy" and "low comedy," always coexistent, have become increasingly difficult to distinguish. While some assert a productive complicity between comedy and modernism, for many these developments indicate a precipitous cultural decline. Antonin Artaud, for instance, writing about the Marx Brothers, considered comedy an avenue of "essential liberation" that had lost its meaning in modernity (*Theater and Its Double* 142–44).

These affinities suggest that comedy and melodrama, far from being incompatible, are intricately interrelated, and no less a figure than Northrop Frye insists upon the accord between them when, eager to differentiate low melodrama from high tragedy, he argues that the former boils down to "comedy without the humor" (167). The two forms have always appeared together in popular culture, and Polanski's combination of them hardly places him at the margins of cinematic practice. Indeed, the genius of the cinema could be said to reside in its successive subversion of cultural stratifications, and many of the great filmmakers realize this ideal at least to the extent that they blend these two modes frequently, in a spirit of popular diversification—think of D. W. Griffith, Erich Von Stroheim, Louis Feuillade, or Fritz Lang's *Spiders* (1919–20); the F. W. Murnau of *The Last Laugh* (1924) or *Sunrise* (1927); the Jean Renoir of *The Rules of the Game* (1939) and *The Golden Coach* (1951); John Ford, Alfred Hitchcock, or Orson Welles in nearly all of their films; or the line of ironic modernist or postmodern comic melodramatists from Douglas Sirk, Max Ophuls, and Stanley Kubrick to R. W. Fassbinder, Pedro Almodóvar, Emir Kusturica, Wong Kar-wai, Lars Von Trier, or Todd Haynes.

Polanski mines comedy and melodrama variously for all these implications and more, but he is especially drawn to these two modes for the way they operate as formal correlatives of his key theme—the fate of rationality and subjectivity in modern experience. To the extent that comedy challenges the rational while melodrama redeems the subjective, both have relevance to these concerns. The most compelling theories of comedy and melodrama conceive these genres as uniquely positioned to engage with or to portray modern crises in the contiguity of inner experience and outer form. When Henri Bergson argued that laughter results from the clash of the organic with the mechanized, he was not only asserting its distinctively modern cast but also proposing an incongruity between subject and object as the basis of comedy. One thinks instantly of Chaplin's whimsical battles with the world of things, or Keaton's improbably unself-conscious mastery of rebelling machines. For Freud, humor marks the ego's triumph over adverse realities through a process of objectification; by projecting itself as externalized superego through the vehicle of the joke, the ego insists that "it is impervious to the wounds dealt by the outside world" (Freud 217). Triumph over adversity is, of course, a basic staple of melodrama, which derives its key features—starkly polarized moral schemes, investitures of emotion in excess of what can be stated, hysterically overexpressive gestures standing in for the inarticulable—from its acknowledgment of modern failures of understanding and enlightenment.

The peculiar emotional textures of Polanski's films owe a great deal to the ways they juxtapose comedy and melodrama. Typically, each mode checks the other: comedy undermines the emotional excess of melodrama, and melodrama disables some of the distancing effects of comedy. Most of Polanski's movies operate on principles of irresolution and frustration, denying clear emotional outlets, as perhaps best illustrated in the suspended or truncated climaxes that end so many of his films. The counterpointed uses of comedy and melodrama—both reliant on formal indeterminacy and strategies of indirection or frustration—work toward mutual neutralization and amplification: Polanski's comedy regularly elicits laughs only to choke them in our throats, while the melodramatic tenor of some of his films evokes pathos only to mock it. The two modes edge into each other with such insinuating force that no response seems safe—any reaction might be, in the next instance, derided, subverted, or otherwise called into question. The comedy is sometimes excruciating, while the melodrama is often funny, and the quicksilver shifts between them are so capricious you can never tell when the rug will be pulled out from under your feet.

At times the comic and melodramatic modes collapse entirely into one another in Polanski's films, allowing no transition between them and conducing to a confusion of response bordering on the hysterical. *Rosemary's Baby* is perhaps the best example of this tendency, as it is at once Polanski's funniest movie and his most emotionally charged melodrama. Like that of *Psycho*—a film Hitchcock claimed to think of as a comedy—the comedy of *Rosemary's Baby* inheres at the level of conception. Though pronounced and unmistakable, it lurks behind the film rather than being easily discernible within it, and it attests to the attitudes of a pervasive sensibility rather than turning on discrete jokes and gags or the accumulation of comic moments. There are no jokes to speak of in the film, just as there are few in *Psycho*. In both cases, a popular genre novel with a straightforward if earnestly sensationalistic approach has been converted into a sophisticated exercise in Grand Guignol camp and quasi-modernist, sadomasochistic black humor, less by virtue of the material—which readily lends itself to straight melodrama—than by virtue of a particular way of understanding the material: through a kind of cosmopolitan disengagement, attuned to the emotional levels of the stories as narrative textures, formal constructs, based on frankly absurd premises.

Yet, like Hitchcock—and in keeping with the double-consciousness of camp, split between surface and symbol—Polanski insists upon an

Conflicting tonalities of comedy and melodrama in
Rosemary's Baby.

emotional investment in the character of Rosemary at least as vivid as
the one goaded from the viewer of *Psycho* for Marion, that film's erstwhile protagonist. The ultimate effect of *Rosemary's Baby* depends on
a simultaneous awareness of the perverse humor infusing the whole
enterprise and the intense pathos surrounding the figure of Rosemary.
Such concurrence often gives Polanski's movies their sadomasochistic
overtones: they're sadistic insofar as they invite us to adopt superior
attitudes of comic detachment toward horrific situations, and masochistic
when they demand that we acknowledge the real effect of these horrors
and even accept our own implication in them.

The final sequence of *Rosemary's Baby* is a tour de force of conflicting tones: As Rosemary comes face to face with the ultimate horror she
has unknowingly abetted—her own child as Satan's progeny, swaddled in
his black-lined crib—Polanski gives the intensity of her emotions its full
due (and all her loathing, repugnance, and mortal terror are powerfully
delineated in Mia Farrow's flawless acting). But he consistently intercuts
comic details of the florid performances of the elderly Satanists who

have from the start played their roles for laughs in beautifully hammy turns that are stylized, exaggerated, and grotesquely mannered. We cut from a straight-on shot of Rosemary's agony to an impish one of a witch mugging uproariously, or another witch briskly smoothing over the nick in the floor where Rosemary has dropped her knife, and these shifts add up to an unmatched sense of elegantly wrought agitation and hysteria. With an anticlimax as willful as it is notorious, the film trails off—as if to acknowledge that after this delirious fusion of warring styles, there is no further to go—in a welter of bathos that is the movie's ultimate sick joke and its final expression of forlorn desolation.

The interplay of comedy and melodrama in Polanski's films can be equally disorienting when these modes alternate, as in a case like *Repulsion*, as when they mingle. The tone of clinical neutrality with which that film observes its lonely, distraught, and misunderstood main character, Carol, gives way to sudden spasms of dark humor, in scenes at the salon where Carol works, for instance, or in the tavern where her boyfriend confers with his obnoxious chums. These scenes border on caricature in their broad renderings of the snooty complacency of Carol's clients, the smug arrogance of her co-workers, or the boorish crudity of the pub's denizens, and they stand so directly at odds with the film's dominant approach—the delicacy, care, and objectivity with which it treats Carol's gradual, ineluctable dissolution—that they sound an overweening note of discord. The alternation between modes is formally stark, with comic elements attending scenes of community and a muted but increasingly sensationalistic melodrama, absent of any humor, shading the sequences depicting Carol's solitude.

At a thematic level, the extremity of these colliding tones defines a gulf between the two realms whose relation the film chiefly concerns—the public and the private, the social world of human interaction and the personal, inner world of individual thought and agency. It is significant that, in *Repulsion*, the outer domain is identified with the comic impulse as a space of drollery, absurdism, and satire, while the inner is identified with melodrama—the space of affect, disavowed fantasy that recurs as psychological threat, or intense but ineffable feeling, blocked and rechanneled as symbol, gesture, or violent action. As so often in Polanski's work, the point is to suggest an increasingly unbridgeable rift between these realms in modern and postmodern cultures, and the clash of comic and melodramatic standpoints enacts this fission with a bleak literalism.

Polanski's varied deployments of comedy and melodrama should be called *post*-generic, to the extent that they ignore or confuse traditional emotional boundaries and abrogate the usual underpinnings and typical effects that these two modes ordinarily entail. Polanski's uses of genre as such turn on the conviction that genre is obsolete, however much its residual forms and lingering simulacra continue to dominate film cultures. He draws on repositories of genre not as a fund of animating mythology—no filmmaker who works with genre could be less interested in the dynamics of mythmaking—but rather in the way a self-sufficient *bricoleur* might use old shoes, wheels, scraps of wood, or bits of wire to fashion an elegant sculpture. His uses of comedy and melodrama, among other bits of generic detritus, depend on a recognition that the old forms no longer work: horror isn't scary, at least not in the way that it once was; comedy doesn't make you laugh; melodrama doesn't make you cry; and even the more formulaic genres of movie lore, as far as Polanski is concerned, might as well never have existed. (That a Polanski Western is unimaginable tells much of what we need to know about this director's relation to traditional genres.[5]) His work expresses little of the kind of loss, especially the loss of confidence in generic forms, that pervaded film culture of the 1960s or 1970s, in genre experiments of the art film (like the travesties of the American crime film or musical in the French New Wave), or the faltering genre pieces of fading Hollywood auteurs in the 1960s, or the bouts of genre revisionism of up-and-coming young directors of the 1970s. On the contrary, Polanski's engagement with genre demonstrates full confidence in its already-accomplished demise, and perhaps for that reason, his work never stoops to defend itself against the mounting liabilities of genre—naivete, sentiment, or other forms of false consciousness—for there is scarcely any real possibility that these foibles (to which melodrama and comedy were especially susceptible) could ever gain the slightest foothold in this director's work, no matter how generically bound it might seem.

Only two of Polanski's movies—*The Fearless Vampire Killers* and *Pirates*—are billed as outright comedies, and these are both spoofs of notoriously melodramatic genres. More to the point, they parody a secondary or marginal genre (the pirate movie) and specialized or idiosyncratic dimensions of a primary one (the horror film), evincing a dexterous eccentricity of response to the forms and conventions of genre. Horror spoofs, from *Abbott and Costello Meet Frankenstein* (1948) to *Carry On Screaming* (1966), took the classic 1930s series of Hollywood horror movies as their point of departure, but *The Fearless Vampire Killers* alludes hardly at all to that tradition, instead drawing on deviant strains of sixties art-horror or exploitation-prone Euro-shockers like *Blood and Roses* (1960), *Black Sunday* (1960), and *Castle of the Living Dead* (1964). Free of the contamination anxiety that began to creep into filmmaking as movies aspired to insulate themselves from the regressive taint of genre—through parody, pastiche, deconstruction, or abnegation—*The Fearless Vampire Killers* matches its models in brazen bad taste and playfully lurid sensationalism and betters them in the beauty of its lush production design. Far from distancing itself from the object of its parody, or positing horror as a quaint throwback awash in corny old clichés, Polanski's movie, more or less, *is* what it mocks: an actual entry in the transnational, postgeneric art-horror cycle, much closer in style and substance to *Spirits of the Dead* (1969) and *Daughters of Darkness* (1969) than *Young Frankenstein* (1974).

Planned by Polanski for many years before it came to fruition, *Pirates* combines the obsessiveness of a pet project with the desultory treatment of an idea whose time has come and gone. By contrast with *The Fearless Vampire Killers,* it trades in a form so diffuse it barely qualifies as a genre at all, with few of the delineating touchstones or definitive staples boasted by the horror genre, and Polanski's arch, strident burlesque does full justice to the dissipated energies of the form. Perhaps because the pirate movie has no real narrative core—unlike horror, which always concerns variations on the themes of resurrection, metamorphosis, and possession—it tends toward an attitudinizing self-parody even at its most staid, as in *Jamaica Inn* (1939), *The Crimson Pirate* (1951), *Treasure Island* (1951), or even that stateliest and least fanciful of pirate movies, Fritz Lang's *Moonfleet* (1955). *Pirates* shares with *The Fearless Vampire Killers* an elaborate production design geared to anatomize the form as pure spectacle. Taken together as meditations on genre, the two films negate any sense of genre as controlling or homeostatic, revealing it instead as profoundly *meta*-static, defined by its malleability and its compound, hybrid status, always in mutation, fractal and tensile, each of its mutations seen as mutually parasitical, feeding off or plundering others—vampiric or piratical.

Perhaps the most stably defined of Polanski's genre pieces is *Chinatown*, the second of his two Hollywood films. If *Rosemary's Baby* did as much as *Psycho* to modernize the Hollywood horror film in the 1960s, *Chinatown* figured crucially in the mid-1970s revival of film noir. Unlike such counterparts as *The Long Goodbye* (1973), *Night Moves* (1974), or *The Conversation* (1974), however, each of which updates noir for a post-counterculture, Watergate-era climate, *Chinatown* trades in a wily, tenebrous nostalgia. In his two forays into Hollywood filmmaking, Polanski occupied both ends of the spectrum along which the reframings of genre in the New Hollywood could be measured—the debunking of the mythologies of genre by new-generation auteurs, and the wistful revivalism of the old guard, trying to restore luster to the traditional models. *Chinatown* initiated the nostalgic vein of the neo-noir, including the remakes of *Farewell, My Lovely* (1975) and *The Postman Always Rings Twice* (1979). Its detailed reconstruction of Los Angeles in the 1930s has some of the aura and the burnish, if little of the fondness, of other contemporary evocations of bygone days, from *The Sting* (1973) to *Bound for Glory* (1975). But just beneath the veneer of this nostalgia is an acrimony that demands we recognize the brutal corruptions of this lost time even as we long to retrieve it.

Taking into account all of the ambivalence, double-dealing, and multiplicity of Polanski's relation to genre, it is still worth asking why, in an era where theoretical renunciations of genre produced a far greater share of cultural prestige, this director should have remained committed to an exploration of generic practice and permutation in the first place. Polanski's career moved in a direction opposite to that of the art-film directors whose reputations grew in proportion to such abjurations—recondite mystics like Andrei Tarkovsky, ascetic formalists like Michael Snow, breakneck extemporizers like Raúl Ruiz or John Cassavetes, to name a few.

Like those of most important filmmakers of the time, Polanski's early films promised to abandon generic structures in the name of film art, yet his work becomes more, not less, invested in genre as it progresses, leaving behind the heterodox approaches of the early films in favor of parsing the heterogeneous genres of his later work. What makes this trajectory especially interesting is the sense in which the structures of genre increasingly operate as correlatives of social systems in his films. As genre developed in the cinema, it fulfilled key dictates of modern social organization, such as the ordering of a potentially chaotic field of individual entities, the collation of such entities within the purview of a larger group, and the recognition of a specific entry chiefly in its relation to a given pattern that exists not as a concrete point of origin (as there is no zero-degree or singular urtext for any particular genre) but as a metaconcept, made perceptible only through action, in the production of the instances that point back to it. To put this more simply: Genre as a system of classification makes individual movies recognizable as products, even though it cannot itself be located except as concept or behavior. In that sense, it replicates formally the structures of disciplinary societies, and genre as such instantiates themes concerning social utility that occupy Polanski more and more in the course of his work. As a reifying or commodifying instrument, it realizes imperatives of social utility in the industry of cinema.

This claim could provide the best reason why Polanski might have chosen to eschew genre altogether, if his work mounts the critique of utilitarianism's legacy I argue it does, but to compare the filmmaker's attitudes to those of another director whose uses of genre reflect similar preoccupations—Stanley Kubrick—suggests why neither ever finally rejects genre, despite their obvious shared disdain for its typical workings and its ultimate implications.[6] Both filmmakers return to genre with an air of sour resignation, as of the indignant structuralist convinced that because human experience is determined at base by received notions and given templates—implacable models, exemplars, ideals, clichés, and prototypes—any resistance to them amounts to naive vanity or reckless folly, if not bad faith.

More explicitly than Polanski's, Kubrick's work is dedicated to exposing the foundational premises of utilitarianism as the source of a modern dehumanization that is perceived to be general and insuperable. The worlds he imagines constitute a Benthamite nightmare of totalized institutions, disciplinary spaces, social engineering, instrumental materialisms, invisibly domineering authorities, and blanked-out, docile citizens. Unlike Polanski, Kubrick is afflicted with a trenchant didacticism; his films present cautionary tales of failed rebellions that serve only to trigger a reflex of self-destruction built into the social system. Because this didacticism is usually tempered by a mordant, countervailing irony, its lessons rarely take hold in the films themselves, where characters either remain oblivious even after the faux-epiphanies they undergo, as in *A Clockwork Orange* (1971), *Full Metal Jacket* (1987), or *Eyes Wide Shut* (1999); or else they are consigned to literal oblivion, following a blithe and fanciful holocaust, as in *Dr. Strangelove* (1964), or a cosmic revelation of uncertain mystic significance, as in *2001: A Space Odyssey* (1968).

Kubrick works through genres successively to show how each—war films, comic melodramas, melodramatic comedies, doomsday fantasies, sci-fi head trips, historical pageants, and even horror movies—operates as a system that is a microcosm of the large social systems it reflects, in which it is embedded, and by which it is produced. Genre in his films formally manifests the films' content—meditating on the monolithic oppressions installed by the utilitarian state—and in the terms of his work, it can be no more abandoned than that state can be escaped. Polanski's conclusions may be as bleak as Kubrick's, but his work typically concerns characters who have literally removed themselves from the social order only to find that its constraints pursue them. On the face of it, Polanski shares little of Kubrick's interest in regimented space—the barracks of *Paths of Glory* (1957) or *Full Metal Jacket;* the hospitals of *Lolita* (1963), *A Clockwork Orange,* or *Eyes Wide Shut;* the hotels of *Lolita* or *The Shining* (1980); the workplaces, bureaus, schoolrooms, prisons, and offices that appear emphatically throughout Kubrick's films. In Polanski's work we see only glimpses of such places: the nunnery in *Repulsion;* the Catholic schoolrooms of *Rosemary's Baby* (seen in nearly subliminal dream-flashes); and the offices, police stations, and halls of records shown briefly in *Chinatown, The Tenant, Frantic,* and *The Ninth Gate.* Though Kubrick pursued the screen rights to Louis Begley's 1991 novel about the Nazi era, *Wartime Lies,* he never made his film of the Holocaust, but if he had it would almost certainly have provided a hellish vision of the death camps—the last word in regimented space and modern institutional horror. In *The Pianist,* Polanski's film of the Holocaust, the camps are never shown.

While Polanski's work conceives of genre as a formal correlative of utilitarian social systems, much like Kubrick's, his more diffuse renderings of generic structures reflect a different sense of the reach and the power of these systems. What interests Polanski is a residual interiority that lingers outside social space, a remnant that the false rationalisms of modernity have failed to dispel but which can do little to resist them all the same. For Kubrick, nothing falls outside the purview of social space, and whatever fleeting appearance of human interiority remains—Alex's love of Beethoven in *A Clockwork Orange*, for instance, or the doctor's troubled, compulsive fantasies of his wife's infidelity in *Eyes Wide Shut*—is only a by-product of the system, made for its benefit or channeled for its use. Part of the greater generic hybridity, fluidity, and indeterminacy of Polanski's films is due to the fact that so many of his characters are literally on vacation from their normal lives, or otherwise at leisure—*Knife in the Water, What?, Frantic, Bitter Moon, A Day at the Beach* (scripted by Polanski in 1969 but directed by Simon Hesera). They are apart from the institutional regulations or social restrictions of everyday life. Others elect to live in remote locations, like the married couples of *Cul-de-Sac* and *Death and the Maiden;* or, like the protagonists of *Repulsion* and *The Tenant,* in a state of isolation that may be debilitating but which they choose nonetheless over the sacrifice of thought, privacy, and autonomy that would come from taking their places in a fully administered world.

In other words, Polanski's films are about individuals who have escaped from the encompassing gaze of the surveillance state only to find that it has followed them into their distant refuge in disguised or mutated form—either because the characters themselves have internalized it, or because any human interaction, however it removes itself from the influences of social control, is still bound to replicate those norms, because they really are everywhere, even where they do not appear to be. Kubrick's movies, in which utilitarian social structures do indeed appear to be everywhere, show how psychosexual impulses underlie these structures so deeply that these impulses are no longer clearly visible, or even particularly relevant except as fodder for jokes. This is certainly true if *Dr. Strangelove* is about how men's phallic insecurities give rise to prosthetic complexes of high-tech weaponry; or if *2001* is about how primal aggressions give rise to mechanized automation; or if most of his films are about how patriarchy destroys us all. Polanski's movies, in contrast, show how utilitarian social structures produce psychosexual impulses of aggression and domination, sadism and masochism, displaced into seemingly private spheres of human intersubjectivity. Kubrick anatomizes his characters in social space, with little attention to their desires or their inner lives, which figure, if at all, as artifacts, figments, or delusions. Polanski reveals the significance of supposedly private experience to public life, especially since the activity of his characters is always exposed to the camera's view, given the inevitable complicity of cinema with the surveillance practices of utilitarian social structures.

If Kubrick's characters demonstrate sexuality of any kind, it is out of conditioned reflex more than individual desire. Even the bouts of married sex in *Eyes Wide Shut* are self-conscious and automatic, while Alex's vile escapades of rape in *A Clockwork Orange* have about them more of Pavlov than of Sade. In the opening scene of *A Clockwork Orange*, as we follow Alex's marauding gang, Kubrick presents their rapes with what he must take to be an ironic giddiness, apparently intending to provoke disgust by adopting the dispositions of the rapist. That he is able to broach such buoyancy at all, even as a conceit, is sufficient proof that he regards rape as a kind of trope, pursued not to vilify the aggression of the rapist or to declare the violation of the victim—both of which appear obvious to him all the same—but to serve as a metaphor for institutional culture, whose totalizing dominion in the social sphere the passing trope is only there to confirm.

Strikingly, both directors return repeatedly to rape narratives, and it could be said of Polanski, for all the difficulty in defining his generic proclivities in some consistent way, that rape narratives prove to be his encompassing concern, as the plots of six of his fifteen features turn on them decisively, while most of the others invoke the threat of rape in passing. A long and dishonorable history further links popular comedy and melodrama through the avenue of the rape narrative, which has tended to distribute its affect according to whether its sympathies or intentions lie with a pseudo-progressive libertinage, and therefore produce "comedy," or with (in Sade's phrase) a "sentimental chastity," therefore melodrama. That there should be a tradition of rape narratives treated comically in the first place—never mind a long one, from Sade through Pope and Swift to films by Pedro Almodóvar or Richard Linklater's Polanski-influenced movie of 2001, *Tape* (called a "date rape comedy" by its director)—furnishes a particularly shameful chapter of cultural history, though melodrama's contrary tendency to conscript representations of rape to elicit ready-made outrages and synthetic sympathies brings little consolation. Polanski's work plays both sides of this dubious middle, providing comic images of rape in the relevant sequence of *Rosemary's Baby* and the opening scene of *What?*, more traditionally melodramatic images in *Repulsion* and *Tess*, and traumatized recollections in *Chinatown* and *Death and the Maiden*. Unlike Kubrick, Polanski remains attuned to the social causes and consequences of rape, as well as to its psychological ramifications, and if there is a saving grace about his treatment of this theme, it is that he views it not as an offshoot of social utility that fades to insignificance in light of the larger structure it merely serves to indicate but as a primary outcome of an instrumentalist society, showing the pervasive effects of social domination in personal life.

If Polanski is incomparably more concerned than Kubrick with human sexuality, he still credits little of the voluptuary or sensualist aspects of traditional artistic representations of sex. A single instance in his films, the kiss between the wife and the young hitchhiker in *Knife in the Water*, is presented with an erotic charge. Every other sexual representation in his work is designed to be repulsive, discomfiting, or grotesque, signifying the invasion and appropriation of sexuality by the demands of social utility. For Polanski, rape is the most utilitarian sex act, the most literal and recurrent example of the usurpation of the private sphere by the forces of social utility. It literalizes a body's "use-value" in the most violent way, and its justification, as brute action, appeals frequently to utilitarian pleasure principles, asserting the rapist's satisfaction as a higher value than the victim's pain, if that is acknowledged at all. The rapes depicted in Polanski's films are often motivated by explicitly pragmatic considerations. In *Rosemary's Baby*, for instance, the husband offers his wife's unconscious body for the carnal satisfactions and reproductive ambitions of the devil because, as he later explains to her, "we get so much in return!" The incestuous rape of *Chinatown* is duly exculpated when the rapist invokes the utilitarian values of convenience, property rights, and superior will, amounting to a privatized, domesticated form of social engineering: in a potent application of Occam's razor, the father decides that he need not trouble himself looking afield for a sex object, as he already owns a daughter who can bear him a child he will love all the more for its origin in such a tightly controlled gene pool. In *Death and the Maiden*, rape is the prerogative of the victor, a predictable by-product of a political conquest with fascistic and explicitly Darwinian overtones—and we should recall that it was Darwin in *The Descent of Man,* laying the groundwork for generations of genocide to come, who eloquently championed "the natural basis of utilitarian morality" (472).

Polanski's films show that rape takes some of the bases of utilitarian social design to their ultimate and logical interpersonal conclusions. Defenders of social utility will be quick to point out that rape is really a perversion of utilitarian concepts, not a realization of them, and that it was, as action, often unseen and unprosecuted before utilitarianism promoted its agenda of rendering actions collectively visible so that they could be ranked and evaluated according to their consequences. Barely stigmatized at key points in history, rape was increasingly criminalized as the influences of utilitarianism grew, and crucial reforms were instituted to answer claims that rape could be defended on utilitarian grounds, if its perpetrators could pretend they were enhancing the greater good. Tort laws, for instance, were revised to account for intentions behind actions, so that someone's intention to have sex could be distinguished from another's intention not to, apart from the act itself.

Essentially a neo-utilitarian call for reform, Thomas Hardy's *Tess of the D'Urbervilles,* the story of a working-class girl's rape by a faux-nobleman, is an important step in this progress, and Polanski's treatment of the story pursues something like a dialectic of the greater enlightenment Hardy's novel calls for. The film makes clear that Tess is visible as an individual only because of her beauty, but that she is invisible as a social entity because there is no reason to take note of her, except to make sure she is working, a proof readily accomplished without excess attentions. After Tess is raped, her beauty is seen to be polluted, her marginal visibility denied. Polanski emphasizes this point by making Angel Clare's rejection of her more fickle than it seems in the book. As a rape victim, Tess is never visible—or, as the film would have it, always visible, but never seen. She can be seen only at the story's end, as a murderer who must die.

Carol in *Repulsion* imagines her own rape in scenes portrayed as vividly as any in the director's work, with a palpable sense of tensed, breathless horror at these violations (though he remains complicit in their imagining). The blunt materialization of Carol's tortured fantasies makes it difficult for the viewer to shrug them off by saying that she is only tormenting herself. It is astonishing that *Repulsion* neither forfeits sympathy for Carol nor tries to earn it with easy psychological explanations, refusing to minimize her own violence. The rape scenes in *Repulsion* are more painful to watch than those in Polanski's other films, even though they are clearly Carol's fantasies. Their awful power comes from the fact that even though they are not "really happening," we are not allowed to forget that what they show really happens all the time. Carol's fantasies enact what the film makes clear are perfectly logical fears. The quality of the film's empathy comes from its *understanding* of her repulsions, not its castigation of them, and we feel the intensity of her sense of violation, the reality of it, even as we recognize the rapes themselves as delusions. In Polanski's films, rape is always a specific injury, however it may be related to overarching social injustices.

This is the case even considering the corrosive ironies of Polanski's work. In *Rosemary's Baby,* the rape scene that marks a narrative turning point is indeed "really happening," as its victim herself cries out in an instant of horrific epiphany: "Oh my God—this isn't a dream, *this is really happening!*" The sequence leading up to this moment of revelation is framed as a virtuoso set piece, pointing back to *Psycho* in its willingness to take such violent action as the occasion for bravura exhibitions of style. The camera glides sinuously over dreadful sights only barely deprived of their full horror by the smooth elegance of its display, like a Kenneth Anger short remade by Cecil Beaton: the syncopated ritual preparations; the well-dressed socialites and berobed priests; the clustered coven of nude witches, all slumped shoulders, wrinkled skins, and saggy breasts, like a gaggle of Weird Sisters out of *Macbeth;* and the sudden appearance of the devil himself, first as nothing but a limp arm groping Rosemary's vulnerable body with an oversized claw—all too obviously a rubber limb from the props department meant to bring guffaws—then as a pair of steely, piercing eyes that in a cold flash freeze our mirth over the corny effect. It is the horrifying sharpness of this gaze that provokes Rosemary's realization that her exotic dream is really a terrible reality, but with a sharp fade the moment passes, and in the next shot Rosemary is engaged in small talk with the Pope while the devil, in flagrante delicto, still energetically pumps away at her.

This outrageous set piece may be Polanski's most telling conflation of melodramatic horror and sadistic comedy. The sequence demands a strong reaction, even as it confounds almost every possible response by quickly juxtaposing it against an opposing one. The situation as a whole is so obviously horrific that the slyly insinuating wit of its treatment seems repugnant, while the scene's calculated shocks are rendered with such an impersonal elegance that they throw us back on helpless laughter as the only way out of the emotional binds in which the film places us. Polanski's blending of genre thus produces not a simple amplification of affect but a wholesale expansion of affective ground. Out of an interest in the fate of the corporeal, he returns to the "body genres" of comedy and melodrama, so called in recent film criticism because they produce the physical sensations of laughter and tears. But with rare exceptions, nobody ever laughs or cries in a Polanski film, and the audience, trying to cope with the vicissitudes of the films' shifting emotional grounds, is often paralyzed between these states. If Polanski's films produce any consistent physiological response, it is a gasp. One comes away with the sense that the maker of these films, confronting a ruined world, does not know whether to chortle or to weep, but chooses in the end a hard, dark laughter over weak-willed tears.

Cul-de-Sac and the 1960s Art Cinema

What is the art of the "art cinema"? The most satisfying reply might be that it encompasses fundamentally different effects, functions, and implications at different times in different places. But even that answer may have to defer to a more basic question: What is art cinema? The first tentative investigations into the matter took place in Anglo-American film criticism—not surprisingly, for the art film is largely an American construct, a way of apprehending European films (especially those not in English) that has no mutual equivalent in the opposite direction. These inquiries occurred in tandem with an especially vigorous renaissance of the art film in the 1960s and 1970s, but some forty years later, we're still asking. When David Bordwell attempted to anatomize the form in 1979, he began with a limited array of examples: *La Strada*, *8½*, *Wild Strawberries*, *The Seventh Seal*, *Persona*, *Ashes and Diamonds*, *Jules et Jim*, *Knife in the Water*, *Vivre sa vie*, and *Muriel*. Though the roster enlarges as he goes on, including two directors from Japan (Akira

Kurosawa and Kenji Mizoguchi) and one from India (Satyajit Ray), the circumscribed compass of this list remains striking: ten films from four countries, ranging over a period of eleven years (from 1955 to 1966).

What Bordwell was doing is probably the best that any critic could do, defining a specific manifestation of the art film, and few would dispute the legitimacy of his impromptu canon. It is not surprising that this era should now seem so definitive, since it is the period during which the designation "art film" began to gain wide currency under the influence of, among other sources, the section called "The Art Film" in Robert Warshow's *The Immediate Experience* (1962). But this critical decade is best understood as part of a diffuse program of oscillations, drifts, and countercurrents that has shaped world cinema practically from its beginning. A broad history might include the *films d'art* movements in Europe and America in the first decades of cinema; the continued efforts of key directors to gain legitimacy for film by appealing to canons of traditional art (*Cabiria, Intolerance, Leaves from Satan's Book,* among many others); and the consolidation of national cinemas of the 1920s that drew explicitly on the cultural prestige of established movements in the fine arts like German expressionism or French impressionism.

Though great works of film art continued to be made, a lull in the development of the art film during the 1930s, as war loomed in Europe, suggested that there had always been an internationalist dimension to the form. At the same time, in this period of relative abeyance, writers like Harry Alan Potamkin and Rudolph Arnheim promoted an understanding of the "art" of the art film as being congruent with, if not identical to, that of the most venerable arts of the ages. After World War II, a new cinema culture fostered by the institution of international film festivals revived the art film and nurtured its successive movements of the next twenty years—principally, Italian neorealism and the "new waves" of France, Germany, and Czechoslovakia. Meanwhile, a few individuals who emerged without the benefit of a matured national cinema to bolster them received due support in these same venues as latter-day types of the lone, mystic artisan from national cinemas that may have been thriving, in some cases, but still had no particular profile on the festival circuit: Carl Theodor Dreyer or Ingmar Bergman, Akira Kurosawa or Satyajit Ray.

At least until this decisive period from *La Strada* (1955) to *Persona* (1966), then, the "art" of the art film was of a familiar kind. It bespoke a tradition that preserved within the commercial cinema vestiges of those values endangered by the age of mechanical reproduction: authenticity, sincerity, personal expression, and uniqueness of form or style, all time-honored constituents of the "aura" of classical art. The cycle of the art film that Bordwell traces may have continued to maintain these values—though the particular features that he isolates are realism, psychological causality, and ambiguity. But two factors distinguish this period from those before it. While the international art film had always defined itself, or been defined, in reaction against the domination of Hollywood on the world film market, Hollywood in the postwar years sustained a series of economic crises that ultimately gave rise to strategies of international expansion.[7] At the same time, the French New Wave—the movement that consolidated this phase of the art film, accounting for three of Bordwell's ten examples—incorporated an intricate dialogue with the Hollywood cinema into its filmmaking practice. At the point where one might have expected stronger resistance to the growing threat of Hollywood's power, a central line of the art film instead made a point of emphasizing the formative influence of Hollywood cinema on its own development.

During this same period, the institutions supporting the art film developed in a manner in keeping with the increasing hybridity of the form. Commentators noted the growing commercialization of important festivals worldwide, while in the United States the functions of the "art-house" mode of exhibition widened beyond the role of making foreign films available to specialized domestic audiences.[8] These broader purposes arose in tandem with a vastly enlarged market base; while the number of foreign films imported into the United States remained relatively stable from 1927 to 1968, the number of venues in which they were shown increased dramatically after World War II.[9] But the fare in these venues was notably various by the end of the 1950s and the early 1960s, when art houses routinely alternated screenings of European art films with exhibitions of American independent or avant-garde cinema, occasional films from outside the Europe/Hollywood matrix (especially from Japan or India), reissues and revivals, and even upscale horror and exploitation movies, with occasional bouts of literal pornography. In the early 1960s, one might have seen Federico Fellini's *La Dolce Vita* side by side with a reissue of *Breakfast at Tiffany's*; Alain Resnais's *Hiroshima,*

Mon Amour in close quarters with John Cassavetes's *Shadows* or Shirley Clarke's *The Connection;* a revival of *The Guns of Navarone* rubbing elbows with Ingmar Bergman's *The Magician;* or Georges Franju's *Les Yeux sans Visage* (Eyes without a face)—dubbed and rechristened with the more prurient-sounding title *The Horror Chamber of Dr. Faustus*—on a double bill with *The Manster,* a low-grade horror film.[10]

The variability of these transactions indicates what we already knew: Like the products of modernist culture more generally, the art film never occupied an exalted province removed from ordinary influences of commerce or exchange, despite its occasional appearance of holding itself apart from these networks. But the art film gains and retains its prestige not only in spite of its unseemly trafficking in the marketplace with lowlier forms of popular culture but in some measure because of it. The status of a particular movie as an art film always owes much to the context of its presentation; a film taken as just another movie in its native context, produced within commercial networks and presented as part of the common film culture, could easily be exported as a specialized art film—this was especially the case in the twenty years after World War II—while just about any foreign-language movie shown on an American screen, whatever its intent or content, might as well have called itself an art film. All the same, even if audiences were immune to the elegant, clinical poetry of *Les Yeux sans Visage* and attuned to the screechy, hysterical pseudo-chills of *The Manster,* it is nearly inconceivable that most viewers would not distinguish between them—if only because of differences of setting, topography, or language. The stew of many different kinds of films to be found on the art-house circuit in the United States during this time had the long-term effect of tempering the uniformity of the art film throughout the 1970s and after, in what some have called its "second wave." But it also had the subsidiary consequence—*pace* Bordwell, and in a classic case of product differentiation—of consolidating the art film as a mode or a style by contrast with the diverse body of films among which it circulated.

What really emerged during the time from *La Strada* to *Persona* was a distinct, exclusionary canon—a subgroup of the art film defined by an ethos of high seriousness, despite the occasional earthy humor of, say, a Fellini. This lineage takes shape less around elements of style and technique than around a whole gestalt of mood, treatment, and tonality.

Think of such signatures as the stark interiors of Bergman, the mercurial but severe, shifting tenses of Resnais, the rigorously unforgiving long takes of Michelangelo Antonioni—each important as an element of style or form, but equally so as an expression of attitude. Especially if we take as the touchstone the work of someone like Bergman—who alone accounts for another three of Bordwell's cases—the art film could be said to comprise themes of great moment, of life-or-death significance, approached with a defining sense of existential dread and handled with gravity, solemnity, weight, low-pitched formality, somberness, and even grimness. This description not only squares with popular parodies of the art film throughout this period (as in television programs like *Your Show of Shows* and movies like *What a Way to Go!* in 1964 or Woody Allen's spoofs, especially the Antonioni parody in *Everything You Always Wanted to Know about Sex* in 1971), it fits nearly every item on Bordwell's roll-call. And even if the list is weighted in the direction of this characterization—as when he represents the French New Wave with three of the least playful examples of that waggish movement—that only certifies the relative validity of the definition.

But the history of any cultural form can be written from many different angles, and it is interesting to consider how our conception of the art film might differ if subject to an alternative slate of films from the same period. To paraphrase Jean Genet: What if, despite the airs of high seriousness attending these films, somebody laughed? Consider the following list, for instance: *Big Deal on Madonna Street* (1955), *Divorce Italian Style* (1961), *Zazie dans le Metro* (1959), *Mon Oncle* (1958), *Fireman's Ball* (1966), *Closely Watched Trains* (1966), *Cul-de-Sac*—even Bergman's *The Devil's Eye,* a terminally stilted comedy of 1960 so slight it can barely hold its place in the master's oeuvre. Or consider this list, even more variegated with reference to provenance and quality: *Les Yeux sans Visage* (1959), *Diabolique* (1955), *Blood and Roses* (1960), *Testament of Dr. Cordelier* (1960), *The Innocents* (1961), *Blood of the Vampire* (1958), *Repulsion,* and—yet again—Bergman's *Hour of the Wolf* (1967). Two eccentric lists, perhaps, but each of these movies, comedy or horror, nonetheless has some remotely legitimate claim to art-film status. All of them played in art houses in the United States at some point from 1955 to 1967, and some are the work of directors (like Bergman, Renoir, Clouzot) whose credentials few could deny. Yet they remain marginal to the traditional art-film template in large part because the genres with which they intersect tend to abjure the high seriousness of the art film as such. Though comedy and horror are often relegated to the sphere of low culture, one could write a kind of shadow-history of the art film through the lens of either genre on the basis of the films named above, or on that of certain directors' fleeting transactions with these genres (like Bergman's or Fellini's) or others' more than incidental connections to them (such as Jacques Tati or Luis Buñuel—or Fellini—in comedy; Henri-Georges Clouzot, Georges Franju, or Carl Dreyer in horror).

What are the roles played by genres like comedy and horror in the art film? The question seems especially pertinent to the decade under consideration, because while it was the period of the art film's transient çongealment into something like a genre in its own right, it was also a time at which the cultural hybridity of the art film, especially its capacity to traverse cultural levels with great tractability, had never been more apparent, though it would become even more so in decades to follow. One need not be Jacques Derrida—nor even cite him—to see how the changing relations of the art film's so-called center to its putative margins were not so much outcomes or consequences of historical processes as crucial determinants upon them. These relations were not initially stable and subsequently called into question in some decisive moment of crisis; they were checkered, vacillating, muddled, fluid, and reciprocal from the start—so much so that one might reasonably conclude, Derrida-like, that there had never really been a center, no "art film" as such, only rotary simulations issuing from a shifting vortex of styles and types with more or less congruence to some imaginary zero-degree of the form. To the extent that comedy and horror are "marginal" elements of particular art films, they underlie this pliant hybridity; to the extent that they have been formative influences, they reveal the very notion of the art film to be little more than a convenient fiction.

Of the key figures in the 1960s European art film, Roman Polanski traded most brazenly in comedy and horror of differing types and at various levels or extremes, most often where these forms intersect with melodrama. Perhaps the most eclectic art-film auteur of the decade, he was—maybe for that reason—most instrumental in opening up the art-film canon and disturbing its established hierarchies, thus paving the way for the putative second wave in the 1970s, of which he is an equally crucial representative.

The first decade of Polanski's career in feature filmmaking, from *Knife in the Water* (1962) through *What?* (1973), provides a virtual typology of the art film of that period, following its permutations often exactly, for all the errant energies of the films themselves. Despite its undercurrent of corrosive wit, *Knife in the Water* is Polanski's most conventional contribution to the form (perhaps earning it its place in Bordwell's catalogue). With its deliberate pacing, downscaled action, and wryly unflinching yet becalmed scrutiny of its trio of characters, the film operates on a plane that all but typifies the form, presenting fairly straightforwardly—though with overtones of ambiguity—a "serious" treatment of a "real" contemporary phenomenon in its depiction of an ordinary marriage gone slightly sour. It also has a clear formalist aspect in its aestheticized treatment of landscape and its psychologically sug- gestive placement of characters in space.

Completing the profile, the film played outside its native Poland under the patronage of rumors regarding state censorship or, at least, government disapproval of the movie's bourgeois characters, and it came accompanied with a condemnation from the Catholic Legion of Decency, presumably for its rather tame presentation of an adulterous flirtation. These circumstances could function as selling points, the first enabling international audiences the self-congratulatory pleasure of chiding other states' repressive regimes, the second imparting a kinky thrill to a given film however austere its treatment of sensational or transgressive materials. In the case of *Knife in the Water*, the film's sta- tus—perhaps even its relative conformity to the norm—was clinched when it won the Critics' Prize at the Venice Film Festival and ultimately certified with a nomination as Best Foreign Film by the Motion Pic- ture Academy in the United States, an acknowledgment that practically guaranteed entry to the official canon. And making the cover of *Time* certainly didn't hurt (see note 8).

Polanski's next three films—*Repulsion* (1965), *Cul-de-Sac* (1966), and, as it was titled in Europe, *Dance of the Vampires* (1967)—departed markedly from these more ordinary standards, and in doing so they con- tributed to the erosion of certain conventions and the transformation of basic aspects of the template. In the wake of state objections to *Knife in the Water,* Polanski left Poland and became, for the next forty years, a constant expatriate. Thus, he pioneered a model of the art-film auteur as international cosmopolitan, a figure that would become especially common in various forms in the next wave (Antonioni, Bertolucci, Nagisa Oshima, Raúl Ruiz). Polanski's films continued to meet with official forms of success in the burgeoning market of the international art film. *Repulsion* and *Cul-de-Sac* won major prizes at the Berlin Film Festival in two consecutive years. Thus, even as Polanski's films were rewarded with such prestigious approval, they continually reshaped the canons that legitimated them.

Each of these three films is characterized by distinct problems of placement, having something to do with their abandonment of the ordinary protocols of nationality in movies. They are, in one sense, "British" films—albeit made by a Polish director—but they are also international co-productions that bring together actors of different nations and handle the whole question of locale with some ambivalence. The South Kensington exteriors of *Repulsion* offer a deglamorized London (like that of contemporary views in films ranging from *The Knack* in 1965 to *Blow-Up* in 1966, also nominally British films by "foreigners") of harried crowds, burnt-out blocks, loud construction sites, and dizzying traffic. The handheld camera that captures all of this may reflect, in its vertiginous movement, Polanski's own displacement as much as it does the disorientation of the film's protagonist, a Belgian émigré played by the French Catherine Deneuve. The remote location of *Cul-de-Sac*—a coastal stretch of Northumberland, complete with decaying castle—functions abstractly as a sort of elemental, geometrical no-place in which the absurdist sadomasochism of the equally abstruse characters plays itself out. The beautifully designed sets of *Dance of the Vampires* mimic a kaleidoscopic fantasia of an Eastern Europe of the mind, but they are so eccentrically stylized as to suggest that the weird, moonstruck geographies they represent are lost to history—if they ever existed—and can be accessed only through myth or imagination.

These problems of placement are not restricted to questions of nationality or geography. Each of these films is difficult to fit comfortably or fully into the ordinary framework of the art film more generally. *Repulsion* may have mounted a careful, exacting character-study of a disintegrating personality, but it also contained shocking portrayals of violence far in excess of the genteel norms of the art film (compare, for instance, the violence of Bergman's *The Virgin Spring*), and the precedent most commonly invoked in discussion of the film is a highly commercial Hollywood movie, Hitchcock's *Psycho*. *Cul-de-Sac* may have traded in the sophisticated absurdism that was just about the only accepted mode of comedy in main lines of the art film, but the movie combined it with broader comic forms not typically found there, often verging on the burlesque. Splitting the difference between the stark quasi-horror of *Repulsion* and the errant comedy of *Cul-de-Sac*, the outright spoof of *Dance of the Vampires* would seem to have had no place in the art-film category at all. But with its baroque settings, international cast, intemperate dubbing, and pan-European sensibility, there was no place else for it. Maybe that was why the American producers—in a tale of avaricious commerce not unheard of in the annals of the art film—recut it and released it under a title worthy of *Mad* magazine: *The Fearless Vampire Killers, or Pardon Me but Your Teeth Are in My Neck*.

In the sense that Polanski's films locate themselves within both central and marginal strains of the 1960s art film, he is a defining figure, yet his sensibility remains difficult to assimilate to ordinary categories. It does not seem right to call *Cul-de-Sac* his most "representative" work of this period, but it articulates concerns that recur throughout his career—most explicitly in *What?*, *Bitter Moon*, and *Death and the Maiden*—and a closer look at it clarifies the complexity of Polanski's habitation of the art film's criss-crossing territories.

Much has been made in discussion of this film of the absurdist dimensions of Polanski's work under the influence of three main practitioners: Antonin Artaud, Samuel Beckett, and Harold Pinter. Such influence has been evident nowhere more clearly in Polanski's work than in *Cul-de-Sac*. Two key players are cast at least in part for their associations with this tradition. Jack MacGowran had appeared on stage in several works by Beckett, and he is duly cast in *Cul-de-Sac* as the comically inert, inept, dejected, bulbous-nosed Albie. Donald Pleasence had appeared in stage and film versions of Pinter's *The Caretaker*, and his acting in *Cul-de-Sac* is redolent of that earlier work. Pleasence's performance is brittle, self-conscious, and weirdly primal all at once, wrought with epicene indignation, hard double-takes, and prissy slapstick turns—a cross between Edgar Kennedy and Franklin Pangborn. In its story of two odd strangers, refugees from a bungled robbery, who arrive at a remote castle and take the occupants hostage as they await instructions from a mysterious leader, the plot combines the variable nonsense-games of Beckett (the film's working title was *Waiting for Katelbach*) with the hovering menace of Pinter. But despite these influences, it is the first of Polanski's films to articulate his own distinctive sensibility in full, with its peculiar mixture of comedy and pathos (as well as Artaudian cruelty)—of an exacting formal precisionism with unapologetic sensationalism.

Although *Cul-de-Sac* has been called a pastiche,[11] it is hardly a patch-work of absurdist clichés. For one thing, the film's key reference points extend beyond the absurdist lexicon. Of equal importance to that of MacGowran and Pleasence is the casting of Lionel Stander, who plays Dickie, Albie's more presumptuous partner. An oddly imposing, gravel-voiced actor, Stander perfectly conveys a slightly effete quality beneath the character's brute sadism, and he brings a range of associations to the film by his very presence. As a Hollywood character actor in the 1930s and 1940s, he was perhaps best known as a latish member of Preston Sturges's stock company, appearing most memorably in Sturges's darkest film, *Unfaithfully Yours* (1948). With his sharp, caustic drawl, Stander's presence in these films worked through a mode of comic excruciation; as in *Unfaithfully Yours,* he often stood at the periphery of troubled marriages as a sort of oblivious, abject third-banana, combining ele-ments of the asexual and the lascivious, of ineffectuality and threat. Echoes of such roles appear in *Cul-de-Sac,* where Polanski relies upon Stander's distinctive presence to expose the palpable sadomasochism of the comedy.

Perhaps even more significant, however, are Stander's associations with a specific history and culture of exile. One of the few heroes of the Hollywood inquisition during the McCarthy years, Stander vociferously and uncompromisingly criticized the House Un-American Activities Committee (HUAC) in his testimony before that panel, and he was promptly blacklisted. During the 1950s and 1960s (in the margins of a new career in commodities trading), he worked mostly in Europe, often in movies that reflected a certain American malaise that took up where some of the more ideologically sophisticated movies from the pre-HUAC era had left off—"spaghetti-westerns" like *Once upon a Time in the West*

(1969), or anomalous items with post-HUAC undertones like Anthony Mann's *A Dandy in Aspic* (1969) or Martin Scorsese's *New York, New York* (1977). *Cul-de-Sac* features Stander's most interesting performance of this period by far, not least because of the way the film's atmosphere · of dislocation resonates with his own status as a signifier of exile.

It has been suggested that the work of blacklisted exiles from Hollywood had been of a piece in the 1930s and 1940s, the years leading up to HUAC (Andersen 183–85). Their work in the period following is even more unified. Films of the 1950s and 1960s by blacklisted directors living and working in Europe—Jules Dassin, Joseph Losey, Cyril Endfield, John Barry, and others—form a veritable genre. They tend to reconstruct the patterns of American genre movies in European settings (as in Dassin's *Night and the City* [1950], Losey's *Stranger on the Prowl* [1954], and Endfield's *Hell Drivers* [1957]) such that the shift in location estranges typical conventions of their genres, creating disorienting alienation effects. Setting is often treated in an abstract manner, with ordinary markers of place downplayed or withheld (as in Endfield's *Mysterious Island* [1962], Dassin's *Phaedra* [1963], or Losey's *Boom!* [1969], movies that use coastal or island locations in a way comparable to Polanski's). *Boom!* in particular, like *Cul-de-Sac*, mixes the rustic with the gothic, assembles a colorful gallery of grotesques, and makes a darkly sadomasochistic roundelay central to its plot. Not incidentally, despite the broadly European provenances of their productions, these films are typically in English, while exhibiting a haphazard babel of accents, a rich polyglossia that gives them a defamiliarized aspect suggesting states of exile even when the movies do not treat that theme directly. Typically, they are infused with a quality of sadness, even bitterness, that exceeds the simple needs or surface implications of their plots, a feeling that circulates apart from the films' literal content as a disjunct strain of free-floating melancholy.

Though marginal to most accounts of the European art film, this series of movies is quite definitive of the period, and the connection of Polanski's film to this lineage is clear not only in the casting of Stander but in the movie's illustration of every one of the attributes noted above. Stander's Dickie in *Cul-de-Sac* is something like a refugee from an eccentric American gangster film—maybe Kubrick's *The Killing* (1956), since he could be described as part Sterling Hayden and part Elisha

A cross between Sterling Hayden and Elisha
Cook Jr.: Lionel Stander in *Cul-de-Sac*.

Cook Jr.—and his headlong intrusion into the rarefied European domain
acts out an aggressive confrontation of differing cultural orders. At one
level *Cul-de-Sac* is a virtual allegory of the 1960s art film, if we conceive
this as an exploded form, still lingering, that abides as a repository for
a diffuse bounty of conflicting residual energies. Judging from this film
and his subsequent work, that is how Polanski himself understands it,
and though his own status as expatriate may differ from the enforced
exiles of directors like Losey, he joins their efforts to forge a new kind
of European cinema that exceeds the bounds of nation and shares their
concern with exile as a theme and their penchant for staging absurdist
tropes of alienation in a mode of sardonic, gloomy comedy, often as a
confusion of nationalities.

Three of Losey's films of the same time were collaborations with
Pinter: *The Servant* (1963), *Accident* (1967), and *The Go-Between* (1971).
To varying degrees, these films explore Pinter's fascination with the vio-

lence of the unspoken. They turn on relationships destructively mediated by unstated desires or motives and on the troubled symbiosis between willfully concealed secrets and unconsciously repressed impulses. Such themes operate more enigmatically in Pinter's dramas than they do in these films, where Losey's baroque, expressive directorial style serves as an animating counterforce. The scripts remain characterized by the oblique, confounding, minimalist dialogue typical of Pinter, but Losey's extreme camera angles and visual distortions bring the subtexts of these dramas emphatically to the fore. In *The Servant* and *Accident,* Losey uses exaggerated lighting and shadow to play up a hothouse atmosphere of repressed homoeroticism, with characters' shadows mingling in symbolic faux-copulations, even as they go on heedlessly uttering Pinter's fey locutions. This schism seems so forthright, so guileless in its way, that it creates a gap between the sly, clever reticence of the scripts and the excess of the mise-èn-scene, a rift that borders on camp. So direct is this contrast—it is key to the success of the collaboration—it could be said that Pinter's plays are mostly about inescapable repression, teased out as civilization's primary discontent without ever being fully revealed, while Losey's films are about the return of the repressed, exposing what lies under the surface with a blunt grandiloquence so extreme it often edges into the comic.

This example indicates the limits of Pinter's influence on Polanski, which is slight. Closer in spirit to Losey, Polanski deploys some of the same techniques of garish wide angles and sometimes exaggerated deep-focus compositions, though Polanski's visual stylizations are sharper, crisper, and more restrained than Losey's. The film's comedy depends not on the menace of the unspoken but on the unconcealed violence of the directly stated, not on the opacities and frustrations of repressed feeling but on the bitter irony of how desire is thwarted even when it is openly expressed. The cruel world of *Cul-de-Sac* (like those of *What?* and *Bitter Moon* later in the director's career) is one in which people say exactly what they think, no matter how heartless, sparing nobody's feelings; and where, for all that—though a will to power motivates this ruthless candor—events pursue their own logic, relentlessly, entirely outside of anyone's control. The characters in this film may try to gain advantage by hiding their interests or intentions, only to find—in moments of grim comic reversal—that everyone already knows them anyway, and the audience is almost always in on the joke. With malevolent, reflexive hostility, those who inhabit this strange, blighted world compulsively and derisively attribute the basest motives and the meanest characteristics to one another, and although these attributions may be fiercely denied, the joke is that they're usually accurate. The ignorance of Polanski's characters is nearly always fodder for mordant humor, especially since we are usually shown exactly what they are oblivious of, and when they try to hide something from themselves, the bleak ironies of their benightedness are typically clear to the audience.

By the time Dickie saunters into this world, it has fallen. From the start of the film everything is awry, and the incongruously trivial sights he encounters in the opening sequence are signs of a world already out of joint. Gravely wounded, he first sees a kite caught in the telephone wires; next, in quick succession, he witnesses a man flying another kite on the beach, and a woman gamboling with a younger man in the grass. Their frank carnality is imbued with sadism from the start, as they throw a scorpion at each other as part of a teasing sexual game. The woman, Teresa, and the older man, George (played by Pleasence), are husband and wife, and the dodgy, circuitous relay of the film's opening immediately allows us to share Dickie's knowledge of the deception their marriage is based on, an awareness that feeds his scorn. In the next scene, Teresa taunts George by dressing him in a woman's gown and applying grotesque makeup to his face. Teresa's open disdain for her husband is immediately evident, as are most of the feelings and impulses of the characters in the film, but it is tempered by a quality of sad distraction, even a current of tenderness. George's passive acceptance of her weary disdain shows his own inert submission. Clearly, this is a world in which things can't get much worse, where everyone is already beaten down, and where there is no point in trying to conceal one's contempt or despair, or anything else, because the worst has already happened.

George's compelled transvestitism enforces the comedy of humiliation even more forthrightly in the subsequent scene, where the couple confront Dickie, who has sought invasive sanctuary in their house. George's efforts to stand up to the intruder are made ridiculous by his garb, which gives Dickie ammunition for rancorous attacks on his masculinity, and the audience is encouraged to laugh at the cruelty of Dickie's assaults and the sick comedy of George's debasement. Transvestitism turns out to be a handy trope for the particular forms of Polanski's comedy, as it will be later in *The Tenant*. On the one hand, Polanski seems to take a familiar delight, fraught with Milton Berlesque low comedy, in parading such images of men in women's clothing, as he appears to find them creepy and funny in some simple and direct way. On the other hand, they point to some of the deepest features of his comic sensibility as well as to the most superficial. He may see his characters as repressed, or as hiding something, but what he thinks is funny, most often, is how obvious what they're repressing always is, or how little is gained by their machinations of concealment. In Polanski's films, transvestitism emerges as a comic vehicle for this attitude to the extent that it reveals men's internalized misogyny not as something steeped in their unconscious but as something worn on their bodies—George's craven, fearful assent to his wife's sadism in *Cul-de-Sac*, or Trelkovsky's irrational fear of becoming a woman in *The Tenant*. The most comic moments in Polanski's films, as well as the most horrific, occur when some inner dimension of consciousness or some internal effect manifests itself on the surface, is made flesh, suddenly, palpably, and potently. His most basic point seems to be that, especially after the worst has already happened, this is the fate of all subjectivity.

In keeping with this propensity, a long comic set piece in the last half of the film involves a preposterous masquerade, the humor of which lies once again in its utter transparency. Friends of George—whom we've seen at the beginning of the film coaxing him to return to the city from his distant hideaway—reappear for an unannounced visit, and Dickie is obliged to pose as the family valet. He acquits this pretense with no concern for plausibility, as a pugnacious parody of servitude, yet the guests are too involved in their own frivolous caprices and self-interested purposes to pay any attention to the obvious falseness of this charade. Polanski's subsequent work is filled with comparable sequences in which characters impersonate others or engage in ludicrous bouts of role playing (as in the desultory sexual games of *What?* or *Bitter Moon*, or the whole plot of *The Tenant*), and the comic point is almost always to show the hopelessness of the effort. In Polanski's films, selves may lack any integrity of their own, but they are never more absurd than when they try to enact otherness, an attempt they cannot commit to in the first place, identity itself being unfixed yet final destiny, and the ultimate joke.

The most basic transactions between self and other in Polanski are fundamentally sadomasochistic, and in *Cul-de-Sac* the main characters are starkly defined along this sharp axis, as either sadists (Dickie and Teresa) or masochists (Albie and George). The lurid sensations of watching Polanski's seemingly fated but still unpredictable, wayward plots work themselves out often lie in witnessing the fickle, probative ruminations of these positions. When the sadist meets the masochist, it is fairly certain that familiar dynamics of domination and submission will result, and these are typically presented in the films as initially pathetic but increasingly hilarious the more they repeat and even reverse themselves. But what happens when sadist meets sadist, or masochist meets mashochist? In *Cul-de-Sac*, the confrontations between Dickie and Teresa are charged with a potential of violence so tangible it's nearly carnal, while the mute, aloof encounters between George and the dying Albie speak of an acknowledgment too profound to be mutual. There is a poignancy in these transactions that derives from the characters' silent recognitions that misery and death are all that await them—a pathos unexpectedly realized in the film's final, haunting shot of a bereft George crouched on a rock as the tide comes in, crying the name of his dead first wife.

The sadistic or masochistic components of comedy have been noted often and may be exemplified across a range of types. The sadistic joke most often revels in the straightforward mishap, the slip on the banana peel, inviting its audience to delight in the misfortunes of others, to find humor in the residual hostility that Freud claims underlies every joke. The masochistic joke—not without its own reserves of sadism—solicits not aggression but passivity, playing out the variables to an exaggerated degree, taunting the audience by forcing them to take pleasure in the deferral of a punchline that ordinarily concerns prostration, debasement, humiliation, or self-punishment.[12] In film comedy, though often interdependent, these extremes may be seen broadly, on the one hand, in the low comedy of the Keystone Kops or the Three Stooges and the high comedy (so high as to be unrecognizable as comedy in some quarters) of Buñuel's *L'Age d'Or* (1931) or *Belle de Jour* (1968); or, on the other hand, in the work of Buster Keaton, Jacques Tati, or Jerry Lewis.

Polanski's films alternately affiliate themselves with sadistic and masochistic positions of embodiment and subjectivity. As in *Cul-de-Sac*, identifications are rarely located stably within or around a single

Sadist and masochist: Francoise Dorleac and
Donald Pleasence in *Cul-de-Sac*.

character—the two key exceptions in Polanski's work being Rosemary and Tess. Because of these shifting identifications, a final position or emotional vantage point on the film's materials is difficult to extrapolate. The films are as likely to be contemptuous of the sadist's violence or the masochist's vulnerability as they are to express some grudging, doubtful admiration of the masochist's chastity or the sadist's aggression. Despite passing affinities with the sadistic aesthetic of a Buñuel or Pasolini, or the masochistic one of a Von Sternberg, Fassbinder, or Bertolucci, Polanski's sensibility never rests at one or the other point of this dualism. The forms of his comedy, in *Cul-de-Sac* and elsewhere, are perhaps the best illustration of a genuinely sadomasochistic aesthetic at work in Polanski's films.

With its combination of verbal prattle, vaudeville pratfall, and shaggy-dog plotting, *Cul-de-Sac* mixes these modes even more promiscuously than they are usually mingled in his work. As we watch the inexorable tide come in around a car on a beach where Albie is stranded at the beginning of the film, we are encouraged in short order to laugh at his predicament, to feel contempt for his helplessness and pity at his fear, to hope for his rescue, to forget about him for long stretches so that the growing extremity of his plight is even funnier when we are abruptly returned to it later, and to admire the merciless cruelty of the cosmic design that could engineer such a nifty prank. The halfhearted masquerades of George and Dickie are also pertinent examples of the film's comedy of sadomasochism. In different ways both involve appropriation, submission, and subjugation—usurping the role of another, internalizing the demand to do so, and subordinating one's own selfhood in the process. (In Polanski's work, this dynamic finds its fullest expression in *The Tenant,* as it is what the film is largely about.) If Polanski's aim is to portray a stifled world where the brutal, endlessly recurrent interplay of sadism and masochism determines everything—and to make audiences confront their own impulses in these directions—his use of comedy in *Cul-de-Sac* and elsewhere is perhaps the clearest evidence of those intentions.

Because the film's comedy is never without its melancholy side, it is less surprising than it would be otherwise when melodrama emerges abruptly as the dominant note of the film's final moments. In the final shots, as the tide comes up again, we see George perched on a rock surrounded by water, his position as perilous as Albie's in the first scene. This final shot fuses the film's absurdism with its pathos in one last gasp. It culminates a comic metaphor likening George to a turtle, a visual comparison that has lurked under the surface throughout the film, courtesy of Pleasence's expertly performed stylization of his own body—emphasizing a thin neck and protrusive, undersized head, a bald pate and a puffy, larval body, like a cross between Citizen Kane holed up at Xanadu and a mock-turtle without its shell. The film's treatment of George is at its cruelest as we take our leave of him, but this last scene introduces a new element—his grief—that we have not seen in this direct way before. This grief is not derided; like the metaphor of George as a turtle, it is presented as what has been there all along, ubiquitous if unseen.

This reference to Kane may seem far-fetched, but in fact Polanski's films of the 1960s bear striking affinities to the late work of Orson Welles in their styles, their sensibilities, and their senses of scale. This is especially true of *Cul-de-Sac,* which amplifies this affinity by combining it with references to the work of Fritz Lang. The balloon trapped in the wires in the first sequence of Polanski's film, for instance, harks back to Lang's *M.* (1931), in which a similar image also points to a desolate world out of joint. George's hobby of "Sunday painting" recalls that of Chris Cross in Lang's Hollywood movie *Scarlet Street* (1945), a film that also turns on a sadomasochist triangle between a milquetoast, a thug, and a femme fatale.

Such allusions to the auteurs of previous generations were common in the international art film of the 1960s, but Polanski's—more oblique, yet more deeply embedded in the patterns of his films than comparable references in films of the French New Wave, for example—express something closer to kinship than to nostalgia or homage. A comparison to Welles is especially telling in this regard, because the careers of these two filmmakers yield striking points of convergence, however improbable these may seem. Welles's late film *The Deep* (shot principally in 1969 and still unreleased) was based on a 1963 novel by Charles Williams but features a plot that virtually remakes that of *Knife in the Water,* involving an increasingly violent interaction among people alone on a boat. Both directors made versions of Shakespeare's *Macbeth,* and it seems likely that Polanski was drawn to that play at least in part because of the precedent of Welles's adaptation. The final sequence of *Chinatown* is clearly modeled on the climax of Welles's *The Lady from Shanghai* (1948): the mythic return to the urban ethnic district and the delirious anarchy of the final showdown. Though Welles's career yields less in the way of the psychosexual dynamics that interest Polanski, both filmmakers are concerned with the way that forms of dematerialized power infuse material, social relations—a theme each is inclined to treat with absurdist or explicitly Kafkaesque overtones. (Welles, of course, adapted Kafka's *The Trial* as an international art film in 1963, while Polanski capped his theatrical career by portraying Gregor Samsa of Kafka's *The Metamorphosis* on stage in Paris in 1988.)

Like Welles's late films, Polanski's movies of the 1960s combined low budgets with virtuoso technique (including Wellesian long takes and deep-focus) in European settings, with international casts and reconstructed genres pieced together with impromptu ingenuity and various shades of burlesque and seriousness, parody and pastiche. Viewed in this light, Polanski's work is obviously closer in approach to Welles's than to that of the classical auteur most often cited as Polanski's key precursor, Hitchcock. This connection has everything to do with Welles's exile from Hollywood. In one sense, Polanski's movies by the time of *Cul-de-Sac* seem already to have entered a post-Hollywood phase, *avant la lettre*. In another, they seem to be a dry run for an unlikely Hollywood career to come, especially in their willful adoptions of English as a lingua franca of sorts—and that may be where Lang comes in. The Langian influence in Polanski's films derives mostly from the works of Lang's Hollywood period, especially those of the 1950s, when he moved toward a more austere style, the sharply geometrical compositions and crisply engineered plots stoked by a new economy. The constant in this dual affinity is exile—Lang was in exile in Hollywood much as Welles was in Europe after his Hollywood stint—and this kinship is conveyed in Polanski's work of this period by means of a style that combines some of the bitter minimalism of late Lang with the baroque yet makeshift excesses of late Welles, producing a meditation on the condition of exile that makes itself known less as an explicit theme than a pervasive feeling.

A similar atmosphere is already felt in films like Welles's *Othello* (1952), *Mr. Arkadin* (1955), *Touch of Evil* (1958), *The Trial* (1963), and *Chimes at Midnight* (1966), or in Lang's *Human Desire* (1954), *While the City Sleeps* (1956), and *Beyond a Reasonable Doubt* (1956). When Polanski absorbs this kind of atmosphere into his own work, refashioned to express his themes of abjection, it also pays tribute to the drastically reduced scales, by contrast to their earlier films, in which directors like Welles and Lang found such stylistic bounty in their late films. By the 1950s, Welles and Lang were making what amounted to B-movies, and the films Polanski made throughout much of the 1960s are modeled in part on their example.[13] Welles and Lang may have been forced into such diminished economies by the circumstances of their careers, but it is worth noting that as early as 1944, when he was still nominally a Hollywood player, Welles sang the praises of the B-movie as a refuge for art amid the commercialism of Hollywood in a newspaper column about a gutsy, adventurous little film called *When Strangers Marry* (directed by William Castle, who later assisted Welles on *The Lady from Shanghai* and produced *Rosemary's Baby*).

Welles, Lang, and Polanski are all integral figures of the revaluation of filmmaking economies that was staged throughout the 1950s and 1960s as a mounting assault on the philistine mercantilism of the big budget. Evident in the most important trends of the European art film of that time, this incursion was also fully articulated in the celebrations of "underground" movies and "termite art" in the work of the American critic Manny Farber, who argued for the superiority of small movies, "termite" films of no prestige and little pretension—incidentally also singing the praises of *When Strangers Marry* (Farber 56). These films he contrasted with what he called "elephant art"—big-budget, middlebrow studio movies filled with a sense of their own importance. It did not take long before Farber's "underground"—a hectic catalog of brutalist noirs and tight-fisted action films—became conflated with the more common conception of the underground as the "experimental" cinema, as defined, for instance, in Parker Tyler's 1969 *Underground Film,* which canonizes not Sam Fuller, Raoul Walsh, and Anthony Mann but an international coterie of avant-gardists. Farber (who wrote admiringly of Polanski's early films) might have been paving the way for the director's abbreviated Hollywood career and its prolonged aftermath, as Polanski's work goes on to conflate these two senses of the word "underground" systematically; but although his films of the 1960s are not as polemical in their subversions of cultural hierarchies as the semiotic inventories of Godard, say, they are nearly as calculated, and they remain important to an understanding of the cultural shifts under way in the international cinema of the day. With its fiercely modest sense of the absurd, its low-key stylistic pyrotechnics, and its emotional and visual starkness, there is no better example than *Cul-de-Sac* of this emerging paradigm—the art film as B-movie.

Polanski in the New Hollywood

On April 8, 1966, the cover of *Time* magazine carried a provocative question: "Is God Dead?" The editors hastened to point out that the query was not theirs but rather "the startling question hurled at a baffled world by the new theologians" (Ellison 21). It appeared in harsh relief in bold print against a jet-black cover because, as the editors explained, no work of art could be found to represent "a contemporary idea of God." The article that followed was very much a product of its time, just as the cover itself quickly became an iconic emblem of the period. Tracing a familiar arc from Nietzsche's nihilism to Beckett's post-nihilistic absurdism, the article went on to bemoan Soviet atheism and Third World primitivism, deplorable circumstances, according to the author, that deprived well over half the world's population of "any expectation of being summoned to knowledge of the one God" (Ellison 22). Despite the article's show of journalistic neutrality, the initiating question was answered, at least implicitly, with a somewhat predictable reassurance.

To ask it at all, however, especially in such stark terms, was already to broach possibilities of negation or doubt, countering formerly dependable ratifications of affirmative culture. The late–cold war rhetoric of the article belies the patent provocation of the cover—which may explain why the former is forgotten while the latter lingers as a sign of the times, routinely reproduced in visual collages depicting the era and collectively recalled, almost mythically, as a salient effect and a portentous turning point. This particular sign evokes that tumultuous and quasi-revolutionary period during which magazine covers came to seem like acceptable and even reliable indicators, if not sources, of general cultural trends—an era in which the disasters of history finally seemed to coalesce into the outward appearance of apocalypse, with ultimate effect severed from localized cause and surface superseding symbol. As a by-product of this emergent society of the spectacle, the "Is God Dead?" cover bespoke a form of pop-spiritualism on the rise, or a malaise traceable to any one of the definitive calamities of the era yet attributable to none of them.

The *Time* cover turns up significantly in Polanski's first Hollywood movie, *Rosemary's Baby* (1968); it is displayed pointedly as a prop in an obstetrician's waiting room. By that late point in the film, the title character has finally come to believe what the audience has known all along: her husband has promised their unborn child to a cult of witches. She is about to discover that her obstetrician colludes in the apparent conspiracy. So urgent is her immediate situation that it is not clear, as she pages through the magazine distractedly, how she reacts to the peripheral sight of the cover, if she notices it at all. It is not presented for her delectation but, in a swift, canny close-up, for ours. Perhaps we are meant to register the range of associations it signifies, the litany of mishaps, each neatly condensed on an adjacent magazine cover of its own—bombs, wars, assassinations, world-historical uprisings and vanquishments—that made it possible for the question to be asked in that time, place, and manner. It is a joke, proposed with an exacting, deadpan calculation that is characteristic of the movie as a whole. In this

Pop-nihilism in *Rosemary's Baby*.

film in which Satan mounts an extended cameo, decked out in the full demonic regalia of a Hammer horror show, it is a noteworthy irony that God fails to put in an appearance of any kind, however perfunctory.

For many, even in America, the question had been pressing, perhaps even answered, long before *Time* magazine ventured to pose it. Together with dozens of authoritative sources, J. Hillis Miller's magisterial study *The Disappearance of God* (1963) dated that circumstance to the nineteenth century; Albert Camus and Jean-Paul Sartre had already undergone translation and worldwide distribution in the two decades previous; and Ingmar Bergman's somber meditations on God's absence had been brought to the limited masses of the American art house throughout the 1950s and 1960s—though *Time* cited Antonioni as the foremost exponent of existential crisis in cinema. In Gabriel Vahanian's 1961 book *The Death of God*—the first paperback edition of which coincided with the *Time* cover story, effectively forming a critical mass of popular discourse on the issue—the author notes many of the causes of contemporary atheism that *Time* enumerated, including the influence of rationalism, the rise of science, and rapid urbanization, among other general features of post-Enlightenment modernity. But Vahanian argued that as long as the new agnosticism remained restricted to specialized realms of theology or philosophy, as during earlier phases of the Enlightenment, it merely repeated time-honored expressions of doubt that were, however anomalous, as old as religion itself. The transference of such ideas into the sphere of culture was a migration abetted by a new secularism of which it was also a cause, and for writers like Vahanian, what seemed new in the era after World War II was that this skepticism came to infuse world culture more generally and extensively than ever before, so that even the most ardent believers would somehow have to confront it. The blunt subtitle of Vahanian's book told it all: *The Culture of Our Post-Christian Era.*

In film—as socially influential by that time as any branch of American culture—1966 also marked the end of what proved to be a final phase in the fitful cycle of Hollywood's blustery romances of piety. John Huston's *The Bible* and George Stevens's *The Greatest Story Ever Told*, enfeebled aftershocks of the florid biblical sagas of the 1950s, showed once and for all that the era of the straight-faced and reverent yet devoutly nondenominational religious opus was past. The makeshift renaissance that was to run its devious course over the next decade in Hollywood relied on the wholesale abrogation of such traditions, and in the triumph of this new skepticism—only a heartbeat away from the culture of agnosticism—whatever residual effects lingered of a former pop-spiritualism were staunchly channeled into epics of visionary counterculture like *2001: A Space Odyssey* (1968); or, in a remote yet oddly parallel mode, films like *Brother Sun, Sister Moon* (1972), *Jesus Christ Superstar* (1973), or *Godspell* (1973); or else they were diffused into the existentialist parables that accounted for just about everything else of note that the first half of the decade produced: *Five Easy Pieces* (1970), *Two Lane Blacktop* (1971), *McCabe and Mrs. Miller* (1972), to name only three representative titles. In *2001*, despite that movie's telekinetic, quasi-theological delirium, God appears as an extraneous, impervious monolith, while in the existential vein God figures only as an absent tormentor, or a tormenting absence. Either way, the New Hollywood edicts that made pessimism and a novel pop-nihilism the determining facets of an emerging vanguard were fulfilled. In the coming years, Hollywood would fortify itself by posing implicitly, in a host of forms, the very question *Time* magazine had made history by asking outright.

Rosemary's Baby

Rosemary's Baby may not be among the first films one thinks of to exemplify the terms, forms, or conventions of the New Hollywood. Those movies might include *Bonnie and Clyde* (1967), *The Graduate* (1967), *The Wild Bunch* (1968), *Wild in the Streets* (1968), *Midnight Cowboy* (1969), *Easy Rider* (1969), *M°A°S°H* (1970), *2001*, or even *Zabriskie Point* (1969)—all crucial gauges of the era and variously pitched hymns to the greening of America. Still, for a movie set within a few square blocks of a small island—in this case, Manhattan—*Rosemary's Baby* reveals as much as any of them about the conditions of the United States following the speedy demise of the Great Society and just before the interminable malaise of Vietnam and Watergate. *Rosemary's Baby* is less inclined toward overt social chronicle than most of the films commonly associated with the central trends of the New Hollywood, and that may be why its documentation of the time is so compelling. Though intricately connected to the film's main preoccupations—which may be broadly characterized as domestic-hipster-gothic—this documentation appears in the margins of those concerns, as a set of given variables that are taken for granted rather than of novel, determinant factors given full attention as subjects for investigation. For that reason, the world on view in *Rosemary's Baby* seems at once more familiar than that of many other New Hollywood films—in its dailiness, its tacitness, its latency, even its odd occasional glamour—and incomparably stranger, ultimately defamiliarized. It is a world of fierce inequities supporting an appearance of security that crumbles on a dime; of inviting, pristine surfaces concealing unimaginable horrors that, once revealed, turn out never to have been fully hidden in the first place; of underlying yet rampant paranoia that proves insufficient to the real extent of the evils it imagines—a world, in short, in which it makes perfect sense to ask whether God is dead.

A young couple arrives in a baroque New York City apartment building overlooking Central Park. They occupy an apartment vacated by the death of an old woman who has left behind an overgrown herbarium and a slate of enigmatically scrawled messages, including this cryptic plaint that draws the special attention of the young wife: "I can no longer associate myself. . . ." The phrase is only as mysterious as the couple themselves; they too lack any background, any framing context against which to understand them, and if they seem instantly apprehensible, it is only because coupling itself is such a familiar estate. We do not know where they have come from, where they have been living before, how long they have been married, or why—except in the usual sense that people do tend to get married. The film rigorously eschews the extensive, naturalizing backstories of its source novel, and in doing so it immediately hits a brisk, unyielding stride, a severe rhythm, dependent on a headlong momentum that comes from being concerned strictly with the surfaces of things. The movie follows the plot of the bestseller it is based on with an uncanny, nearly unwavering fidelity, but once it strips away the book's novelistic trappings—exposition, psychology, interior monologue—it places itself in a completely different order, to which the equipments of traditional fiction are largely irrelevant. It becomes less about devils, witches, and Satan's brews than about everyday bedevilments, ordinary obsessions, diurnal possessions. Whether the starkly "natural" proves to be even more horrifying once it turns out to contain the improbably "supernatural" remains to be seen. The movie is really about the relation between the falsely rationalized and the merely given.

Another way of putting this is to say that *Rosemary's Baby* is a film about being pregnant. To think that it is one of the few such films in the history of the cinema is a striking perception, considering how normal, natural, and widespread the phenomenon of pregnancy is generally taken to be. Despite this common understanding, the Hollywood Production Code had for decades looked with chagrin at representations of pregnancy and flatly abolished images of childbirth, suggesting how divergent and prone to legislation conceptions of normality really are. The comparatively forthright treatment of the physiology of reproduction on view in Polanski's film is an index of its currency in the context of the New Hollywood. Not only does the movie, like so many New Hollywood films, bring into prosaic view a sight formerly outlawed—in this case that of the pregnant female body, presented in tandem with deceptively casual discussions of menstruation, miscarriage, and abortion. It also reveals what is at stake when that body, installed as an apogee of the natural, is subject to forms of utilitarian social control. According to this film, such naturalization *is* that control, and the fact that Rosemary happens to be giving birth to the devil's spawn only exacerbates a contest over dominion of the womb presumed to be a function of the same norms that produce the foregoing oppression.

The couple, Guy and Rosemary Woodhouse, soon take up with the Castavets, an older, eccentric pair who live down the hall. Almost at once, it is clear that these funny, fussy oldsters are really latter-day Satanists, that they have designs on the younger couple as beacons of fertility, that they secretly—and apparently quite easily—recruit the ambitious young husband to their cause with promises of untold success, and that they thus engineer the impregnation of Rosemary by the devil himself in an elaborate ceremony of ritual rape. Presented in a meticulous, building-block method of narrative construction, these events occupy the first third of the plot, depending for their accumulative impact on a sharp-edged but objective neutrality. Often discussed as an exercise in the unreliability of subjective cognizance, the movie certainly mines the heritage of the paranoid gothic, especially as it edges into the territory of domestic horror, in texts from Charlotte Perkins Gilman's *The Yellow Wallpaper* (1891) to Henry James's *The Turn of the Screw* (1898) and beyond—not to mention movies like *Suspicion* (1941), *Dragonwyck* (1944), *Cry Wolf* (1947), and *The Secret beyond the Door* (1948).

But Polanski's film makes little sense if we discount the straightforward, bluntly unemphatic treatment of its horror plot. The film's effects depend upon the audience's foreknowledge of the terrible conspiracy to which Rosemary is in thrall—as surely as those of *Psycho* rely on our presentiments of that movie's "secret" (that Norman Bates *is* his own mother). Both films point beyond the simple novelty of their plot gimmickry by considering the possibility that secrets are less horrifying in what they conceal than in what they reveal when they are known in advance. The "secrets" of *Rosemary's Baby* are almost entirely rhetorical; from the start, the audience is cued to see through them and invited to participate in the excruciating irony of the fact that Rosemary is the only one who can't. The movie's horror lies not in Rosemary's paranoid imagining of ills that are not there but in her inability to imagine the evils everywhere around her, however instantly visible they are.

Rosemary's Baby thus reverses the conventional logic of the paranoid gothic in tales like *The Turn of the Screw* or *The Yellow Wallpaper.* All three are stories of women's victimization, but the terms differ radically. In James's narrative, a young governess takes a job at a country house and soon begins to imagine she sees ghosts of a dead valet and a former governess haunting the mansion and stalking her little charges. In Gilman's, a wife recovering from illness is confined to her bedroom by a well-meaning but fanatically condescending husband and starts to envision shapes in the patterns of the room's wallpaper, which gradually form themselves into the image of an entrapped woman seemingly bent on violent liberation. As products of a pre-Freudian, fin-de-siècle awareness of the powers of unconsciousness, both stories supply implicit explanations with clear social ramifications—the governess's sexual repression, the wife's domestic oppression—but their meanings depend on a confusion between reality and projection, on maintaining the probability that the characters' visions are warped fantasies or perverse hallucinations. The best to be said for them is that, read progressively, they suggest how inequitable social arrangements of class and bourgeois marriage make women see things.

Whether it is more or less progressive to show how such arrangements *prevent* women from seeing things, that is certainly the tack of Polanski's decidedly post-Freudian variation on the same themes. So little interested is the director in the forces of the unconscious that he hastily dispenses with a crucial subplot of Ira Levin's novel, an extended treatment of Rosemary's lapsed Catholicism that serves as an underlying explanatory motivation, parallel to the backstory of the governess's cloistered childhood in a sheltered parsonage in James's tale. The evils of Polanski's film need not be resolved through any such recourse to psychology, sociology, or even gynecology. They are right before our eyes, presented as brute, material fact, and the only question is how to distinguish them—if at all—from the everyday world of which they are a part.

Polanski's reversal of the traditional logic of the paranoid gothic produces suggestive implications for the film's cultural politics, which may best be described as postfeminist, post–civil rights, and preliberation. It is not clear whether or not Rosemary has read Betty Friedan's *The Feminine Mystique,* a bestseller of 1963, but as a glimpse of the bookshelves confirms, she owns both volumes of the Kinsey Report. The fact that her preferred reading material is Sammy Davis Jr.'s autobiography *Yes I Can* (1965) may suggest a spirit of countercultural enlightenment that refuses to yield to the new dogmas on the rise. In its account of Davis's ascent as a black, Jewish entertainer, that book relates a history of racism and anti-Semitism, but it preserves American mythologies of the triumphant individual by suggesting how slight an adjustment of the social compass was required to accommodate the new needs of civil rights.

The film gives some indication of primal fears about racial otherness lingering under the characters' modish equanimity. A party Guy and Rosemary throw for their hipster friends is a very multicultural affair, part swinging fete and part Warholian factory. Like similar festivities in films such as *Blow-Up* and *Midnight Cowboy,* it is meant to serve as an index of changing mores—it's a Come-Dressed-as-the-Free-Spirit-of-Sixties-Counterculture party—and the film's visual style shifts accordingly in this scene to a faux-verité mode, with handheld camera and freewheeling cuts. Planned as meticulously as the couple's pregnancy, this party's guest list is as stylishly color-coordinated as the décor of their apartment, nonwhites appearing to serve mainly as the fashionable ornaments of a raised consciousness. The same cannot be said of the building's black elevator operator, portrayed as both servile and hostile, who turns a contemptuous gaze at Rosemary in a quick, oblique, unexpected close-up as they ride the lift up to the apartment, and who later haunts her nightmares, clad in a sailor suit of pristine white and snarling ill-tempered commands.

Rosemary herself mixes heavy doses of the New Woman of 1960s liberalism with occasional throwbacks to the old-style wifeliness of bygone days, and her marriage combines the imperatives of up-to-the-minute egalitarian couplehood with periodic regressions to the Dark Ages. Her short, pleated skirts and vernal frocks, frilled or polka-dotted, split the difference between the garb of a modern Miss and the uniforms of a Catholic schoolgirl. The tenor of her interactions with her husband is established in the first scene, as they are shown the apartment by a quirky, fastidious custodian (played by the B-movie veteran Elisha Cook Jr.). Her role is to chortle appreciatively at the private jokes Guy directs at her, tactfully mediate the boyishly impudent jibes he aims at others, tend to the official business while he romps playfully in the background,

and accept with coquettish delight the frisky slaps to the behind he deliv-
ers impetuously from time to time. Although Rosemary demonstrates
some marginal feminist consciousness—she is the one who initiates sex
on their first night in the new apartment—she appears perfectly content
to remain a "homemaker," and a surprisingly large share of the film is
dedicated to showing her decorating the apartment or tending to the
daily chores. Her husband takes her domestic ministrations for granted,
as his entitlement and her duty. On the morning after he has colluded
in her rape by the devil, he rouses her from bed to get his breakfast,
retorting, "Like hell I will!" when told to eat out, and imparting what
looks to be an especially stinging slap to the rump for good measure.

In sketching the contours of this relationship, Polanski's film shows
itself to be unusually mindful of its historical moment as a period of
transition. More typical products of the New Hollywood locate their
own putative radicalism in their registration of social change that they
typically present as already accomplished, if insufficiently accepted or
recognized. *Rosemary's Baby* depicts a social sphere in a state of change,
fraught with emergent and residual energies, where it remains an open
question whether the forces of the new will triumph or dissipate—or
even whether they are anything more than passing fads or fancies, concealing the same old arrangements, ideas, compacts, and structures. Part
hipster, part square, Rosemary and Guy demonstrate the compatibility
of countercultural attitudes with atavistic aspirations of the Eisenhower
era. They want to live the life of the mod and, at the same time, have a
big family in a secure home. As the film shows, these ambitions coexist
as comfortably as the horrifically supernatural does with its everyday
counterparts.

They are compatible in part, in the terms of the film, because what
they have in common is their amenability to trends in their status as "lifestyles." Of the films of the New Hollywood, *Rosemary's Baby* is among
the most eloquent treatments of the new lifestyle-ideology, since it is
chiefly concerned with the domains of home and family. Even more to
the point, it is about "building a home"—especially in a place inhospitable
to that end, a big city where space is at a premium, privacy is largely
unavailable, and property is mostly for rent, not for sale—and about
"starting a family," especially at a time when the traditional domestic
ideology, while still firmly in place, can also be seen, more and more,

as the iniquitous covenant it always was. In this context, what the main characters of *Rosemary's Baby* clearly inhabit are lifestyles, as opposed to lives. Their dress signifies their status and their self-image—Rosemary as ultra-ultra kewpie doll, Guy as neo-beatnik gone straight—and they spend their time acquiring furniture and accessories as seen in the latest magazines. The film keeps a running tab on their activities as consumers, itemized in the pert, dissociated, yet self-satisfied announcements they dispense throughout the film. "We went to see *The Fantasticks!*" Rosemary declares, apropos nothing, as she submits to a blood-test for her obstetrician. "I got that shirt that was in *The New Yorker!*" Guy asserts, out of the blue, repeating a second later, "I got that shirt that was in *The New Yorker.*" "I've been to Vidal Sassoon," Rosemary affirms, returning home with a radical new hairstyle that places her somewhere between austere fashion plate and Falconetti in *The Passion of Joan of Arc.*

In the course of the film we see one admittedly extreme ritual of witchcraft—the rape scene—and countless rituals of homemaking: Rosemary doing the laundry ("Pardon me, but I have to add the softener"), Rosemary arranging the throw pillows, Rosemary measuring out the wallpaper, Rosemary assembling the shelves—and proudly displaying them, like a stock TV housewife, to her unimpressed husband. The point is not that these two forms of ritual amount to much the same thing, though both depend upon clichés of the popular imagination. Rather, the film draws attention to the common role of consumerist acquisition underlying "building a home" and "starting a family" in the age of the lifestyle. For every sprightly montage of interior decoration in the first half of the film there is an equally lively sequence to answer it in the second half, showing the duties, practices, observances, and rites of maternity. Despite the exuberance with which these are undertaken, they assume an edge of bitter poignancy because their uselessness is so obvious from the start: We know, as Rosemary does not, that the worst has already happened.

Though hardly unresponsive to the manic-depressive mood swings of the material, Polanski's camera looks on these orgies of getting and spending with a cool gaze that seems like a mordant acknowledgment of the vanity of human endeavors. Absorbed in the busy futilities of her domestic life, Rosemary pursues the given roles of wife and mother-to-be as if they were sufficient constituents of a real identity, but as so often in

Polanski, the immensity of the character's obliviousness overshadows any possibility of a willed consciousness. The fits of acquisition that occupy much of the film emerge as substitutes for a disavowed superstition and defensive effects of a pseudo-rational mentality. As a comment on the fate of rationalism in contemporary life, *Rosemary's Baby* may be the most lucid statement of that crucial theme in Polanski's work as a whole. As nearly everywhere in Polanski's films, its fate is to disappear in ubiquity—to show itself everywhere and therefore to be nowhere. As Hegel forecasted, in the absence of spirit (or following the death of God, as the case may be), objects assume primary importance as the substance of reality as such. Bereft of inner endowment, they are simply there, testaments of an objective world outside of the self, alight with arbitrary significance but empty of the subjectivity intrinsic to a thing made, induced, contemplated, or valued. In Polanski's work—so paradoxically committed to a precise account of the objective, and never more than in this film—objects have a stubborn obtuseness that is exactly what makes them available for demonic projections. The fact that reality, proposed as a given set of objects, is always and only itself does not mean that it cannot be taken for what amounts to evil, however banal its guises. It means, precisely, that it can be.

To the extent that the objective *is* the rational—or might as well be, in the modern world—it forges conditional hiding places for the occulted, or even, as in this case, for the occult. The narrative of *Rosemary's Baby* depends on an intricate set of relations between objects and events, a series of connections determined by a rigorous and barely submerged logic. Consider the following plot points: In the basement laundry room, Rosemary meets Terry, a young girl who has been taken in by the Castavets. Expressing her gratitude to them, Terry shows Rosemary a pendant they have given her as a pledge of their devotion. In the next scene, Guy and Rosemary return home to find police gathered in the street around Terry's battered corpse. They learn that she has thrown herself from the seventh-floor window. That night they hear Minnie Castavet's shrill voice beyond the bedroom wall: "I *told* you not to tell her—I told you she wouldn't be open-*mind*ed!" Shortly afterward, Minnie presents the pendant to Rosemary as a gift. This sequence of events is tightly constructed around a causal logic that is only slightly eclipsed, and especially in retrospect—though the unswervingly straightforward motion of the narrative leaves little room for backward looks—the actuality behind the oblique plotting is all too clear: informed of the coven's intention to inseminate her with the devil's offspring, Terry has balked and been killed, after which the coven chooses Rosemary to replace her.

Lightly veiled though these events are, the point once again is less the diabolical intrigue of the concealment than the perfunctory nature of the covering. So little concerned do the witches appear to be with hiding their fiendish ceremonies, they carry on with them, full throttle, just behind Guy and Rosemary's marriage bed. The wall that is all that stands between the young couple and these horrors is a thin partition covered in a sickly, jaundiced paper gilded in florid arabesque—strongly recalling the yellow wallpaper of Gilman's tale. Barely serving to divide the rooms, the partition actually connects and mediates, and an uncanny shadow cast upon it from time to time suggests, because of its indeterminate origin, that this insubstantial barrier can literally be seen through. In Polanski's films, though the things of the objective world provide a full complement of possibilities to obscure—behind, beyond, beneath, within—their eerie transparency remains their most striking feature. Even the pendant, presented to Rosemary after Terry's death, is the symbol of a sinister transference so obvious it might as well be stamped on the object's surface, and the charm is lucent enough to reveal the uncomely fungus it contains, exuding an abhorrent reek that would surely be masked if its benefactors were really concerned to hide anything. Instead they chirp, "You get used to it!"—a telling phrase, since the film is ultimately about how it is possible to adjust to the most unspeakable horrors.

A significant rise in popular interest in the occult, as well as in resurgences of old-fashioned superstition, was noted by many cultural commentators in the years after World War II, and by 1968 a watered-down form of pop-Satanism was all the rage. In its least diluted forms, as practiced by figures like Aleister Crowley or Anton LaVey, it organized transgression into ritual as an assault on traditional deism. Such thoroughgoing manifestations of actual devil-worship made their mark on the times; Crowley's 1930 autobiography was republished to some note in 1969, while LaVey founded the Church of Satan in San Francisco in 1966 and published *The Satanic Bible* in 1970. But neither Crowley nor LaVey garnered wide adherence until their precepts were repackaged as anti-establishment postures of libertine rebellion, sexual liberation, or bland, proto–New Age spirituality. This transition occurred through vehicles like the Crowley-influenced Church of Scientology—attracting celebrity followers from its inception—or the assimilation of satanic imagery into the iconography of pop music. Crowley's face, for instance, appears on the cover of the Beatles' *Sergeant Pepper* album (1967), and the Rolling Stones' song "Sympathy for the Devil" also reflects Crowley's influence. In the end, the occult influenced the American imagination mostly as style—a kind of chichi neopaganism, generating paraphernalia to be found in trendy specialty shops or glossy mail-order catalogs, and certifying consumerism as the real American religion.

This boom in the market for things occult was accounted for, variously, by a general postwar malaise and a decline in traditional religious belief, enabling a displacement of spirituality, remade as superstition. Theodor Adorno's dour commentary on this phenomenon in 1952 is so pertinent to the present context that Polanski's film—as well as much of his work in general—could be taken as a virtual gloss on it. Not surprisingly to anyone familiar with his work, occultism was, for Adorno, a regressive reaction-formation to the emancipation of humankind from nature's dominance, converting the mysteries of nature into determinant sectors of an administered mass culture, amounting to a profusion of prepackaged curios and freakish sideshows to be sold to the gullible. As in the prevenient dialectic of enlightenment—wherein fully systematized knowledge conquers the threats of nature but thereby blocks true self-consciousness—so occultism emerges as destructive pseudo-knowledge, an account of reality founded in a terror of reality, a perversion of the "natural":

> By its regression to magic under late capitalism, thought is assimilated to capitalist forms. . . . Occultism is a reflex-action to the subjectification of all meaning, the complement of reification. If, to the living, objective reality seems deaf as never before, they [individuals in general, just as much as occultists] try to elicit meaning from it by saying abracadabra. Meaning is attributed indiscriminately to the next worse thing: the rationality of the real, no longer quite convincing, is replaced by hopping tables and rays from heaps of earth. (*Stars Down to Earth* 129)

Often castigated as paranoiac, Adorno is a theorist of paranoia as a by-product of modernity. Once all zones of experience have been charted, managed, measured, and stratified, he avers, the denatured objects still littering that landscape are made to frolic like so many magicians' rabbits or doves, so that their already-accomplished destruction need never be acknowledged. Emptied of real significance, they speak to each other as if through a medium's crystal ball that stands in for the absent God, with the significance of a false affinity governed only by the happenstance of their random configurations.

Polanski's work too deals with structures of paranoia understood as debilitating and inevitable by-products of modernity. The difference is that where Adorno is concerned with exposing mass delusions (though he harbors little hope of correcting them), in Polanski's films just about any conviction—or any lack of conviction, for that matter—is founded in misconception, delusion being seen as the basis of belief itself. Thus there is little to choose between committing to one true faith, accepting a verifiable fact, holding to a chimerical reality, or wholeheartedly believing a deception. Belief and skepticism, for Polanski, are attitudes with a parallel logic of their own, quite distinct from the realities they claim to construe. To that extent, they embody "the subjectification of meaning." According to Adorno, in the modern world "spirit is dissociated into spirits and thereby forfeits the power to recognize that they do not exist" (*Stars Down to Earth* 129). The most elegant paradox of *Rosemary's Baby* is that we are asked to view superstition in just this light, and then to accept the generic contrivance that the witches *do* exist. The latter conceit is subject to some passing doubt in the course of the film but coolly verified once and for all in the final scene; in context, this scene presents a chilling consummation of the film's treatment of human alienation from an indifferent reality that pursues its own opaque purposes, a condition seen as so pervasive that it is impervious to proofs or confirmations. Doubt reality or credit illusion, distrust the visible or believe the evidence of your senses—in the world of Polanski's films, more pessimistic in their way even than the philosophy of Adorno, it all comes to the same thing. The worst will still happen, because it already has.

It is not until the final scenes of the film that Rosemary begins to express even a vague awareness of the plot against her. Even upon learning that her neighbors are descended from notorious Satanists, even with the prompting of a skeptical friend who leaves a series of obvious posthumous clues after he has been dispatched by the coven, Rosemary remains oblivious. It is only when she haphazardly ciphers the meanings of a few chance objects in relation to one another—the pendant, a swapped necktie, a missing glove, and (in a nod to Hitchcock's *Suspicion*) the inscribed tiles of a Scrabble game—that she finally draws the unavoidable conclusion. Kept at a distance for two-thirds of the film, paranoia creeps back in with a vengeance in the delirious last stretch, when everything that had seemed simply adventitious suddenly appears linked up with everything else in a sinister chain of coincidence allowing no way out, a mechanism so complex that, despite its inordinate logic, it cannot be understood except in terms of a foundational irrationalism. According to Adorno, such morbid perceptibility is nothing but common experience in the administered, post-deistic world, where "people even of supposedly 'normal' mind are prepared to accept systems of delusions for the simple reason that it is too difficult to distinguish such systems from the equally inexorable and equally opaque one under which they actually have to live out their lives" (*Stars Down to Earth* 115). For her part, it seems that Rosemary just can't win, as we are invited to consider her delusional only in the few minutes of the film in which she finally awakens to the unthinkable reality we have been inwardly enjoining her to grasp all along. That being the case, it would seem that, in the logic of the film, we can't win either.

The "subjectification of meaning" happens when objects are alienated from the subjects for whom they might formerly have constituted a given, immanent, nondiscursive rationality. After that, meaning—which might have inhered within objects—can only be conferred on them from without, in the manner of that aggrandizing reification that, says Adorno, is its complement. Just as reification endows the immaterial—work, exchange, value—with a gross substantiality in the service of capital, so this subjectification takes objects as the instruments of its program, no longer a grandiose, divine master plan but a series of intermittent, localized, and conflicting schemes. That this has occurred goes without saying in all of Polanski's films; it is, in large measure, what they are about. If the subjectification of meaning is seen as the inevitable consequence of the death of God, or the concerted withdrawal of any conceivable deity from the world, the films are still too cold-bloodedly dedicated to rendering that outcome to lament the absence of God—à la Bergman, say, whose tortured epicedia amount to a naked plea for some deity to be restored, at least as an idea. That impulse or wish is inconceivable in Polanski, where everything seems far too matter-of-fact to be an aftermath and too far gone for redemption.

The dazzling and trenchant stylishness of *Rosemary's Baby* lies in its emphasis on the surface of things. The saturated colors, the crisp textures, the hard, sharply focused light that seems to have no source and cast no shadows—these elements conspire to proclaim that we are in the world of the now, that modern world of chic fashion and glittering commodity, where everyone knows, as Rosemary herself remarks, "there *are* no witches, really." Especially in the first half, the tempo of the film, relentlessly brisk yet unhurried, strictly trains this concentration on the outer world through the clean, incisive editing, so curt that the soundtrack, also fiercely controlled, can barely keep up with it. Sounds overlap from shot to shot with such bluntness, yet with such seeming casualness—the film helped to make such overlapping sound an overnight cliché in the New Hollywood—they seem to be simply another part of the external objects, indurate yet crystalline, that make up the general surround. The film moves forward with a steep drive that does not pause to concern itself with inner dimensions, which are relevant only to the extent that they foster the subjectfication of meaning, turning insensitive objects into pointed, indicative, graphic, if ambiguous, signs—a pendant into a talisman, a wall into a screen, a toaster into a mirror, an airplane into a portent, a book into a palimpsest.

The subjectification of meaning might seem to give a great priority to dimensions of human subjectivity, endowing it with the power to animate things with a new significance, but in fact, for Polanski as for Adorno, it is only further residuum of damaged life, the function of a constitutive solipsism, an insulated selfhood diminished and panic-stricken by its banishment from the objective world, seeking vengeance by imposing itself on what it can no longer comprehend. Chiefly concerned with the fate of subjectivity in the modern world, Polanski illustrates its oblivion in *Knife in the Water* and *Cul-de-Sac* and its implosion in *Repulsion*, suggesting that it is destined, in its exile from outer reality, for evacuation or collapse. As an essay on the mutilated subjectivities of mass modernity, *Rosemary's Baby* examines both possibilities. Presented for the most part as comical grotesques, nowhere more insistently than in the final scene, the witches enact a series of gratuitous clichés that are nothing but straightforward reversals of the tenets of Christianity, no less ridiculous for being performed in the service of an actual embodied—and quite ludicrous—demon. Their rituals are satirized not for being profane or sacrilegious but for being inane and banal, right out of old horror movies.

Amid this loony pageant, sensitive and earthbound Rosemary, with her touching aspirations to normality and ordinary happiness, is the only one in whom some semblance of inner life lingers. If the mechanized pseudo-rationality of the modern has abrogated the interior spaces of selfhood, all that is left is action—to talk and to do—and in Polanski's films, that is mostly what we see. Surrounded by characters typical of Polanski, in that they are benumbed yet energetic figures who can only act, Rosemary also thinks, feels, hopes, and dreams. Her demeanor thus recalls that of Carol in *Repulsion,* whose stubborn yet fragile interiority at first seems freakish simply because it appears to exist, then becomes genuinely horrific because it apparently no longer can. Polanski's probing, intransigent camera is equally stubborn in its compulsion to find this interior and render it as mute spectacle, but the film's stringent despair comes from a sense of its own failure, ending where it started, with a fixed and adamant image of the space beyond or within Carol's eye as pure, impalpable darkness.

From the start, by most measures, Rosemary is a more recognizable kind of person than Carol, a circumstance that could make her all the more frangible if taken to signify the standardized or the commonplace. Her dreams are repositories of random memory, trifling fantasy, and collective fancy. She dreams of yachting with the Kennedys and hobnobbing with the Pope, and though the experience of being raped by the devil momentarily breaks the prophylactic tissue of these protective hallucinations, it is quickly assimilated to allow the dream to go on as usual—or the ritual to proceed as if it were a dream. Polanski's relative lack of interest in these dreams' content is evident in the handling of the first one, Rosemary's memory of her participation as a child in a swindle in a competition at Catholic school, and of her subsequent confession to her complicity. In the novel, the scene is a key part of the subplot involving Rosemary's Catholicism, her guilt, and her longing for absolution, and the action is presented clearly through extended exposition. In the film this subplot is all but gone, and the dream is inexplicable and enigmatic. The scene begins with a close-up of Rosemary, seeming fully awake, staring at the wall above the bed. A shifting series of images appears on the wall, ending with a close-up of a furious nun and a quick pan to a gruff worker, to whom Rosemary, still lying awake and looking up from below, whispers urgently yet almost inaudibly—"I told Sister about the windows and she eliminated us from the competition!"—as the camera tilts vertiginously and the scene quickly fades.

Unsettling and disorienting, these dreams appear as fleeting, quicksilver projections, volatile and kaleidoscopic images of estranged consciousness. In realizing them, Polanski insists on the sense in which they appear to exist outside of Rosemary, just as she is apart from them, gazing up at them from her bed with the dazed curiosity of a detached spectator. They illustrate a converse principle to the subjectification of meaning: the objectification of subjectivity. In the world of Polanski's films, solipsism answers the paranoia it produces; once things are cloaked in the significance his characters give them, consciousness itself cannot escape the inevitable consequence of this condition. Stripped of spontaneous being, compelled to a doomed self-sufficiency and compensatory but futile acts of will, it too becomes a thing, no longer justified simply in its self-surrender to a deity but subject to the same uses, manipulations, and exploitations that haunt any other object. Like Carol's hallucinations in *Repulsion*, Rosemary's dreams are fevered visions that torment her with the half-knowledge that she cannot escape into herself. That private, interior province has already been invaded, deprived of refuge, and forced outside. That the space of dreams has somehow become horribly permeable, letting demons out and monsters in, is further evidence of the dissolution of a boundary that, even if it was never really there, might have preserved an order in which things could be just what they were and people could dream in peace.

"This isn't a dream—this is really happening!" Rosemary cries in the midst of the longest, slyest, vilest, and most baroque of the film's dream sequences, when she is confronted with the piercing eyes of the devil. (Rumor had it that the devil was embodied by none other than Anton LaVey himself, who was also said to have served as a "consultant" on the film, but tantalizing as this gossip may be, all relevant parties deny it.) It is an instant of explosive self-awareness that comes to nothing. In the next shot—horrific yet comically anticlimactic—Satan copulates with her strenuously, as she, peering over the devil's palpitating shoulder, conducts a prim colloquy with the Pope. In Polanski's work, these moments of self-consciousness never amount to much, pointing to an inescapable double-bind: though the realities and outcomes are always more terrible than anyone could have guessed, the director's characters are endlessly castigated (often in a spirit of sardonic glee) for their obliviousness and paranoia. Even paranoiacs have enemies, Polanski's films attest, and even if the worst horrors prove to be incontrovertibly true, that does not mitigate the crazed fantasies by which we have conceived them—or from which we have projected them, since what is bluntly and physically real still lends itself to tortured imaginings. Often considered an explorer of the fine line between reality and illusion, Polanski is little interested in that well-scrutinized divide. He is less concerned with a confusion between dream and reality—in the manner of the surrealists, for instance—than with showing that the final choice of which is which, momentous as it can seem, does not matter much in the end.

For all that, Polanski's demeanor in *Rosemary's Baby* only *seems* heartless, and the power of the film's ultimate effect derives from counterpointing this appearance of cruelty against an intensity of empathy for Rosemary—an intensity unequaled in Polanski's work, if only because not attempted, until *Tess*. Rosemary's forced impregnation is the film's primary example of the ruinous breach of the divide between subject and object, inside and outside, and the delicate treatment of her abiding, remnant interior life is perhaps the clearest indication in Polanski's work that he might be inclined to defend subjectivity were he not convinced that doing so would be sheer naivete.

From the start of the film, Rosemary's aspirations to normality are treated as touching and vaguely hopeless. The extent to which bureaucratic mechanization has trickled down into everyday life can be seen in the fastidious care with which Rosemary plans, makes appointments, circles dates on the calendar, tallies lists, orders her days. The pat, chipper, and slightly defensive reply with which she answers repeated inquiries into her husband's not-yet-successful acting career—"He was in *Luther* and *Nobody Loves an Albatross,* and he does a lot of television and radio"—is not unlike her stock response to nosy questions about whether she wants children. She does, of course: three, to be exact, two boys and a girl—and "it would be nice if the first one were a boy."

As a theme, pregnancy is so tied up with ideas about interiority that it seems inevitable that Polanski should have taken it as a subject. In doing so, he exploits the conflation of secular and spiritual discourses in constructions of American motherhood. In the language of cliché, each pregnancy is a "miracle," a "blessed event," yet it is also a bodily function with a vast industry of support and regulation built up around it, spawning a mass of commodities as plentiful as those supplied to Better Homes and Gardens. Rosemary's "maternity" clothes can be every bit as stylish as her everyday wardrobe only because the business of fashion implements a market niche geared especially for the mod pregnancy, for the new mother that the New Woman will still inevitably become. The self-help books Rosemary reads for information on the physiology of gestation provide a form of empowerment that might conceal or outweigh those books' status as a line of goods as vendible as the cribs, dolls, and rocking chairs that Rosemary and Guy acquire in the same avid spirit of consumerist bliss with which they furnish their house.

The production of an expansive commercial market based on motherhood, the film makes clear, depends not on challenging the spiritualized vocabularies it might be seen to endanger but on sustaining them, and Rosemary never seems to doubt that her pregnancy is a sanctified extension of her inner life. In the first half of the film, she talks to herself, in the second half, to her unborn baby, and the two forms of address are strikingly congruent. The more her pregnancy isolates and pains her, the more she turns for comfort to her sense of the being inside her, even when her only remaining comfort is to try to save the child—as in the heartrending moment when, trapped and in labor, she is held down on her bed by the witches, and she cries out to her baby, "I'm sorry, my darling, forgive me!" What she does not know, what gives her plaint its special pathos, is that it is already too late, that the baby cannot be saved, that her insides have already been plundered. Pregnancy may make interiority literally, materially visible, but it does not make it any more apprehensible, except by those who would exploit it.

Rosemary's pregnancy repeats her pattern of trying to normalize her life by ordering it. Hers appears to be an ordinary middle-class pregnancy, expertly self-managed and mediated by the latest advances in status, marketing, and technology. Her celebrity obstetrician ("He was on *Open End!*") discourages Rosemary's managerial zeal, directing her away from the self-help books she reads, but she devours them anyway—and later, after learning of this, he scolds her, vindicated: "And all it did was worry you!" What we watch, in the course of this film, is an exceedingly well-planned and painstakingly administered modern gestation period. It is also an excruciating exercise in dramatic irony. We know what she doesn't: the worst has already happened, and yet Rosemary goes on, blithely planning, managing, and ordering in her prim, self-custodial complacency. The plot replicates in the sphere of private life the operations of modern societies that build their complexes of bureaucratic officialdom, supposedly to stave off further destruction, whether knowingly or not, upon the foundation of their own ruins.

Chinatown

Polanski's second and final entry in the New Hollywood heat differs from *Rosemary's Baby* in being reversionary instead of revisionist. *Chinatown* is the slickest, smoothest film of Polanski's career, a precise simulation of a meticulous, dispassionate job for hire, until a fervent coda in the final ten minutes reverses the temper of what has gone before. *Chinatown* is at the opposite end of the New Hollywood spectrum from *Rosemary's Baby:* its setting is Los Angeles, not New York; it takes place in a vaguely romanticized past, not a defamiliarized present; and it trades in an ambivalent nostalgia, presuming to revive instead of revamp a hoary old genre. Yet *Chinatown* elaborates its pastiche of film noir as a critique of the old Hollywood ideologies, and like *Rosemary's Baby,* it is about the functions of evil in everyday life after the rise of modernity and the death of God.

Considered in terms of genre, what is most striking about the film is how little it resembles visually any of the main touchstones of film noir that it evokes thematically. Shot in the glossy tones of Technicolor, *Chinatown* shares little of the dark, dense, black-and-white expressionism of the genre's 1940s cycle. Compared to contemporary neo-noirs like Robert Altman's *The Long Goodbye* (1973), Polanski's film resists almost perversely any hint of the chiaroscurist palette—until that final scene, which reverts with a bleak sense of abandon to a more typically noirish style. In place of the grainy night-shooting of Altman's film, *Chinatown* features sun-drenched deserts and cityscapes and moon-washed night-scapes with a crisp, metallic, sapphirine tincture. Under the influence of Raymond Chandler, many 1940s noirs were set in California—*The Maltese Falcon* (1941), *Double Indemnity* (1945), *The Big Sleep* (1946), and secondary examples like Andre de Toth's *Pitfall* (1948) or Douglas Sirk's *Shockproof* (1950)—and sometimes these films generated their frissons by showing how little illumination is cast on the darkest events by the light of day, with the washed-out floods of the studio often standing in for the California sun—a crucial exception being the blanched exteriors at the beginning of *Double Indemnity*. With its preponderance of loca-tion shooting, and scene after scene set in an intense brightness that is burnished and blistering, *Chinatown* goes those movies one better by placidly displaying the corruptions that take place in broad daylight.

As a form of "blood melodrama"—in Graham Greene's striking phrase—film noir melded the primal imagery of sex and violence from popular entertainment to the concerns with subjectivity and depth psy-chology of modern art. This combination produced a strain of vernacular modernism, as James Naremore argues in his trenchant study of the genre, characterizing the link as follows: "Like modernism, Hollywood thrillers of the 1940s are characterized by urban landscapes, subjective narration, nonlinear plots, hard-boiled poetry, and misogynistic eroti-cism; also like modernism, they are somewhat 'anti-American,' or at least ambivalent about modernity and progress" (*More than Night*, 45). Indisputable as a description of what we might call the high noir, Nare-more's explication is less applicable to a film like *Chinatown*. Especially noteworthy in this light is the film's complete avoidance of the subjective dimensions or techniques that are staples of the genre, such as voiceover, skewed narrative perspectives, or point-of-view camerawork. Placing the action in the 1930s—historically before the advent of the golden age of noir—*Chinatown* seems in an odd way as forward-looking as it does atavistic; its modernism resides in a particular way of understanding the past. With its caustic nostalgia, Polanski's film portrays a mythic point of origin that renders subjectivity and agency alike obsolete.

The myth in question is well known—that of Oedipus—and a long line of critics interpreting Polanski's film have seen that legend as an explicit intertext. Despite this persisting line of thinking, the Oedipal undercurrents of *Chinatown* are not immediately obvious. The plot concerns a slick, slightly oily private eye named Jake Gittes who is hired to follow a city official suspected by his wife of infidelity. In short order, Gittes discovers a much larger crime, a plot to divert water from a drought-stricken valley to enable a profitable annexation of this land by the city and to secure entrepreneurial ownership of public utilities. Behind this convoluted scheme is a tycoon with the mythically inflected name of Noah Cross, and as Gittes discovers the extent of the plot, he becomes increasingly involved with Cross's daughter, Evelyn Mulwray. The plot twists: Hollis Mulwray is the name of the official Gittes was following, but though Evelyn is his wife, she is not the woman who hired the detective to trail him. That woman turns up dead, Hollis is murdered, and it becomes clear that Gittes has been enlisted as a pawn in the larger conspiracy. Though this summary omits crucial turns, it conveys something of the willful intricacy of the narrative, which culminates with the final revelation that Cross and Evelyn have produced a daughter together.

This disclosure of incest forms the basis of the claim that *Chinatown* is "an Oedipal text,"[14] but this argument typically departs from the more general sense, promoted by Raymond Bellour and others, in which Hollywood cinema is said to build upon Oedipal foundations. Bellour argues that the main thrust of Hollywood cinema is to reinforce patriarchal attitudes by compulsively narrating tales of male ascensions to power and a "proper" masculinity. This triumph is predicated on resolving blockages or fixations that are linked to hostile or rivalrous relations with actual or surrogate father figures: once these are overcome, the hero achieves a climactic identification with symbolic fathers and learns to embody patriarchy himself. The 1940s cycle of film noir figures prominently in these formulations, especially by way of Bellour's analysis of *The Big Sleep*. Yet few would argue that *Chinatown* is an Oedipal text in this sense of the phrase. If anything, the film systematically deconstructs such foundations, depicting a world polluted and destroyed by patriarchal control, exposing the symbolic father as evil incarnate in the figure of Noah Cross, and insisting on the ultimate failure of Jake Gittes to assume some final position of patriarchal authority.

The death of the woman, however—a common generic feature of noir—remains constant. If classical Hollywood routinely sacrificed women in the name of patriarchal triumph, the New Hollywood sacrificed women to underline its newfound sense of patriarchal oppressiveness. Clearly, this continuity demonstrates a misogyny that persists as a remnant of the Oedipal underpinnings of Hollywood *tout court*. Still, the primarily psychosexual attributions of this argument seem misplaced when applied to *Chinatown*. In some literal sense, as suggested above, Polanski's film is *anti*-Oedipal. One could advert to Deleuze and Guattari in their more dystopian moments to work out the argument systematically with reference to concepts like the body as "desiring machine": In *Chinatown*, sex is little more than reflex, passion a game that mistakes "molecular" motives for "molar" universals. And like Deleuze and Guattari, Polanski always insists on enigmatic dimensions of consciousness that exceed or escape controlling discourses, such as those of psychoanalysis. If, in the end, they cannot escape, they still try, even when it means death—as it does for Evelyn Mulwray.

In another sense, *Chinatown* is Oedipal to a fault. It is not the Oedipus of Freud, however, but of Sophocles, whose definitive rendering of the legend emphasizes the portrayal of a diseased polity. In that tragedy, it is ultimately discovered that the community's ills are founded on the transgressions of its leader, but because these are unwitting, the play ultimately serves as a commentary on a fate so inexorable, it metes out punishments for actions regardless of the intentions behind them.

Returning to *Chinatown* after reading the critics, one is struck by how little the movie emphasizes its psychosexual subplot and how much it attends to civic intrigues. Several commentators have remarked on the importance of the relation between these levels of the plot, but most argue that the incest plot trumps the water plot.[15] Most of the film, however, concerns municipal wrangling surrounding public utilities of water and power—an odd plot emphasis, come to think of it. Much is made in comic terms of Gittes being out of his element investigating such matters, by contrast to his usual bread-and-butter work of following errant husbands and wives. That work is treated with wry humor from the first scene, in which a client laments comically over photographs of his wife's infidelity. The water plot, meanwhile, treated with unstinting, portentous gravity, shows scene after scene of the detective probing sluices, roaming deserts, staking out reservoirs, and wandering riverbeds. All these investigations are fruitless, but they are especially futile if we

Water and power: Jack Nicholson as Jake Gittes in *Chinatown*.

assume that the explosive revelation of the final moments eclipses the plot that has consumed so much of the film.

What is clear is how the incest plot, once revealed, disrupts the classical structure of the narrative that has been so carefully preserved, even to the point of bringing back at the film's climax the cuckolded husband from the opening scene to resolve even this minor subplot. Until the last scene, the story's progress, though enigmatic in its way, is also quite linear, proportional, stably pursued, and causally determined. Early in the film, when Gittes touches a nerve while questioning Evelyn, he attempts to appease her by saying, "It's nothing personal, Mrs. Mulwray"—to which she replies tartly, "It's *very* personal, Mr. Gittes." By exposing just what is "personal" in this situation, the revelation of the incest plot forcibly upsets the film's equilibrium, spinning it into a realm of anarchic devastation in its final moments. Certainly the apocalyptic power of this climax merits the claim that the incest plot has been the underlying cause of everything all along, even if it is granted only a few minutes of actual screen time. Equally clear is the fact that this disclosure resolves or forestalls nothing: disaster follows anyway. As in Sophocles, and contrary to Freud, the final revelation is destructive, not curative.

It is well known that Polanski insisted on changing the original ending of Robert Towne's script. In Towne's version, Evelyn triumphs over Cross in a final showdown when she shoots him—a climax Towne recycled in a different form in his own later film, *Tequila Sunrise* (1988). In Polanski's film, Evelyn is killed by a cop's bullet as she flees with her daughter, who is subsequently taken away by Cross. As in most of Polanski's films, the abortive attempt at escape cannot succeed because the worst has already happened: the ending implies a Sophoclean fate that irrevocably connects the water plot and the incest plot. In the name of Manifest Destiny and property rights, Cross has defiled his daughter and raped the valley. (The historical events on which the film's plot is based were popularly known as "the Rape of the Owens Valley" from 1933 on.[16]) These dual violations compromise the distinctions between public and private action because there is no way to rank Cross's private lust and public greed as moral depredations, even when both have been rendered equally visible.

Polanski's style is held in check throughout much of the film so that its power is all the greater when it comes back with a vengeance in the final scene. It is one of a sequence of macabre street scenes in Polanski's work, like the one in *Rosemary's Baby* outside the apartment building when Terry's suicide is discovered, or in *The Tenant* when Trelkovsky tries one last time to flee his imagined captors. Often these scenes concern last-ditch efforts to escape that fail horribly, and in *Chinatown,* the final scene builds to a delirious pitch of anarchic calamity in which an irrevocable loss of human agency is felt as palpably and hopelessly as it is anywhere in this director's work. The whole scene has a Möbius-strip anxiety, images calibrated with a crisp, deep focus, even though all the action is staged in the extreme foreground, leaving little in the depth of field but an enveloping, eerily luminous darkness, the camera tilting from face to face, action to action, body to body, each contorted yet still, like figures in an El Greco painting. The general effect is of chaotic action and complete paralysis—of all hell breaking loose and rigor mortis setting in at the same time—and the action seems predetermined yet totally accidental, as when the cop shoots Evelyn. When Evelyn pulls the gun on Cross, the camera dips wildly to show the gesture only seconds after it is completed: we register the spasm of her movement before we see its cause, as if to suggest the potent force of her action and its utter futility in the same moment. Her death is the only event staged in depth, with a long shot of her far-off car, the stuck horn wailing.

Polanski's principal service to the New Hollywood was to coax it into some semblance of adulthood by giving it a powerful shot of old-world nihilism mixed with an up-to-the-minute stylishness. Less radical than *Rosemary's Baby*—which went some distance toward reinventing the horror film—*Chinatown* displays this combination at first in the form of a seemingly familiar throwback. While *Rosemary's Baby* springs full grown from its maker's head as a full-fledged novelty, *Chinatown* starts with a cute anachronism—a view of the Paramount logo from the 1930s—and makes its way to a conclusion that provides one of the most compelling examples of fatalism in American movies since Von Stroheim's *Greed* in 1924. The film shows its own awareness of how it enacts this inexorable progression by concluding with a coyly bookended image of the modern-day Paramount logo. By the end of *Chinatown*, it could really be said that the New Hollywood had finally arrived, though it was destined to depart quickly. Even after the success of *Rosemary's Baby*, Polanski's second American film—some six years later—could still have been only the start of an illustrious Hollywood career. Instead, perhaps fittingly, it was the end of one.

Polanski and the Art Film's Second Wave

To call the period after the cresting of the *nouvelle vague* the "second wave" of the art film is an obvious misnomer, given the long and various history of that cinema. Yet, without wishing to exaggerate its influence, the New Wave does inaugurate approaches, disseminate themes, and popularize sensibilities without which the subsequent developments of the international art film in the 1970s and 1980s would be difficult to imagine. In a book called *Second Wave* (1970), Ian Cameron justifies this designation by alluding to the special status of the New Wave and the revival of international film culture that followed it:

> In the wake of the New Wave . . . has come more formal discussion about the cinema than there has been since the abortive theorizing of the

twenties. This process undermined many of the preconceptions about film which had been accepted equally by the "commercial" and "art" cinemas. . . . The New Wave has provided not so much the inspiration for the films described in this book—many of them were made before their directors had seen films by Godard and the rest—but has created the pre-conditions for their acceptance. And, in any case, the spirit in which these films were made paralleled, if it did not actually echo, that of the New Wave. (5)

According to Cameron, these films managed to escape the values that tied capital-intensive cinemas like Hollywood to a mass audience. Thereby, they were able to confront realities of contemporary experience in new ways unimaginable in popular commercial cinema or even, increasingly, in the New Wave itself. And that, says Cameron, was the birth of the "second wave."

The films of the New Wave were animated by a distinctive social consciousness, but it was often infused by a palpable anxiety regarding the films' own position in the marketplace. As early as *Hiroshima, Mon Amour* (1959), this anxiety is seen in one character's deceptively casual epigram: "They make films to sell soap—why not a film to sell peace?" A fear of selling out underlies Godard's work especially—most obviously in *Contempt* (1963), about a crass American producer trying to buy the services of a serious writer to make a dumbed-down movie version of Homer's *Odyssey*—and this fear could be said to have been what ultimately put an end to the movement. Godard denounced his Italian disciple Bernardo Bertolucci for going Hollywood with *The Conformist* (1970), and he broke with other colleagues, including François Truffaut, after vitriolic accusations about the growing commercialism of their work. Despite the New Wave's constant incorporation of reference points from popular culture, the films of the movement retain a devoutly modernist disposition that often elevates the materials they seemingly embrace by assimilating them into a context of parody, intellectualism, and self-reflexive critique.

The second wave aligns itself with a more postmodern disposition. The locus of production moves ever further east from Western Europe—to Poland or Yugoslavia (in the work of Dusan Makavajev or Jerzy Skolimowski, two of Cameron's principal exponents)—or away from Europe altogether, to Japan, South America, or Canada. These films adopt a free-ranging internationalism to complement their resolute postcolonialism (as in the films of others cited by Cameron, like Bernardo Bertolucci, Ray Guerra, Glauber Rocha, Gilles Groulx, and Jean-Pierre Lefebvre). Though these films, like those of the New Wave, often draw upon pop-culture references, as in Makavejev's wildly encyclopedic *WR: Mysteries of the Organism* (1971), they do so less in a spirit of parody or pastiche than of inclusiveness or affiliation. Little concerned with protecting themselves against forms of cultural contamination, these films express almost no fear of selling out, either because they're pretty sure nobody's buying anyway, as in Makavejev, or because they see no problems with articulating their ideas via the logic of the marketplace, as in certain films of Bertolucci or Nagisa Oshima—or the later work of Makavejev.

A decisive feature of this wave is precisely that it is *not* a movement but rather a condition or a situation, so that these films often seem even more freewheeling than their New Wave counterparts because they are less bound to shared aesthetic or cultural aspirations. The New Wave may have set itself against the Tradition of Quality, but this second wave proceeds as if there were no such tradition in the first place. By comparison to the self-reflexive, formalist modernisms of the New Wave, these films move toward a carnivalesque diffuseness, reveling, at times, in bad taste or in a developing "trash" aesthetic that is both cultish and more directly communicative, in its way, than the work of most art cinemas that precede it.[17]

Just as he was a key figure in the art film's initial postwar phases, so Polanski is central to this second wave. While the director's themes remain relatively constant, the tone and the treatment shift slightly, at least to the extent of exaggerating certain features of his earlier work. If the first ten years of his career showed proclivities toward disreputable material, these were often balanced against a decisive social or cultural critique. In certain of Polanski's later films, these proclivities are pushed to an extreme—beginning with *What?*, the film that initiates this phase of his career—while often leaving behind the imperative of a modernist critique to legitimize them. Polanski's movies continue to be difficult to "place" nationally, yet they are almost always seen in a negative relation to Hollywood filmmaking—as the work of other figures in this second wave are not, because they are perceived not as renouncing Hollywood but simply ignoring it. In Polanski's case, however, his Hollywood stint leaves its mark on the rest of his career, so that various narratives of decline, triumph, or pathos that attach themselves to his name after *Chinatown* alternately figure Hollywood symbolically as the pinnacle he can no longer achieve, the unholy crucible from which he has managed to escape, or the adopted home from which he has been exiled yet again. Each of these narratives has some truth to it, and from 1973 on, Polanski's films enter a kind of self-consciously late phase, embracing the carnivalesque and eschewing the overt "progressiveness" of the former art-film movements, to which he had belonged only marginally in the first place. In both these phases, paradoxically, his marginality turns out to be what makes him so central, and his work of this period becomes, in its way, post-Hollywood *and* post-art cinema.

What?

The film that initiates this phase of Polanski's career is *What?*, a casual, jocular, anarchic movie trying hard to be a sunny romp, a buoyantly transgressive sex comedy, in spite of its own devigorating counterweights of cynicism, insouciance, sour capriciousness, complacency, and half-hearted dolefulness. A minor work, it is also a turning point for Polanski, especially when viewed in retrospect, in which light it initiates a second wave, a late phase, of his career, with resonances that are echoed in the rest of his films—forecasting the buxom frivolity of *Pirates* or the blithe debauchery and even some of the darker undershades of *Bitter Moon,* or predicting the feckless delirium of *The Ninth Gate.* Though critics had accused Polanski of betraying his talents by dabbling in genres unworthy of them, *What?* is the first of his films—and by no means the last—to bask in its own disrepute and lowness, like a lizard in the sun. No film he has made was received with a greater sense of outrage. (As usual, the American reviews were especially vitriolic, when the film was reviewed in the United States at all.) From start to finish it is a perverse exercise: a flat rejection of the ordinary terms of reputability; a film by a director who wants to be a libertine and a dilettante—or at least to be seen as one; the *jeu d'esprit* of a filmmaker capable (to resort to an appropriately grandiose rhetoric) of mustering a light hand but not quite of obscuring a heavy heart.

The New Waves of the 1960s art film in France, Germany, and Czechoslovakia were often frank sexually without ever being especially erotic or carnal. The key directors of these movements were disinclined by temperament or ideology to portray sex simply as a physical pursuit—whether because they romanticized it, like Truffaut; vilified it as a by-product of bourgeois consciousness, like Godard; loathed it as a facet of human folly, like Fassbinder; all but ignored it, like Herzog; or treated it as earthy, plain, and ordinary, like many of the Czechs. In dating a second wave of the art film, no factor is more important than the greater freedom of representation of the late 1960s and the 1970s, made available by such events as the obscenity trial in the United States in 1968 of Vilgot Sjoman's *I Am Curious (Yellow)* (see De Grazia and Newman 297–303). Found acceptable in court by virtue of "redeeming artistic merit," Sjoman's promiscuous medley of sex and sociology certified an international market for movies situated in an uneasy middle position between art and exploitation, prompting through the 1970s a spate of quasi-pornographic films with marginal artistic pretensions (like the films of Radley Metzger, or items like *Emanuelle* in 1974), as well as works by bona-fide art-film directors with newly aggrandized sexual content. In this cycle may be numbered the late films of Pier Paolo Pasolini, Luchino Visconti's *The Damned* (1969), *Fellini Satyricon* (1969), Alejandro Jodorowsky's *El Topo* (1971), Dusan Makavejev's *Sweet Movie* (1971), and Bernardo Bertolucci's *Last Tango in Paris* (1972), among many others. The somewhat more latent sexualities on view in earlier phases of the art film had given rise to occasional speculations about the new paths film might pursue if these undercurrents ever came to the surface, but once realized, they often elicited uneasy musings about whether the new art film was an authentic exploration of human sexuality or a cheap ploy to turn it to lascivious advantage at the box office.

In this context, *What?* plays as much like the porn film Buñuel never got around to making as the one Polanski nominally did. Its atmosphere is spry and teasingly wicked, its meandering structure simulating a typical porn narrative with the action coyly suspended in a sybaritic limbo, as if to suggest it might turn hardcore any minute. Yet, despite a voluptuary lushness of surface, the film is essentially chaste, a daft morality play on the depravities of sex. Playing on *Alice in Wonderland*, the idea is to cast a young woman—somewhat incongruously supplied with the

Anglo-American name of Nancy—in a house filled with profligates and lechers and to exhibit her wide-eyed yet matter-of-fact reactions to the displays of licentiousness and defilement she constantly happens upon. These debauches are relatively tame—a bout of straightforward sodomy dressed up in a cloak of exotically colored feathers, a little bit of fey sadomasochism, the loopy exploits of a fellow called Mosquito, played by Polanski, who hoists a phallic but pith-less harpoon.

The woman herself is not quite the pure maiden of blue-movie lore, whose successive debaucheries fulfill lurid fantasies of male heterosexual domination. Like that prototype, she spends much of the film fending off unwholesome advances resulting from her own hypothetically inadvertent acts of sexual exhibitionism. Yet if Polanski's film adds anything new to its venerable conceit, it is to render the figure of the innocent sexpot as a creature of the spirit and the intellect. The house she wanders into is a luxurious villa exorbitantly adorned with modern art, and while most of the other habitués are completely heedless of these surroundings, she is highly respectful of them. In the first scene, trying to explain her situation to a gruff maid, she notices a painting by Francis Bacon hung on the wall, but when she appreciatively identifies it, the maid thinks she's talking about cured pork, then ferociously swats a fly that has landed on the canvas.

Like most art films dealing with sexuality, Polanski's subverts the usual assumptions of pornography even as it adopts some of porn's basic iconography and putative sensual appeal. The monomaniacal sex drives of characters in porn are typically taken as both a fact of life and a utopian promise, while in this vein of the art film they are treated as excrescence of vanity and betrayal of spirit, though rarely denied as primary motivation. Like Buñuel, Polanski is wryly amused by the kinky sex and kicky fetishes he conjures up not because they're so odd, but because they're so common. In Polanski's films, sex is indicative of desire that cannot be sated—that is to say, in the terms of these films, any desire—and it is deeply private to the extent that it subsists in specialized and highly individual fetishes, but public and social to the extent that this is true of everyone. That is also why, in films like *What?* and *Bitter Moon*, sex is destructively self-perpetuating and insatiable. In both cases, fantasies of sexual satisfaction are provoked when one character agrees to accept and to enter into the fetishism of another. But these fantasies are dashed when the fetish ultimately proves to be so "personal" that no one else can really participate in it.

In the film, the villa belongs to a character called Noblart—a name that suggests the irresolute allegory archly underpinning the whole enterprise. A fading patriarch, Noblart has spent a lifetime accumulating the aesthetic artifacts that clutter the house, but in his declining years he has rejected the sublimations of art. As one of his minions gnomically puts it, "He would rather eat an actual apple than look at a picture of one." When Noblart's obsequious nephew finagles to procure Gericault's epic canvas *The Raft of the Medusa* to add to his uncle's collection, it is declined with this tart admonition: "Having spent his whole life preferring the image to the object, recently he's found that he prefers the object to the image."

Far from being noble, art represents a severely degraded category in *What?*, a futile corollary to the reprobate sexualities of the film's characters who, surrounded by art, ignore it, exploit it, abuse it, or mock it. Yet if art is nothing but a feeble substitute for the experience of reality in the film, sex is nothing but the delusion of direct contact with that reality, gussied up with costumes, ornaments, and fripperies that make it nothing but an adjunct of art. Summoning Nancy to his chamber, a dying Noblart expresses his preference for the object to the image by asking to see her breasts and her genitals. For her part, Nancy has painted one of her legs blue in a bid to turn herself into art and escape her status as object. Yet she obliges the old man, and he dies, ecstatically satisfied.

Though the film is never really in danger of detouring into pornography, it does seem to conceive of itself as an anatomy of the form, and it shares basic concerns of that genre—namely, the idea of human intercourse as essentially material and bodily, unencumbered by affectional ties. The comic conceit is to titillate with the promise of porn—that everyone is only sexual—then show how sexual satisfaction is rendered impossible by that very promise. Polanski himself embodies this tension in his appearance as Mosquito, who brandishes his harpoon as a phallic substitute yet sneers at anyone who draws the obvious conclusion, "*You* probably think it's something *sexual!*" As a meditation on pornography, the film cannot be called consistent. It rehashes familiar celebrations and condemnations of pornography: that it liberates and that it exploits. Soon before making the film, Polanski appeared as a talking head in a sensationalistic documentary about the European porn industry, *Confessions of a Blue Movie Star* (1971; dir. Karl Martine). His comments shuttle between freethinking acceptance and moralizing disdain. Answering antiporn crusaders, he trundles out a familiar line, that film "only reflects" reality, only serves as "a mirror on the world." The next minute, he vilifies porn as a stairway to hell. About the sadism of some pornography, he says, "The next step is to kill someone for real." The cheerful muddle of *What?* takes this confusion to its logical end.

As a meditation on art, the film is even less coherent (if possible), but as a realization of the new tendencies of the art film it is telling. Whether consciously or not, the film follows a tradition perhaps best represented by Godard's *Contempt,* with which it has much in common: the same producer, an impromptu quality, a philosophical bent as epigrammatically speculative as it is half-baked, an international cast conducive at once to a cult of celebrity and a chastisement of stargazing, a quality of lewdness that expresses self-contempt as forcefully as it poses as wicked satire, a genuinely acerbic wit underlying its excruciating complacency, and most literally, a seaside setting. In the case of *What?* this setting is a villa owned in "real life" by the producer of the film, Carlo Ponti, who had earned Godard's wrath as a co-producer (together with the even more philistine Joseph E. Levine) of *Contempt.* In light of these parallels, one might see *What?* as the anti-*Contempt;* since *Contempt* had already fashioned itself the anti-everything—against pornography and against moralizing attacks on it, against prostitution and against self-righteous denunciations of it, against modernism and against mass culture, and most of all against movies and against those who are against them—it is unclear just where, after *What?*, Polanski leaves the art film. It is clearer, perhaps, where it leaves him: After Polanski's rape case, the movie was cut and recirculated under a new title: *Roman Polanski's Diary of Forbidden Dreams.*

The Tenant

Polanski was forty-three years old when he completed *The Tenant* in 1976, but though the film is the work of a relatively young man, it has the feel of a terminal summation—along the lines of Jean Cocteau's *Testament of Orpheus* (1959), from which it cribs a few choice images. Like *Rosemary's Baby, The Tenant* is a meticulously faithful adaptation of a prior source (the French cartoonist Roland Topor's 1964 novel *La Locataire Chimérique*) that manages, in spite of this fidelity, and in keeping with persisting tenets of the art film, to yield all the appearance of being a "personal" work. A share of that appearance lies in the revisitation of uncannily familiar images and tropes ranging from the broadly generic to the idiosyncratically local, from a plot constructed around a sinister apartment building populated by creepy neighbors, with obvious shades of *Rosemary's Baby,* to the image of a grasping hand reaching mindlessly yet doggedly from behind an armoire, a haunted replay of a charged moment from *Repulsion.* Such echoes and resonances make up the whole film, yet though it was widely accused of enacting an unwholesomely premature self-parody, it is not exactly that. Rather, it formulates a sly pastiche of the elements of the director's work that the public, critics, and audiences had seized upon as the most distinctively "Polanskian," and it assembles them into a truculent meditation on the nature of the personal. Not surprisingly, the point is to suggest that the personal, far from inhering as an inner essence of the individual, is really an expression of otherness and the province of others.

Though Polanski's basic concerns and principal themes had always been clear enough, critics noted something elusive about his work nearly from the beginning of his career. Reviewing *Rosemary's Baby* in 1968, for instance, Stanley Kauffmann noted that as he migrated from the art film to Hollywood, Polanski had been "teaching us how to regard him" (84–85). Kauffmann meant that the director was instructing audiences to lower their artistic expectations, to consider him a mere entertainer, but he could easily have been referring to the variety of Polanski's endeavors, the evident range of his work in spite of its apparent consistency. As a virtual anthology or recitation of moments from the director's previous work, *The Tenant* is the first, and perhaps the only, of his films that makes a conscious bid to be a sort of commodity that might be called "a Roman Polanski film." Probably for that reason, it maintains a reputation as the director's most "personal" work. Yet it gains this personal quality—and brazenly courts self-parody—by acceding to the most overt, even the most superficial characterizations of his work, and in that sense it is not so much *self*-parody as it is a parlous caricature of the general conception of what "a Roman Polanski film" ought to be. The film is fraught with the strange glee, the derision, the self-loathing, the sense of paradoxical freedom, and the sadness of a man submitting to his own public image, and this dimension becomes especially striking when one considers that the plot concerns a character who seeks to escape from a web of paranoia by turning himself into a grotesque parody of what others want him to be.

Played with cunning trepidation by Polanski himself, Trelkovsky is a Polish émigré, a naturalized French citizen living in Paris who rents a small apartment after its previous occupant, an Egyptologist named Simone Choule, mysteriously throws herself from the window. Once he moves in, he finds himself, despite his near-pathological timidity, the object of errant and fitful hostilities from the landlord and the other tenants, old-world Europeans in decline or hapless transients of indeterminate origin. Though there is no sign of any viable community among the residents, who seem to harbor the same enmity toward one another as they do toward the new occupant, Trelkovsky gradually begins to imagine that they are joined in an inexplicable conspiracy to transform him somehow into the previous tenant. They demand that he behave like her, adopting her daily habits in place of his own—drinking chocolate instead of coffee, smoking Marlboros instead of Gauloise cigarettes. As his feverish perception of this plot escalates, he even begins to dress as a woman, and it seems he is doomed to follow the unfortunate destiny of the previous tenant.

As embodied by Polanski, Trelkovsky remains an unreadable presence, distinctly redolent of Kafka's gallery of ciphers, bereft of any meaningful past and deprived of interior life, doomed to a dire future that merely reenacts another tragic past in a remorseless, unstoppable loop. In keeping with Polanski's usual procedures of adaptation, matters that are quite direct in his source material are obscured in the film simply by being rendered literally. The first line of the book runs as follows: "Trelkovsky was on the point of being thrown out in the street when his friend Simon told him about an apartment on the rue des Pyrénées" (Topor 3). Like the novel, the film begins with a scene in which Trelkovsky is shown the apartment by a belligerent concierge (Shelley Winters), but Polanski's characteristic elision of any antecedent narrative circumstance makes Trelkovsky even more inscrutable than he already is in the book. We are given no sense of his prior history, there is no friend Simon, and the location of the apartment is unstated. Indeed, Polanski goes out of his

Absurdist isolation: Polanski as Trelkovsky in
The Tenant.

way to make Trelkovsky's past, such as it is, enigmatic. Asked in the first scene how he heard of the apartment, Trelkovsky tergiversates: "I heard about it from a friend—I mean, a relation." When Trelkovsky begins to take on the identity of Simone Choule later in the film, the cut that discloses his sudden transvestitism is strikingly abrupt, especially because it follows on an epiphanic scene showing Trelkovsky's realization of the extent of the plot he imagines against him, whereupon he mutters to himself, "I'll show them!" In the novel this sequence of action is clearly motivated, as Trelkovsky resolves to give the appearance of becoming Simone to lull his tormentors into a false security: "He might have to go on for a little while longer, letting them think the transformation was taking place, so they would have no cause for suspicion" (88). The effacement of this relatively straightforward motivation makes the film perversely abstruse, rendering Trelkovsky's vow of resistance comically ineffectual.

As piquantly absurd as it is straightforwardly absurdist, this plot is treated with a corrosive, insidious irony, as if it were best understood as a gnomic yet stolid and impudent gloss on Polanski's themes rather than an actual performance or illustration of them. In truth, no Polanski film can be called "personal" in the sense of being directly self-revealing, but *The Tenant,* perhaps the most flagrant gesture of aggression against the audience among all of Polanski's films, initiates a tendency in some of his later work (*Bitter Moon, The Ninth Gate*) toward a scabrous self-reference that actually conceals the self in a webwork of vagrant citation. Quotations of Polanski's own work are strewn throughout *The Tenant* with an impious, puckish disdain, so that the film plays as a kind of masochistic acquiescence to his own public image staged as a sadistic joke on the audience. It is as if this director, so staunchly resistant to biographical approaches to his work, were giving in to the inevitability of such interpretations while simultaneously venting his scorn for them. In its stubborn opacity and equivocal perspicuity, teasing and blunt, *The Tenant* all but demands that it be read biographically, only to block the achievement of any conclusive meaning along those lines or, for that matter, any others.

Bitter Moon

As an anatomy of marriage, *Bitter Moon* is as detailed as *Knife in the Water,* as vitriolic as *Cul-de-Sac,* as undeflectable as *Rosemary's Baby.* During the months when it slowly made its way as a highly disreputable item through the art-film circuits in 1993–94, one of its chief competitors was *Four Weddings and a Funeral* (released in the United States early in 1994), a fatuously genial romantic comedy with which it shares two main actors (Hugh Grant and Kristin Scott Thomas). That film earned its exorbitant popularity by celebrating heterosexual coupling as the apogee of the gloriously natural, in a tone by turns earnest and risible, and it was not above sacrificing a token gay character—to nobody's surprise, the beneficiary of the titular funeral—to the cheerful din of its anserine message, an otiose reaffirmation that audiences embraced enthusiastically. It is no wonder these same audiences were less enthusiastic about Polanski's opposite number, portraying desire as fickle obsession, sex as sadomasochistic folly, and marriage as outright impossibility.

To these ends, *Bitter Moon* goes one better over the director's previous forays. The films of Polanski named above tend to show how desire, or some even less tangible and more demonic force, always broaches the sanctity of monogamous couplehood, which is never seen as very secure to begin with. To demonstrate this premise, they recur to a sort of zero-degree principle of triangulation, intruding a third party into the exigent dualism of the couple's orbit—the student in *Knife in the Water*, the crook in *Cul-de-Sac*, even the devil in *Rosemary's Baby*. The plot of *Bitter Moon* craftily exceeds this minimum by bringing two very different couples together for purposes of drolly tendentious counterpoint. Nigel and Fiona (Grant and Thomas) embody clichés of straitlaced Britishness, complete with unshakeable resilience and stiff upper lip, while Oscar and Mimi (Peter Coyote and Emmanuelle Seigner) hurdle a gamut from American crassness to Eurotrash debauchery. Brought together for a luxurious cruise aboard an ocean liner—a plot conceit that points back to *Knife in the Water*—they prod one another's characteristic postures to the breaking point.

Drawn to Mimi inexplicably, Nigel is collared by Oscar—a sort of crazed Ancient Mariner redivivus, confined to a wheelchair that might as well be an albatross around his neck—and forced to listen to the wild, intricate tale of Oscar and Mimi's past, an insalubrious story Oscar recites with a sarcasm that belies the narrative's bitter compulsion. At first repelled, Nigel grows more and more engrossed in the story, returning to hear more of it—a little like Guy in *Rosemary's Baby* going back for more of Roman Castavet's bombastic theater lore—as it becomes ever clearer that the tale is really a kind of last testament, both scatological and eschatological, an act of renunciation that might be purifying were it not suicidal.

The story is illustrated in four interlocked flashbacks that do equal justice to the sour romanticism and the jocular cruelty of the narrative. Even at the start, while Oscar breathlessly evokes the first flush of his adoration for Mimi, the imagery emphasizes the triteness of what he's saying, and as the story degenerates into a Bataillean orgy of malignity, the visual text mockingly recalls these earlier depictions of their supposed bliss. For instance, an early shot of Mimi framed against the window of a bus is charged with a dreamy erotic allure, the delicacy of the lighting casting an aura about her as she watches Oscar with a gaze that seems innocent yet frankly desiring. After the sadomasochism of their relationship has begun to emerge, the same shot is repeated in reverse, this time from Mimi's point of view, with Oscar framed against

Bataillean sex games: Peter Coyote and
Emmanuelle Seigner in *Bitter Moon.*

the window of an airplane. In another example, Mimi and Oscar pose
early in their courtship for a faux wedding portrait that is crassly paro-
died late in the film, when they actually marry. In both cases, the film's
visual rhetoric—at odds with Oscar's verbal text—suggests a reciprocal
relation between romance and debauchery.

The film's spirit is reminiscent of the work of the French avant-gard-
ist (and not so distant philosophical cousin of Antonin Artaud) Georges
Bataille. In its cool, insulated wit, the movie follows the example of
Bataille's theoretically inclined erotic fictions, and in its treatment of
community it pursues a Bataillean consideration of the role of transgression in the formation of social bonds. (If ever there were a director
who could film Bataille's *The Story of the Eye,* it's Polanski.) The idea
of community is a theme often touched on in Polanski's work but rarely
treated at any explicit length, and it is subject here to a muted satire.
The film implies that marriage and community are socially coextensive
yet literally incompatible. Both are tied to "restrictive economies" (in
Bataille's phrase) that produce energies they cannot account for within
their own systems. For Bataille, any such system will always be rup-

tured by its own excesses and, in trying to maintain itself against them, will demand convulsive expenditures and losses in the form of sacrifice and self-destruction. Paradoxically, in Bataille's formula, stagnation is all that guarantees the order on which continued connection among human beings depends, while all that creates genuine human relation and community—sexual ecstasy, sacrifice and self-sacrifice, laughter—is destructive of that order. Similarly in *Bitter Moon*, "normal" marriage is pure hypocrisy, while the shared, escalating transgressions of Oscar and Mimi, beyond the prim rationalities of ordinary life, are presented as the true fulfillment of natural desires. Yet these excesses lead clearly to death through one route and back to stagnation through another. When the two women come together at the end of the film, it appears to be the only way out of the impasse—to refuse the confinements of hetero-sexuality, to define and exceed a new boundary. But it is not a way out; it too leads to death. The ending of *Bitter Moon* is the most truncated in Polanski's work, yet it has an odd quality of reconciliation about it. It suggests the beginning of community in Nigel and Fiona's reunion and in their strangely heartening interaction with a young Indian girl that ends the film. If what the film means to show is how, Bataille-like, the possibility of community is founded on violence in the theater of sacrifice—in Nigel's murder of Mimi and his own suicide—this seems only to underline the true basis of such community: our common destiny in death.

Death and the Maiden

Bitter Moon stands in close relation to Polanski's subsequent film, *Death and the Maiden,* insofar as both concern an unreconciled relation between past and present. In *Death and the Maiden,* a woman encounters the man she believes raped and tortured her years before, during her captivity as a political prisoner under a totalitarian regime, and the drama derives from the clash between her fierce certainty about his identity and his desperate, futile, and increasingly angry denials. Considering these companion pieces in the larger context of Polanski's career, it is striking how little the influence of the past is felt in Polanski's other works, especially by contrast to these two films. Nearly without exception, Polanski's characters are creatures of an impervious present who live without reference to any of the edicts, uses, or benefits of the past, and the narratives they inhabit take place almost entirely in the precipitous realm of the immediate. This is not to say that Polanski has been uninterested previously in the relation between past and present; on the contrary, it could be placed among his foremost concerns. Before *Bitter Moon* and *Death and the Maiden,* however, the past recurs in his work largely as an absent principle, a structuring absence—ignored, denied, or voided—that appears to hold little sway until the moment when it seeks an ineluctable revenge for its exclusion.

Consider *Repulsion,* an anomalous instance in Polanski's early work in which the past impinges, however minutely or obliquely, on the narrative's otherwise remorseless present tense. The famous last shot of that film moves in on a photograph of Carol, whose final breakdown we have just witnessed in painstaking, protracted, second-by-second detail. The photo shows her as a young girl, the onset of madness already apparent in the rage and contempt of her expression as she gazes at the man we assume to be her father. We are compelled to this assumption as much by the logic of deduction and the prevalence of Freudian cliché as by the film's exacting, severe reticence on the matter, and the camera's approach to the picture is halting yet relentless, with the sententious urgency of a revelatory final verdict. Earlier in the film, willfully deviating from the action, the camera almost reveals this photo prematurely, roving toward it just as the image discreetly fades to black. In fulfilling this unfinished gesture, the climactic disclosure is rendered even more portentous: At least in the encrypted form of this starkly visual emblem, the past is always already there, contained visibly in the present, but unseen—not an explanation, exactly, but an omen.

Until *Bitter Moon*—the only one of Polanski's features to contain a flashback of any kind, let alone to follow such an intricate flashback structure—Polanski's films had insisted emphatically on their own temporal presentness. Indeed, many of them are literally films about the anxieties and pressures of living not only in time but in a tedious, unforgiving present, at once monolithic and mercurial. His most characteristic films simulate pronounced effects of real time—prolonged continuity, extended durations—to evoke the monotony, repetition, and perpetuity of daily life in repose and under siege: this can be said of most of *Knife in the Water,* all of *Repulsion,* long sections of *Cul-de-Sac, Rosemary's Baby, What?,* and *The Tenant,* and the first third of *Frantic.* Typically, they are films about the diurnal as much when portraying the constraints and modalities of the everyday as when chronicling the threats that attend those limits and infuse those passages seemingly as a matter of course. In *Knife in the Water*, Polanski refuses to omit the minutiae of boating—the hoisting of jibs and mooring of sails, the hard-won balance of rudders, the constant struggles with gaffs, jacks, and spars—nor to elide the journey's progress, which (as in scenes such as the one where the erstwhile sailors must tug their boat through a dense thicket of reeds) always entails an excruciating traversal of space under the unbending authority of time, even when the journey's goal is leisure. It is not so much that Polanski refuses to omit such details but that he insists upon stressing them, and his films are full of hapless journeys unfolding over time, while the incessantly ticking clock that is a staple of his soundtracks delineates an essential feature of time in his films: eternally present, even while gliding off into an ever-elusive pastness, it is constantly slipping away, yet will never stop.

Bitter Moon and *Death and the Maiden* are about the conversion of the past into narrative in a manner that serves particular motives of the present. In the case of *Bitter Moon*, these motives are scarcely explicable, while in *Death and the Maiden* they are the familiar ones of a classical revenge play, exculpation or the prosecution of justice. Eschewing the flashback as a means of rendering the past as a direct image, *Death and the Maiden* turns on conflicting accounts of a past that can never be verified by the presumed objectivity of visible evidence—though already in *Bitter Moon*, the blatantly stylized visual correlatives of Oscar's garrulous, bilious narrative seem hardly more reliable than the tale itself. Thus, the later film, even more powerfully than the earlier one, points up the real import of Polanski's concern with past and present: the failures of memory to confront or to grasp the foregone catastrophe that is history.

In Polanski's film, as in the play by Ariel Dorfman on which it is based, the dramatic situation relies on an obvious contrivance. On the day that a lawyer, Escobar (Stuart Wilson), is appointed to head a tribunal investigating the crimes of a former regime in a newly democratized South American country, he is accompanied home by a doctor, Miranda (Ben Kingsley), whom the lawyer's wife, Paulina (Sigourney Weaver), quickly recognizes as her former tormentor. In an evident state of panic, Paulina flees in Miranda's car, but subsequently emboldened, she drives the car over a cliff and returns to the hilltop cottage she shares with her husband, brutally taking the doctor prisoner over Escobar's ineffectual objections. The remainder of the drama counterpoints Paulina's outraged accusations against Miranda's equally fervent rebuttals, the theatrical conception of the piece made considerably less programmatic by the constantly, subtly shifting allegiances it elicits from the audience. Now Paulina seems duly justified in her violence by the extent of her trauma, now spurred to injustice by the psychological damage she has suffered, now little better in her vigilantism than those who tortured her. Now the doctor seems to be an innocent victim, now an obvious criminal, now simply a desperate captive struggling mindlessly to escape, beyond good and evil in the frenzy of his will to live.

Like so many examples of didactic dramaturgy, *Death and the Maiden* lends itself to more ambiguous readings than its structure might suggest. Polanski emphasizes this ambiguity by shifting tones repeatedly, even by playing up the schematic qualities so that the decidedly overdetermined reversals of power among the characters—as in a road-company tour of *Sleuth*—take on broadly comic overtones from time to time. In Dorfman's play, the righteousness of Paulina's crusade is clearer from the outset; Polanski complicates it by, among other means, showing Paulina's wreckage of the doctor's car (an act that takes place offstage in the play and is therefore subject to the same vagaries of testimony as all other claims) and her subsequent blithe denial of it. Thus, in this film so concerned with the contest of truth and falsity, Polanski deliberately gives this character the only claim that proves irrefutably to be a lie (until the final monologue). Especially by contrast to the more even playing of the two men, Sigourney Weaver's performance brilliantly complements the overall design of Polanski's direction in its nimble, renitent variability, shifting on a dime from the shame and sorrow of a victim, to a victim's fury, to a prosecutor's unwarranted wrath or merciless, lacerating chastisement, attuned all the while to the current of voluble absurdism Polanski discovers in the play's intentions.

Despite this complication of the material's ambiguities, Polanski zeroes in on a dimension, neglected or unnoted in the best-known productions of the piece and all but ignored in the text itself, that lies nonetheless right on the play's composed but fallow surface. It is clear from the film's treatment that *Death and the Maiden*, for Polanski, is mostly about the irreducibility of Paulina's violation. We are meant to see early on that neither of the men, for all their fulsome pledges of sympathy, really sees what it has meant to her, and this obliviousness earns her deserved contempt, justifies her most extreme actions, and instigates the film's strange, discomfiting edge of comedy. Polanski has atomized Dorfman's work into a study of three bodies lodged in space and time, each babbling their demands to the rights of any human, but one of whose claims clearly trumps those of the others in some unmitigated way.

After establishing his hidebound allegory, Dorfman bids for greater dramatic complexity by granting each of his characters some legitimate say, and the play's suspense dictates that the outcome could go any way—the doctor might *not* be the rapist, or (if the point is to vilify vigilante justice) it might not matter. In Polanski's version there is scarcely a moment's doubt that Paulina has every right to her unswerving certitude. It is viewed as ineluctable, not irrational, a justified response to an offense that cannot be redeemed, punished, or avenged, nor lessened by any of the symbolic gestures toward justice by which an unstinting present bids to overcome an unchangeable past. Polanski opens up the play briefly—in the scene of Paulina's flight—only to close it down, depending on the traditional bias against "filmed theater" to make the atmosphere of the play more claustrophobic simply by committing it to film. Nowhere else in Polanski's work, except possibly in *Repulsion*, is the constriction of a space-time continuum felt so palpably: the sense of being stuck in a body, at the mercy of the crude customs of a given place, arbitrary and inescapable, with hour upon hour to be gotten through.

As in the play, Paulina has nothing but scorn for the tribunal her husband has been elected to lead. In Polanski's film, what earns her vituperation is her conviction that even if the proceedings were not to be simply a show trial, they would still falsify the experience of her trauma by refusing to acknowledge its irreducibility. In spite of this conviction, however, it matters very much in the film whether or not Dr. Miranda (perhaps named, ironically, for the legal case in the United States delineating the rights of the accused) is guilty. It is crucial that he is, and that he admits as much in the end. Shot in a single take, with an unflinching gaze that grants no pardons, the doctor's confession constitutes the only moment of actual catharsis in all of Polanski's work.

Chamber plays: Sigourney Weaver, Ben Kingsley,
and Stuart Wilson in *Death and the Maiden.*

But the moment, however prolonged, is fleeting. The final scene of
the film repeats the first: In a concert hall, Paulina and Escobar sit side
by side, listening to a string quartet play the piece by Schubert that gives
the film its title. The atmosphere is tense, close, airless, Paulina's nervous
gaze shifting to note Miranda seated with his family in the same hall. Has
Paulina accepted his expiation, or the impossibility of true justice? Has
she come to terms with having to inhabit the same social space as her
former tormentor? The symmetrical structure repeats a framing device
that recurs often in Polanski's work—the repetition in the final shots of
the first shots, suggesting an unbreakable cycle, an eternal return. One
finds this technique as early as *Two Men and a Wardrobe*—the men
emerging from the sea at the start and returning to it in the end—and
in most of the films to follow. By reverting once again to this framing
structure in *Death and the Maiden,* Polanski leaves larger questions of
justice emphatically unanswered. All we know for sure is that we end
where we began.

After Art Cinema: *The Ninth Gate* and *The Pianist*

That *Bitter Moon* has anything in common with *Four Weddings and a Funeral* can be taken as a gauge of the altered profile of the art cinema of this time. The notion that the 1970s inaugurated a second wave of the art film implies a revival of its avant-garde potentialities, but it is equally plausible to point to a growing commercialism about the form as its defining feature during this period. Polanski's work had long been regarded as too commercial to be avant-garde and too avant-garde to be commercial. From *What?* on, his career shuttled from a quasi-skin-flick (*What?*) back to big-budget Hollywood production (*Chinatown*), back to the pop Euro-modernism of *The Tenant*, on to international productions like the epic costume drama of *Tess* or the galumphing parody of *Pirates*, the pseudo-Hollywood potboiler of *Frantic*, the Bataillean orgy of *Bitter Moon*, and the redeemed respectability of the adaptation of *Death and the Maiden*. These variations suggest an ambivalent attitude toward commercial cinema and an indifference to prevailing assumptions about "quality"—an attitude worth considering in relation to the tireless polemics against the Tradition of Quality that shaped the French New Wave.

During this same period, perhaps because it could never be predicted whether the next Polanski film would be regarded as scandalous or classy, Polanski's every film began to be seen as a comeback of sorts. *What?* was a return to the tradition of his European films after his Hollywood foray, *Chinatown* an even more auspicious return to Hollywood after that European detour, and so on. Even *The Ninth Gate*, a movie so avowedly frivolous that some critics declared the end of the director's career (and not for the first time), played a role in this dialectic, paving the way for unprecedented accolades for *The Pianist* as a triumphant return to form.

An arch, sly tale of the search for a rare book adorned with satanic encryptions, *The Ninth Gate* has a whimsically globe-spinning structure (with delicate shades of Hitchcock's *North by Northwest*) that moves from an insular New York–of-the-mind to a Europe so dizzyingly permeable that one may not even notice the many unhingings, at a literal level—the baroness in Paris, for instance. But because these disjunctions or dislocations are lodged so deeply in the movie's sensibility, they register at other levels, as evocative of fin-de-siècle Europe as they are of post-Hollywood. Shards of Hollywood style linger as figments or fragments of an imploded aesthetic—vague allusions to Hitchcock and others, a wildly convoluted horror-show plot, or a radically displaced Johnny Depp, affecting to play a milksop book collector as a noir-boiled tough guy. But the allusions are overwhelmed by an insinuating self-referentiality that would seem more narcissistic if it were not so enervated by strangulated parody, and the whole thing culminates in an extended set piece that dares to acknowledge its own preposterousness yet still tries to achieve its grandiose frissons. The feeling of entropy that circulates through this movie does not reflect a lack of energy; it reflects a state of mind that assumes that everything has already been lost but that this condition is too entrenched, too familiar, and too general any longer to be mourned.

The offhanded way the film registers what it is really about—the end of an idea of Europe—as a kind of afterthought in the margins of its horror plot is a sign of its odd sense of mastery. The technical achievements of the film are unimpeachable and strangely casual—the precise manipulations of film stocks and of differing visual textures, the complex layering of sound—and though they're recognizable as Polanski's, they have little of the forthright virtuosity of his Hollywood period. They're tossed off, not as if they were easy but as if they'd already been perfected and have therefore become marginal. In Polanski's recent films, a certain commitment to a theoretical crudity has manifested itself, comparable to something like the late style of Flaubert. That Old Master's work is worth invoking because the late films of Polanski—formally stringent and misanthropic, yet oddly empathetic—seem so redolent of it. In his late works, Flaubert adopted a coarseness of style that expressed his ultimate estimation of humanity and—more to the point—his final rejection of the artifice usually called on in art to conceal the crudity of human experience. Yet this coarseness remained infused, to extraordinary effect, by the clinical elegance of style and sophistication of technique that Flaubert had already achieved. Something like this goes on in the late Polanski. His stylistic signatures remain consummate even as he often plays them down, and his occasional resort to absurd plotlines still has its absurdist valence. And even if this work sometimes comes off as slumming—as in *What?* or in *Pirates* or in *The Ninth Gate*—it's the playful, plaintive slumming of one who's already been through it all.

There's nothing playful about *The Pianist,* of course, even though the film's climax turns unexpectedly on a joke. Wladyslaw Szpilman, the title character, has been hiding from the Nazis in increasingly desperate circumstances during the final years of World War II. A Nazi officer discovers him but, instead of turning him in, commands him to demonstrate his artistry at the piano. Following this performance, the officer advises Wladyslaw to remain in hiding and even gives him his own coat. Thereafter, with uncertain motives, the officer returns in secret with food, helping to sustain Wladyslaw as the Russians advance to retake Poland from the Germans. On their arrival, Wladyslaw emerges from hiding wearing the officer's coat, only to be assailed with gunfire from his would-be liberators, who mistake him for a Nazi. When he cries out that he is Polish, they desist, but one of them shouts, "Then why the fucking coat?" And then comes the joke, with Wladyslaw's simple and straightforward reply: "I'm cold."[18]

Until this point, the film has maintained such a somber tone that this line is often greeted by audiences with disproportionate laughter. It is the one moment of release in a film that is resolutely committed to representing a condition of total oppression with a matter-of-fact astringency, and even this easement, like the truncated catharsis at the climax of *Death and the Maiden,* is only momentary. Any impulse to glory in Wladyslaw's survival is cut off by the film's surprising turn, in its concluding minutes, to a concern with the fate of the Nazi officer, Hosenfeld. No sooner has Wladyslaw been freed than we lose sight of him. The next sequence shows captured Nazis imprisoned in a makeshift stockade as liberated Polish Jews troop past them, shouting enraged invective and recrimination. The officer who helped Wladyslaw emerges from the crowd, his face bloody, and calls out to a friend of Szpilman's, asking him to convey to Wladyslaw the message that he has been jailed. We understand that Hosenfeld hopes Szpilman will now aid him in turn. In the following scene, Wladyslaw appears on the same site, apparently willing to attempt some intervention on the officer's behalf, but the stockade has been moved. Subsequently, we see Wladyslaw at the piano as two final notes on screen tell us that he resumed his musical career successfully, while all that is known of Hosenfeld is that he died in a Soviet work camp in 1952.[19]

This emphasis is especially striking in light of the film's silence on the fate of Wladyslaw's family. As we know from Szpilman's memoir, all of them were killed in concentration camps. That Polanski's film elides this painful fact should not be interpreted as simple evasion. In fact, it could easily be read as a gesture of fidelity to the book, since Szpilman's son, in a foreword to his father's memoir, notes that the author never spoke of his family (Szpilman 7). Overall, the absence of any depiction or even any sustained reference to the death camps in the film is felt more as a staunch refusal than a moral failure. Because of this abstinence, even while the film is made up entirely of overt manifestations of anti-Semitic violence, it is haunted by the unspoken and the unseen. However wrenching the brutalities depicted, we must still be aware that other horrors, perhaps unimaginable, lurk elsewhere. The film retreats from the idea that the representation of ultimate horrors would somehow reveal the essential evil of the camps—the strategy pursued by a film like *Schindler's List* (1993), where such horrors serve a cathartic function, mounting successively to a nearly unbearable crescendo that paves the way for a subsequent redemption. In *The Pianist,* Polanski devoutly resists the ranking of horrors, and he is no more concerned to prove or to document the abhorrent reality of the camps than he is to conquer the unrepresentable. The reference to the Nazi officer's death under Stalin does not raise questions of moral equivalency between Hitler's and Stalin's regimes so much as it insists we remember that large-scale inhumanity did not end with the Third Reich. As Polanski's films suggest, it may never end.

Before Steven Spielberg decided to direct *Schindler's List,* he offered the project to Polanski. Whether Polanski turned it down or was prevented by other projects from taking it on is not clear. What is evident from the films, however, is how much more in keeping with Polanski's work as a whole are the materials of *The Pianist* than those of *Schindler's List.* Both narratives are stories of resistance and survival. In the novel by Thomas Kenneally that forms the basis of Spielberg's film, a German entrepreneur assists Jews in escaping from the Nazis. Szpilman's memoir tells of how a random chance for escape separates Wladyslaw from his family and throws him back on his own resources as he is forced to hide in solitude. *Schindler's List* is a story of individual evil, embodied in the figure of a sadistic commandant whose defeat signals that of the Reich itself, and of individual heroism, celebrated in climactic tributes to Oskar Schindler. *The Pianist* turns on happenstance, the arbitrary event of Wladyslaw's escape, framed against a context of totalized authority that brings to bear in homes or in streets something of the same horror that it institutionalized in the camps themselves. Just as so many of Polanski's films concern how individuals evade society's totalizing gaze only to discover it fixes them all the same, so *The Pianist* is about an escapee from the camps who nonetheless lives in a state of perpetual dread. *Schindler's List* is about the horror of the camps, which it portrays as compellingly as any film, even if it concludes with an array of bromides about the triumph of the human spirit. *The Pianist* is about the horror of life once the camps have been conceived.

In the world the film represents, violence lurks everywhere, as an omnipresent possibility, and it explodes intermittently, brutally enacted with a quick, casual efficiency. Each killing, though part of a murderous social system, is also a horrifically unique event, a specific injury. As viewers, we are never permitted to inure ourselves to it or to prepare ourselves for the next incident because—like the violence represented in *Macbeth*—it comes always a shade more quickly than expected. Though each act of violence is portrayed in its full horror, a share of that horror comes from how little commemoration—namely, none—each death calls forth. A shot, a fall, and then it is done. Walking along one day, Wladyslaw sees a boy trying to wriggle under a wall into the street, apparently to escape a tormentor on the other side of the fence. Wladyslaw helps the child complete this escape but finds, as he aids him in trying to stand, that he has died in the split second of Szpilman's intervention. Wladyslaw leaves the corpse in the street and, weeping, strides on his way. In another scene, during a roundup, a young woman asks meekly where they are being taken, and the Nazi officer who is herding captives promptly lifts his revolver and shoots her in the head. She falls out of the frame and is not seen again. In yet another scene, when a group fleeing the Nazis is strafed and slaughtered in the street, what is emphasized most powerfully is the suddenness of these deaths and the lack of any repercussion or aftermath. Even after Wladyslaw's family is whisked away, when he manages to escape, they are not heard of again. In no sense does the matter-of-fact, unforgiving briskness of these representations mute their power. The film portrays the nature of grief and loss in a context of systematic violence and murder, when there is no time to grieve for any victim even while, in a larger sense, there is nothing but grief in every quarter.

The Pianist was received with almost unanimous acclaim, winning the Palme d'Or at the Cannes Film Festival and a number of Academy Awards in the United States, including a previously elusive honor for Best Director. As "important" as *The Ninth Gate* is "frivolous," *The Pianist* shares with Polanski's previous film a sense of that ambiguous mastery that has come to typify the director's late work (as evident when he's slumming as when he's going for broke) and to express a particular quality of *belatedness* in Polanski's late films. These films amply represent modern currents in cinema: they make use of bankable stars, high-concept strategies, and cutting-edge technologies, including the so-called digital ones that are supposed to render cinema obsolete. Yet if these movies are resolutely international, they still don't seem to be a part of the global atmospheres or hegemonies of modern film—they're too hermetic and private to bid for that kind of commercialism, even if they adopt some of its trappings.

Because of how Polanski's films tend to shift so restlessly among cultural levels, and because an auteur's status usually depends on consistency, the director might be considered, from a certain perspective, a little out-of-it—or at least, still very hard to pin down. But it is not the surface features of contemporary film culture that Polanski's movies reject; indeed, they embrace such features with apparent zeal. They refuse something deeper: the sensibility that underlies that surface, or the milieu that produces it.[20] Polanski's late films culminate themes of fetishism or sexual fantasy and paranoia that run through his work, but more than ever, these themes are treated with a remote, formal attitude, culminating in the departure of *The Pianist*. If Polanski ever felt personally implicated in the themes his work explored, then on the evidence of these films, he does not any longer. The movies are "personal" less in their commitments than in their detachment, their defining qualities of estrangement. From *What?* through *The Pianist* and *Oliver Twist*, these films are at once avidly sensual and unstintingly distant. They are linked in the unflinching gaze that they share, curious, steely, but not unforgiving, even of itself, fully mastered but not irreproachable, as when one looks back on an enterprise one still cares about and completely understands but no longer expects or even hopes to participate in; or as when—much the same thing—one has come to terms, at long last, with mortality.

Rendering Classics: *Macbeth* and *Tess*

"Like everyone else I was disappointed by *Tess*," wrote François Truffaut in a letter of 1979 (*Correspondence* 502). Though Truffaut does not expand on this passing observation, we may surmise that his disappointment followed the general critical consensus. According to that line of thinking, a staid adaptation of a classic literary text was exactly what neither Truffaut nor "everyone else" had hoped for or expected from Roman Polanski, especially at that point in his career. In another letter, three years later, Truffaut professes unequivocally to "adore" Polanski's work as a whole (*Correspondence* 546), and his reaction to *Tess* is apposite not only because it indicates his recognition of that film as, for better or worse, a departure for Polanski. Truffaut's own filmmaking practice had undergone a marked shift during the 1970s, when he produced a series of period pieces derived from more or less highbrow literary sources: *The Wild Child* (1969), *Two English Girls* (1971), *The Story of Adele H.* (1975), and *The Green Room* (1978). Considering that Truffaut's early reputation as a critic in the 1950s depended on fierce polemics against the domination of French cinema by old-fashioned literary sensibilities, some critics took this opportunity to accuse Truffaut of making the sort of films he had inveighed so passionately against. Were Polanski and Truffaut, these two *enfants terribles* of the European art film, now reverting to the same kinds of superannuated and traditional movies to which their own earlier work had stood in such powerful contrast?

Putting aside the individual qualities of the films in question, works like Polanski's *Tess* or Truffaut's *The Story of Adele H.*—the aesthetically closest to *Tess* among Truffaut's costume dramas—stand as decisive test cases for the role of the "classic" literary adaptation following the belated advent and ultimate entrenchment of a modernist cinema. In previous eras of film history, such films might have been taken to task for insufficient fidelity to their sources. They might have been criticized for betraying the populist spirit of movies by going highbrow, or the serious traditions of literature by subordinating them to the vulgarizing forces of mass culture. In discussions of the "proper" relation of literature and film, virtually up to the time of the French New Wave, these were the principal models of understanding that held sway. Thus it is especially interesting to note that *Tess* and *The Story of Adele H.* were commonly chided, especially among members of the putative critical vanguard, for being too faithful, for breaking with the modernist skepticism of tradition and regressing to the psychological realism of the nineteenth-century novel.

This reversal in critical disposition may be credited in part to Truffaut himself. However, it is worth recalling that he never really opposed the making of films from literary sources. Surely aware that a plurality of all films in the first half-century of cinema had clear precedents in literature, he must have known that such opposition would have been a fool's errand. Rather, he attacked specific means of adaptation, rarely falling into the naive presumption of an essential divide between the media of literature and film. In the essay most pertinent to these concerns, "A Certain Tendency of the French Cinema" (1954), Truffaut makes a statement that was all but heretical in the face of the discourses of fidelity then dominant: "I'm not at all certain that a novel contains unfilmable scenes, and even less certain that these scenes, described as unfilmable, would be so for everyone" (227).

In many ways the French New Wave was as literary as its antecedents, but one of the movement's goals was to reverse the traditional cultural hierarchy that placed literature above film in the pantheon of the arts—from which, as often as not, film was excluded in any case. Considering the contempt for the old-style Tradition of Quality unanimously held by the new generation of auteurs, one might have expected them to reject the practice of making movies from books altogether in their filmmaking, but nothing could be further from the case. Nearly all of the most important works of the New Wave's first flush were adaptations; what had changed were the kinds of books being filmed. Instead of venerated highbrow classics or other legitimated prestige pieces, filmmakers like Truffaut, Godard, and Claude Chabrol turned to potboilers and seemingly disreputable bestsellers. The work of Truffaut's first decade includes films based on fiction by American genre writers like David Goodis, Ray Bradbury, and Cornell Woolrich. Godard adapted a crime novel by Dolores Hitchens (*Band of Outsiders;* 1964) and gave much of his work of that early period a pulp-fiction spin, often with direct reference to American pop culture. Chabrol adapted the work of genteel middlebrow writers like Charlotte Armstrong into placid, brittle thrillers with a modernist edge.

Often such adaptations were theoretical gestures, ostentatiously subjecting a minor work of literature, however hackneyed, to the auteur's imaginative transformation of it in cinematic terms. The choice of literary text was as often determined by semiotic cultural backgrounds as by the specific book in question—as was the case with Truffaut's adaptation of Woolrich in *The Bride Wore Black* (1968), chosen less for Woolrich's distinction as a writer than because Hitchcock had filmed his work in *Rear Window* (1954). In nearly every case, a larger question of cultural value was at stake. Influenced by Alexandre Astruc's elaborate analogy between camera and pen in "Le camera-stylo" (1948), these directors issued a polemical call for the cultural equivalency of literature and film, illustrated by the practices of their work. On the one hand, they could be said to have used literature like chattel, as so much "material" from which to spin their webs of celluloid, the literary source, however unsophisticated, ultimately transcended by the auteur's cinematic artistry, which usually converted such works of genre fiction into a springboard for bouts of the self-reflexive playfulness that was a hallmark of their hard-boiled modernism. On the other hand, their work remained devoutly literary—allusive, sophisticated, and highly literate—and they obviously loved the energy, the immediacy, and the cultural transparency of the ostensibly lowbrow works they often exploited.

Buoyantly questioning the superiority of literature to film in theory and in practice, these filmmakers succeeded in challenging that hierarchy to the extent that their work exemplified in film a full-blooded modernism that had previously been restricted in the annals of cultural chroniclers to literature and the fine arts, and the films of the French New Wave ultimately revived serious interest in the supposedly uncultured writers they took as their models, like Goodis or Woolrich. As a consequence of this challenge, any cinematic adaptation of a literary classic for years to follow was placed under suspicion from the vantage point of film art. In reaction, national cinemas still largely indebted to the literary canon convulsively modernized their approaches. The British cinema—a contradiction in terms, in Truffaut's well-known declaration, an insult that targeted precisely its heavy dependency on literary sources—underwent a sea change with examples like Tony Richardson's *The Charge of the Light Brigade* (1966), John Schlesinger's *Far from the Madding Crowd* (1967), and Ken Russell's *Women in Love* (1969), each of which willfully imposes a self-consciously modern sensibility on its already vaguely modern source. A current of feral satire infuses Richardson's version of Tennyson's poem, while in Schlesinger's film, post-Freudian psychologies are brought to bear on Thomas Hardy's novel. Russell was the most voracious and reckless of these adaptors-as-creators—excepting possibly Nicolas Roeg, who largely followed the New Wave model of plundering lowbrow or middlebrow culture for his material—bringing the same style of kaleidoscopic misanthropy to bear, no matter what the source.

Rosemary's Baby is the first adaptation of Polanski's career, but of the twelve films he has made since then, eight are adaptations. Not only is the practice of converting literary sources into cinematic versions prevalent in Polanski's art, it recurs as a fairly straightforward procedure, marked by qualities of literalness, even of great fidelity or faithfulness to the sources. In this sense, Polanski's manner of adaptation differs from the precedent of the New Wave, or from those of auteurist cinema more generally, in which a prior text is willfully subordinated to the spectacle of the auteur's transformation or conquest of it, showcasing the triumph of the director's personal signature above any dictate to adhere, whether slavishly or respectfully, to the outline of an original. Despite the verbatim transcriptions of Polanski's methods of adaptation, however, his films do not transmit an unusual sense of allegiance to their sources—by contrast to, say, the tough-minded fidelity of Carol Reed's films of books, or the conscientious rigor of David Lean's, or the fussy pedantry of Merchant/Ivory's.

To understand Polanski's attitude toward sources, as well as toward adaptation as a cinematic practice, it is worth considering the role of allusion or borrowing in the films he has made from original scripts. Movies like *The Fearless Vampire Killers*, *What?*, or *Pirates*, all pastiches of well-known genres, marshal a heady range of references to create their delirious atmospheres of free-for-all burlesque. Though the remaining five of Polanski's features not based on literary sources achieve varying degrees of originality, most also point to clear models, if not to specific sources—1940s film noir in *Chinatown*, or the Hitchcockian thriller in *Repulsion* or *Frantic*. At least from *Rosemary's Baby* on, Polanski's work expresses a keen interest in film as a sort of visual repository in which figments from the popular imagination make contact with images of an individual nightmare, partaking equally of the archetypal and the redoubtably idiosyncratic. In light of this view of film as a composite medium, always intersecting with and borrowing from criss-crossing repertories of word and image, Polanski conceives of his sources from a relatively neutral standpoint, less as cultural totems to be honored than simply as models to be dealt with straightforwardly.

Nowhere is this understanding of adaptation more apparent than in Polanski's first two film versions of classics, *Macbeth* and *Tess*—the cases that have proved most problematic for critics chiefly concerned with the question of whether the filmmaker esteems or bastardizes his venerated sources. Typically, Polanski's choice of sources has been determined either by their popularity—the bestseller *Rosemary's Baby*, the Broadway hit *Death and the Maiden*—or their perceived congruity with his own sensibility, as when he turns to novels that straddle a line between Euro-modernism and pop, like those on which he based *The Tenant*, *Bitter Moon*, or *The Ninth Gate* (the source for which, *The Club Dumas* by Arturo Pérez-Reverte, is more "Polanskian" than the film Polanski made from it).

Especially in his handling of "classic" material, Polanski turns to literary sources as another way of pursuing his concern with the fate of subjectivity in the modern world. His methods of adaptation ruthlessly strip away almost everything that is not immediately visual, including exposition, authorial commentary, psychological detail, and interior monologue. In short, the director dispenses with the very techniques that led many commentators, from Erich Auerbach to Ian Watt, to claim that modern literature had created a new kind of human depth. In his filmmaking practice, Polanski counters this claim with the proposition that cinema invented a new kind of human surface, and his adaptations especially enact a literal clash of that depth with this surface.

Macbeth

Considering the first of Polanski's adaptations of literary classics, an obvious question presents itself: Why *Macbeth*? Shakespeare's tragedy of murderous ambition has clear relevance to Polanski's recurrent themes, and one could imagine the diabolical coupling of the tragedy's main characters treated as a sly inversion of the unwitting pact between Rosemary and her collaborationist husband in Polanski's previous film, another example of virtue submitted to evil through a marriage made in hell. Among Shakespeare's plays, *Macbeth* is second to *Hamlet* as the one most concerned with the relation of action to self-knowledge, and its tragedy derives from a violent severance in that relation: "To know my deed 'twere best not know myself" (II.ii.72). The play considers familiar Shakespearean themes such as the confusion of shadow and substance, or the conception of identity as performance. These themes, often pursued separately in the plays, are twinned in *Macbeth:* "Life's but a walking shadow, a poor player / That struts and frets his hour upon the stage" (V.v.24–25).

Polanski's treatment realizes Shakespeare's theme concerning the rift between action and reflection by shifting repeatedly and emphatically, throughout the film, to voiceover during the soliloquies of Macbeth and Lady Macbeth. This pattern is made even more important by the fact that the play is cut in such a way as to minimize dialogue and maximize monologue, so that for much of the film, we see the main characters talking mostly to themselves. The preponderance of soliloquy in *Macbeth*—taking up nearly a fifth of the whole play—leads Polanski to amplify further its role as a technique in relation to the tragedy's larger themes. *Hamlet* is about an instance of anterior violence, the murder of the king before the play begins, and a subsequent failure to respond to it; *King Lear* is about an initial stubborn resolution, Lear's denunciation of Cordelia, that also paralyzes further action. In both plays, soliloquy stands between action and thought, either as tortured reflection on what one cannot do or painful recollection of what one has already done. Of the major tragedies, *Macbeth* is the one in which ultimate action is undertaken most decisively—the first murder occurs at the start of the second act—and for that reason, as well as because they are shared by two main characters, the soliloquies take on a more rhetorical character than in most of Shakespeare's plays. Strikingly, in *Macbeth,* soliloquy accompanies action rather than standing apart from it; the soliloquies serve less as intervals between thought and action than as actions themselves—oratorical feats of self-persuasion, exculpation, and condemnation. In Polanski's film, language itself becomes the "walking shadow." It is alternately shadow and substance, shifting indiscriminately from inside to outside—from monologue to voiceover—and moving arbitrarily from actualized speech that is still thought because the characters are talking to themselves to thought that remains a form of speech because it can be heard. In Polanski's *Macbeth*, speech and action collide as language becomes a kind of speech act that can, like poetry, make nothing happen.

Polanski's use of the voiceover has been fiercely criticized in part because of widespread disdain for voiceover as a cinematic device, but Polanski exploits the technique, and perhaps even the low esteem in which it is held, to present language itself as dual, sometimes shade and sometimes substance, but never both at once. For all of Shakespeare's dark poetry, the failures of language are perhaps his most persistent theme, and never more so than in *Macbeth*. In this play, language fails as symbol because it cannot communicate, so larded is it with conflicting motives. Its fate should thus be to take its place as just another object in a too-material world, just another set of instruments to be put to use for self-gain or self-justification. But it fails in that office, too, because even though it is tantamount to so many severed thumbs or horned toads simmering in the vast cauldron of public speech, it is still deprived of the flesh and blood it would need to be substantial. The stark, random shifts from speech to voiceover in Polanski's film are alienation effects that reveal the film's language, for all the beauty of its poetry, not as a conduit between public and private parts of the self, between thought and action or matter and symbol, but as a bodily effect that is stuck in one part or the other without the capacity to mediate between them.

In the play, language is already a thing, as when Macbeth finds that he cannot speak the word "amen": "I had most need of blessing, and Amen / Stuck in my throat" (II.ii.28–29). To hear Macbeth tell it, it might as well be a fishbone as a benediction. Throughout the play, the grimmest conceptions are almost instantly realized as the bloodiest events, with no need of mere words to bring them about. The subversion of justice on which the play is based takes the form of a sharp linguistic inversion—"Fair is foul and foul is fair" (I.i.11)—but the play as a whole concerns how little symbol influences matter, how little language influences action. Metaphors become grotesque realities (especially in

Polanski's film, where the bear Macbeth likens himself to turns up as an actual animal), while bodies are nothing but flesh and blood stuck in a base world, however they try to elevate themselves through thought and speech. A metamorphic principle infuses the play's savagery, as thoughts become deeds, words become things, and things turn into smirched totems, like Macbeth's severed head.

In Polanski's film, this metamorphic principle is taken to dizzying extremes. The play is built on stark polarities: Macbeth moves quickly from being a trusted soldier to a bloodthirsty heathen to a guilt-ridden noble back to a brutal killer, finally ending in his equally sudden apotheosis as a tragic figure. Though richly shaded with psychological detail, this feverish Manichean atmosphere may account for the play's being commonly considered Shakespeare's most melodramatic tragedy (Verdi, for instance, called his 1847 *Macbeth* opera a "melodrama"). What underscores the melodrama in Polanski is that the film is not about liminal spaces, border states, the blurred line between waking or sleeping, or any of the other such readings that have attached themselves to the play.[21] In its nightmarish vision of a world in flux, the film eliminates any middle ground. Though everything is constantly changing into something else, these mutations happen in a flash, with no process of transformation. Shadow and substance are not degrees along a spectrum but wholly different phenomena, of separate orders.

The dagger that appears before Macbeth, taunting him with murder, begins as a whimsical, floating figment, a shimmering special effect out of *The Thief of Bagdad,* then converts in an instant to a solid, usable weapon. Banquo's ghost appears either as a flickering, transparent illumination or a firm, stout body, with nothing in between. The witches are either fleshly old crones or disembodied incubi, their brews stews of gory body parts that quickly turn into nothing but misty vapors. For Polanski, the point seems to be that in this world there is nothing between shadow and substance; thought, feeling, conception, and motive exist in a different world from flesh, blood, matter, and act—and it is the latter world in which we have to live. It was Polanski's countryman Jan Kott, in *Shakespeare, Our Contemporary* (1964), who argued most influentially for an understanding of Shakespeare as an honorary modern by pointing to what he saw as Shakespeare's prototypical nihilism, his sense of alienation as a factor in the formation of human subjectivity.

The eerie naturalism of *Macbeth*.

Polanski "modernizes" *Macbeth* by fiercely anatomizing the alienation of symbol from matter that leaves every body at the mercy of material forces amounting to a pervasive and arbitrary violence, with no recourse to the sublimations of language.

Polanski's *Macbeth* points back to Orson Welles's 1948 film version by stripping away much of the play's psychology and bringing its primitive edge to the foreground. Yet Polanski's version avoids any hint of Welles's expressionistic style, which provides a ritualized surround that amplifies the bitterness and pessimism of Welles's treatment but also locates the action in an exotic, otherworldly, mysterious region. In an approach closer to the one Welles followed in his later Shakespearean pastiche *Chimes at Midnight* (1966), Polanski plays up the extreme naturalism of his settings, the grassy fields and rutted roads and muddy lots, the rolling hills and clear skies, the dank castles and close barns, all shot crisply and clearly. The light that guides fools to their dusty deaths is just an ordinary sun, and even when Birnam Wood comes to Dunsinane, the effect is one of a vivid discernibility, not of a mystical ascent. As a consequence of this naturalism, the brutality of the play emerges more starkly than in any other film version, however restrained the violence. Polanski insists we acknowledge that the violence he places on view is the violence of the real world, despite the Elizabethan trappings. Unflinchingly carnal, the film is also completely nonsensual: because the carnality is never erotic, the intense emphasis on bodily presence translates into a terrible, hovering anxiety concerning how prone these bodies are to injury. When Lady Macbeth appears in the nude, our only thought is of how vulnerable her body looks in its nakedness. Polanski's treatment is never Olympian but always immediate, direct, unafraid to get down in the muck, and despite its air of sad resignation, the film forces us to see the blood as real. In this film Polanski has taken seriously the play's hortatory line, "The heavens, as troubled with men's act, / Threaten his bloody stage" (II.iv.5–6)—and answered in kind: *Let it come down.*

Tess

Following the brutality of *Macbeth,* the delicacy of *Tess* may seem at first glance more genteel than it really is. Perhaps for that reason, the film's initial critical reception internationally echoed Truffaut's disappointment that Polanski chose to mount an apparently traditional costume drama instead of mining the savage fatalism underlying Hardy's proto-modernist novel. In a way, though, it is precisely the delicacy of Polanski's treatment—straightforward and bracing, fastidious without being too meticulous—that most forcefully conveys the filmmaker's attitudes toward the material. Lowering the pitch of the book, Polanski converts Hardy's florid testament of mourning into an ardent but subdued expression of melancholy—if not the only sustained act of sympathy in all of Polanski's work, certainly the only one of his films in which a drama of sympathy provides the dominant emotional note.

Freud's distinction between mourning and melancholy opposes progression and fixation: grief resolved, for Freud, finds its proper articulation in mourning, while grief without end, that cannot be worked through, trails off into melancholy, interminable, ubiquitous, and ineffable. Polanski's *Tess* is suffused with mysterious melancholy in just this sense, at nearly every level—in the images, austerely composed but lushly textured; in the saddened comportment of the actors; in the conduct of the narrative, stately and minute. The story's tempo follows a kind of lugubrious momentum—a carefulness, a reticence, then a sudden lunge forward—as if its narrator were unpersuaded that his invisibility from the scene of the action were sufficient exemption from responsibility for the grim implications of its foredoomed outcome.

Something of the same feeling accompanies the exertions of Hardy's narrator, who steps from the wings at strategic intervals to address the reader with direct commentary on the action, demanding pity for Tess in her ineluctable plight. As often in Hardy's fiction, the reach for tragedy is abetted by the tools of melodrama, and it is difficult to evade the element of prurience in Hardy's project of imagining plots of unrelieved bleakness so that his narrators can bemoan the unceasing injustices the author himself has conjured and visited upon the hapless creatures of his own imagination. Hardy's hoped-for vindication is the plea of most fiction that is bedeviled by the problem of its own didacticism, the defense that such injustice is widely abroad in the world and must be adequately shown to be properly understood and forestalled. (This same justification makes Hardy's fiction an unlikely literary realization of a Benthamite logic.) A fervent commitment to this purpose enables the psychological density of Hardy's novels, testifying to their variable sensitivities, to give way ultimately to the Olympian declamations and cathartic orations through which they resolve themselves. Polanski's rendering is largely free of the fits of self-justification that typified the realist novel of Hardy's day; it dispenses with exhortations meant to acquit the plot and resists the heady emotional range of the book, meant to temper the tragedy and make it palatable even to those it would accuse. Bleaker even than Hardy's, Polanski's unremitting version offers exactly one scene of apparent happiness. It follows Tess's rape.

Recent critics of Hardy have been especially attuned to a dilemma in which the novel is enmeshed. The narrator's explicit intent to exonerate Tess is repeatedly foiled by his collusion in the social assumptions that victimize her. To redeem her purity against her defilement, he evinces a valor mitigated by the sense in which the attribution of such purity is likewise the prerogative of her rapist. The intrinsic drama of Hardy's novels is one that escapes the contemplation of their own self-scrutiny, that of the dialogue between Hardy's own blindness and the narrator's staunchly repelled but ever-welling guilt regarding his complicity in the heroine's fate. Like even the least sophisticated adaptor, Polanski has the advantage of being still more modern than his source and therefore able to assume, at least rhetorically, a measure of enlightenment in his audience that Hardy could not, even if Hardy's work increased the degree of such enlightenment to an extent that Polanski's film did not.

Accordingly, the melodrama of the pure maiden debauched by the leering noble lingers as an eidetic vestige behind the film, not a determining condition. Hardy's novel bears the provocative subtitle *A Pure Maiden*, but Polanski's Tess is far less pure from the start, far more effortlessly earthy in her plainspoken sweetness, while his aristocrats, though as oblivious as ever, are less overtly rapacious. Where Hardy hoped to broaden and reform Victorian conceptions of female purity, Polanski's film implies that it might be better, all in all, for people *not* to be pure, or at least not to have the essences of their being conceived or compelled as such. Though all of the film's sometimes oceanic sympathies flow in the direction of Tess, its identifications remain channeled formally through the viewpoints of the men whose violent incomprehensions nullify her.

Basic to Hardy's novelistic practice was a conventional claim to omniscience, including the pretense of entering Tess's consciousness as freely and readily as those of the male characters, Alec D'Urberville or Angel Clare. Without the dogmatism of a flat repudiation, Polanski eschews any such pretense. Though Polanski's film is at least as invested as Hardy's novel in the production of women's suffering as morally edifying spectacle, it is mainly concerned with the tragic impossibility of its own apprehension of Tess's subjectivity.

Hardy's narration moves effortlessly from painterly contemplation of Tess's body to equally assured revelations of her inner states: "Her face had latterly changed with changing states of mind, continually fluctuating between beauty and ordinariness, according as the thoughts were gay or grave. One day she was pink and flawless, another pale and tragical. When she was pink she was feeling less than when pale; her more perfect beauty accorded with her less elevated mood; her more intense mood with her less perfect beauty. It was her best face physically that was now set against the south wind" (121). For all the agony the book expends over the figure of Tess, there is scarcely a moment's doubt on the narrator's part of his capacity to grasp her plight better than she ever could herself: "Being even now only a young woman of twenty, one who mentally and sentimentally had not finished growing, it was impossible that any event should have left upon her an impression that was not in time capable of transmutation" (121).

Tess's viewpoint serves continually as a structuring principle of Polanski's film, but its treatment contrasts with the masterly slippages of Hardy's narrator. Again and again in the course of the film, Tess's point of view initiates key sequences, only to be abruptly suspended, curtailed, or interrupted. The first such sequence occurs during her journey to Stokes, where she has been sent to live in the household of presumably rich relatives after it is discovered that her family bears their noble name. At the start of this sequence, several shots are introduced from Tess's perspective. In context, however, these shots depart from traditional point-of-view editing, which typically relies on a three-shot pattern: a view of a character looking, a cut to what she sees, and a final shot returning to the initial view of the character. Repeatedly, in *Tess*, Polanski dispenses with the last shot of this triad, suggesting only a fleeting promise of access to Tess's subjectivity that is subsequently blocked. In the scene of Tess's journey, for instance, we cut from a shot of Tess gazing upward, to an apparently subjective pan along the roadside treetops, clearly coded as her literal viewpoint. Instead of returning to the initial shot, however, Polanski cuts sharply to an extreme long shot of Tess in which it is clear that she is not looking at the trees at all. The effect is to undermine our sense that we have entered Tess's perspective, to evoke doubt that we could share her point of view, at least as this film mediates it.

This pattern of incompletion remains consistent throughout the film, time after time holding out the possibility of greater intimacy with the character, then withdrawing it suddenly, without fanfare, as if to insist it was never a real possibility in the first place. Often, in the course of a sequence otherwise rendered objectively, a single shot intrudes that suggests a dimension of subjectivity, but it remains disconnected formally from any circuit in the overall pattern of editing that would enable us to associate it clearly with Tess's point of view. In an early scene between Alec and Tess in a carriage, in which Alec pursues his seduction, the camera angles alternate among shots of both characters and close-ups of each, the rhythms constricting to portray a mounting anxiety as Alec arrogantly advances while Tess sullenly withdraws. A sudden cutaway shot shows the head of the horse pulling the carriage, an unmotivated

Through the gaze of others: Tess and her infant.

shift that suggests an emotional dissociation that can only be Tess's but remains unattributable to her through any ordinary route. When Tess and Angel marry, a similar cutaway shot glimpses the Bible held by the minister performing the ceremony. Such stray, overexplicit details, strewn throughout the film and unmoored from the traditional rhetoric of cinematic point of view, give rise to a sense of a free-floating subjectivity. It is as if Tess's point of view permeates the film, fully visible yet unreachable.

In the structure of the plot, Polanski amplifies and sharpens elisions that are smoothed over with boldly essayistic forays in Hardy's more discursive narration. After Tess is forcibly impregnated by D'Urberville, she recedes from the film suddenly, following a mysterious long shot where she appears to vanish into a mist, and she is next seen, after this absence, from an insuperable distance, through the eyes of workers in a field who watch as she feeds her baby. From this point on, Tess is presented almost always at a distance, as the object of others' hostile, pitying, uncomprehending looks, and the vestiges of her subjectivity, glimpsed only in the margins of the film's increasingly corrosive lyricism, signify what has been lost. Near the end of the film, when Tess returns to Alec, another pronounced gap rends the narrative, and the next time we see Tess, she is outwardly changed, virtually unrecognizable, the remnants of her maidenhood consumed by an appearance of pseudo-aristocratic harlotry. The effect is shocking—made all the more so by its weirdly clever deferral through a relay of viewpoints that lead us back to her, slowly, but with all the grim inevitability the film has accumulated. We follow Angel Clare in his search for her, share the random gaze of passing townsfolk, and finally settle into the perspective of a bemused but inquisitive landlady (played with comic shadings by Patsy Smart of "The Benny Hill Show" and the *Carry On* films), a peripheral character whose viewpoint is given more sustained weight in the final sequence than Tess's is granted in the course of the whole film.

The result of all this should turn the treatment of Tess into a textbook case of fetishism—the "lack" by which she is construed overcome by fixing her under the camera's objectifying gaze. Many of the film's images of Tess, caught in supernal light and charged with a strange, ineffable intensity, can indeed take their place in the lineage of cinematic fetishism defined along a spectrum from Josef Von Sternberg's films of the 1930s with Marlene Dietrich to Alfred Hitchcock's *Vertigo* (1958). Most such cases turn upon a male projection of feminine enigma, ranging from the masochistic pleasures of Sternberg's haughty yet forlorn exhibitions of Dietrich's mystique to the manifest sadism of Hitchcock's participation—at once giddy and pained—in the conversion of Kim Novak into the ghostly, irretrievable Madeline. In such cases, the character of the fetish depends on the extent and quality of the woman's complicity in the construction of her own image. Dietrich's evident pleasure in being fetishized supplies much of the masochistic ambience of her films, while also empowering her ultimate subjugations of the men whose narcissistic delusions cast her in that role. Novak is pure victim, dupe of the villains and the putative heroes, whose positions gradually merge under the haphazard influences of her own helpless mediation. At both ends of this spectrum the fetishistic gaze is an extremely self-conscious one, but while Dietrich clearly shares in and conditions the self-consciousness of the Sternberg films, Hitchcock in *Vertigo* aspires to an agonizing recovery, even mastery, of damaged sexuality. Though it is never achieved, this aspiration demands that Novak remain outside the inner circle of the film's own tortured refinements.

Closer to Hitchcock's than to Sternberg's, Polanski's fetishism of Tess falls between the poles, most resembling an unlikely touchstone—the work of Max Ophuls. Another director much concerned with the sufferings of women, likewise portraying them in melodramas forcibly restrained to reach a higher prestige and produce an even greater emotional pressure, Ophuls in films from *Everybody's Woman* (1936) to *Lola Montes* (1955) presents obsessive images of besieged femininity in which his characters become increasingly aware of their own entrapment in these cycles of fetishism but still cannot break out of them. With Hardy-like fatalism, Ophuls repeatedly returns to stories of women whose initial empowerment is insufficient to liberate them from the oppression of patriarchy, and his sorrowfully fetishized images—compulsive as the endless duplicates of photos of the title character spewed from a copying machine at the start of *Everybody's Woman*—attest that the director, for all the depth of his sympathies, cannot break out of the pattern either. From this mutual ensnarement, these reciprocal networks of transference and identification that produce in equal measure feelings of fervency and failure, come all the most powerful elements of these films' emotional textures: like Polanski's *Tess*, Ophuls's films enact melodramas of sadomasochism in that the characters come to some clear realization of how they could escape and why they can't; while the director, for his part, portrays this wrenching dilemma as the human condition itself, from which he could extricate the figures of his imagination only at the expense of his own tragic vision.

The novel, especially in the nineteenth century, produces new forms of interiority in the same moment it inevitably denies them by externalizing them, making them social, public, and visible. Polanski's adaptation of Hardy proceeds with some awareness of this paradox. In an eloquent essay on Hardy, Elaine Scarry reads his work as an account of the transactions of embodied consciousness with the material world: "Man and world each act on the surface of the other; each alters the other's surface either by adding new layers to it or subtracting layers from it. . . . What is at first an interior and invisible aspect of consciousness . . . is lifted out into the world of visible action . . . and now that visible but continually disappearing action acquires an enduring sign of itself in the materialized persistence of a smoky film" (Scarry 51).

With this emphasis on bodily surface and the transmuting of interior space in modernity, Scarry could be describing Polanski's whole corpus. For Polanski, the inventions of new forms of individual consciousness in the modern world (the bourgeois individual of the classic novel, the unconscious of Freudian lore) must be understood in relation to the objectifications of the self that emerge along with them. *Tess* is ultimately a chronicle of denied subjectivity and failed identification. The tragedy of the film is that Tess, though she is a creature of thought and feeling, still cannot succeed in her efforts to defend some vestige of her inner life. She is fated to become only what she is seen as.

Hardy often reflects the same understanding in his treatment of character, as in the cases of Jude and Little Father Time in *Jude the Obscure* or, preeminently, Tess herself. Bleakly fatalistic, all three characters exemplify a disposition of melancholy that is presented explicitly as a response to modernity, which in turn is variously portrayed as an already accomplished ruination, a pseudo-enlightenment that obstructs real self-fulfillment. At the end of Hardy's novel, Tess has been executed, and Angel Clare and her younger sister visit the site of her killing. The tone of the scene is grievous but cathartic, even strangely reassuring, with an odd sense of triumph attending its tragic overtones. What Hardy proposes as redemption (the book's final section is titled, however ironically, "Fulfillment"), the reader can easily experience as affront, as Tess's sister, brought into the novel to suggest that her type is not dead, that something of her survives, is also clearly there to take her place in some sense that, for a reader who is mourning Tess, could seem to betray her memory. Though the novel too mourns Tess, it implies that we have, through the medium of her suffering, learned enough not to victimize her likes in the same way henceforth. To return to the Freudian distinction in which melancholy is a pathological fixation, a stunted and unfinished form of mourning, the climax of the book yields the successful completion of Hardy's mourning over the melancholic Tess. In Polanski's adaptation there is no aftermath, and there is no catharsis. The film enacts a more complicated set of identifications, as it refuses bitterly to complete its own acts of mourning in the name of narrative closure. Stopping at a point of stasis, of leaden immobility, with the backdrop of a reconstructed Stonehenge evoking a parallel condition of timelessness, the film refuses to supersede the melancholy of Tess by any gestures toward redemption, even while knowing that this melancholy—or whatever traces of it the filmmaker may share—can neither save nor redeem her, nor make her truly known to us.

| | |

For versions of classics, *Macbeth* and *Tess* boast an array of unusual intertexts. Of all Polanski's films, these two seem to be the least "personal" due to the nature of their sources. Yet none of his films, including *The Pianist,* have attracted more explicit commentary on their alleged autobiographical content. *Macbeth* was the director's first film after the murder of his wife Sharon Tate in 1969, while *Tess* was the first film he made after his flight from the United States upon being charged with rape. Granted that the plot of the latter film reveals some striking parallels with the rape case, one could still speculate that Polanski's choice of these projects in the wake of these incidents was motivated by a desire to take refuge in classically literary materials. Yet scarcely any reviewer failed to assert some direct connection between the films and the traumatic episodes supposed to have given rise to them.[22]

In *Tess,* Polanski appears to encourage such connections with the film's dedication: "For Sharon." These words stand alone at the end of the opening credits, scrolling slowly, mournfully, over the film's first image. To suggest that the words bid for pathos may seem like a cynical reaction, but it is not incompatible with experiencing whatever pathos they may impart. Indeed, Polanski's dedication goes some way toward accounting for the intense melancholy of the film's emotional climate, its doleful address on the plight of a figure recognized from the start as irrecoverably lost. (Though the words of the dedication may appear to address the lost beloved, it is worth noting that they read *for* Sharon," not *"to* Sharon," and thus register the loss they signify with the smallest nuance.) As a public declaration, this dedication also commands a certain sympathy, connoting a rhetorical purity in the notion of an undying love that persists even after death, and it proposes, in effect, that the film's narrative of the rape of a young woman be understood chiefly in relation to the director's loss of his wife, not in relation to his own violation of a thirteen-year-old girl. Whatever its intents, the dedication serves as a reminder of Polanski's past role as victim, presenting the film as an elegy instead of a gesture of expiation.

The director had to be aware that his more recent status as predator was likely to overshadow the public memory of his own suffering, as was indeed the case in many reviews of *Tess,* few of which mentioned the film's dedication. Considering these films together as symbolic responses to events of Polanski's life, it is striking that in *Macbeth,* the film that follows the Manson murders, the primary identification is with the murderer, while in *Tess,* the film that follows Polanski's own crime, the primary identification is with the victim of rape. If the earlier film is an act of exorcism and the latter an act of atonement, these shifting identifications make sense. More important, they provide a way of understanding the links among sadomasochism, fetishism, and melancholy in Polanski's work as a whole. In a classical Freudian framework, fetishism is a function of sadism, melancholy of masochism. Male fetishism, in particular, overcomes castration anxiety by objectifying the threat of woman, while melancholy derives from a refusal or inability to complete a proper mourning, internalizing trauma as an incessant yet ultimately glorified dejection.

Because the positions of sadist and masochist combine and shift in Polanski's work, this model, while marginally pertinent, is difficult to sustain in analysis of his films. In Polanski's work, fetishism is as likely to be linked to self-punishment as melancholy is inclined to transmute on a dime into cruelty. The whole point of *Tess* is to brandish the failures of the film's own self-justifying efforts to identify with the victim, whose portrait is conveyed via a fetishistic gaze as enchanted as it is self-contemptuous. The worst brutalities of *Macbeth*—such as the killing of Macduff's son, for all its quietness one of the most lacerating acts of violence in cinema history—are presented most regretfully, with a sense of the filmmaker's sadness that he cannot hold off the violence of the world and is thus obliged to show it in its ugliest light.

Such dynamics can be seen throughout Polanski's work, but it is worth considering a final set of strange intertexts for Polanski's classic adaptations—namely, his fashion shoots for *Playboy* and *Vogue*. In May 1967, *Playboy* ran "The Tate Gallery," a portfolio of nude shots of Sharon Tate "personally photographed" (as the accompanying copy informs us) by her director on the set of *The Fearless Vampire Killers* (called in the article simply "The Vampire Killers"). This spread is an intertext of *Macbeth* if we assume that the blood so copiously shed in that film darkly commemorates Tate's killing, and if we further recall that *Macbeth* was bankrolled by the Playboy Corporation. Even clearer intertexts are to be found in similar shots Polanski took of Nastassja Kinski just before she played Tess, images that appeared in *French Vogue* of December 1976, in an issue "guest edited" by the director himself. Both of these features tell us something about the heady cocktail of sadomasochism, fetishism, melancholy, and identification that infuses Polanski's work. The photos are straightforwardly fetishistic in the manner of their genre, but the most striking depictions show the women withdrawing from the gaze of the camera, trying to cover themselves, folding their bodies into positions as modest as their nudity permits. More straightforwardly eroticized than any images in Polanski's films, these yet resist and undermine their own qualities of sensuousness.

That the models' contortions are reticent rather than teasing in the familiar style of such pictures is suggested by the expressions on the women's faces, sincere even amid the obligatory coyness, by turns pleading, impassive, and exasperated, if compliant. Their poses constantly emphasize bodily discomfort and vulnerability, recalling the nude shots of Francesca Annis as Lady Macbeth. Considering that those shots were

Too much the fashion plate? Nastassja Kinski
as *Tess*.

dismissed in some quarters as nothing but *Playboy*-style lewdness—and that other critics chided Kinski for being too much the fashion plate to portray Hardy's heroine convincingly—these spreads may not be such far-fetched intertexts after all.

In one image, Sharon Tate is splayed on her back across a wrought-iron scaffolding atop spear-like protrusions certainly sharp enough to penetrate her flesh. In others, she is posed among banks of snow, her nudity belying the implied cold. As the camera moves closer to her, shot by shot, she averts her eyes. At every turn, the photos are bent on making the viewer aware of the psychic costs of these pictures—of the indignities of being in them and even, in some sense, of consuming them—though such convictions were obviously not powerful enough to cause their author to refrain from producing them in the first place. The photos enact a drama of sadomasochism perhaps always implicit in the act of photography, recalling some of the work of Helmut Newton, who transformed fashion photography by incorporating visual conventions of pornography into his work. Like Polanski in these cases, Newton shot his models in discomfiting positions that yet showed the models as coolly indifferent to that implied sadism. Newton's work became increasingly explicit about its own sadomasochism as his career developed, even to the point of his appearing as an abjectly desiring figure in his own shots alongside models who blithely ignore his wildly incongruous presence.

Polanski's photos mimic the style of pornography that titillates by refusing the viewer full visual access to the model's body. In this way, they fetishize the impossible desire to possess the figure in the photograph. At the same time, they do not let us forget how exposed the women in them are. Tate and Kinski seem willfully, archly, posed in every shot—*directed,* that is, as opposed to acting on their own—and neither seems complicit in her own imaging, yet the images constantly obstruct the conventional visual pleasures such photos would seem intended to provide. If this implies a self-critical attitude on the part of the photographer—a melancholy or masochistic identification with the models' status as object, even as they are sadistically rendered as such—it does little to mitigate the fetishism the images continue to connote. Around the time of the *Vogue* shoot, presumably in much the same way and for the same purposes, Polanski also photographed the young girl who, soon after, would be his accuser.

Discovering the Figural in Polanski's Films

The final shot of Polanski's first feature, *Knife in the Water,* shows a car stopped at the intersection of two roads. The first shot of his third film, *Cul-de-Sac,* shows a car creeping across an expansive desert embankment, a terrain unmarked by significant milestones or guideposts. The shots are linked, if at all, only in viewers' thought or memory, and they are quite concrete images, as opposed to being overtly abstract, and in the ways that cinematic images typically avail themselves of a rhetoric of concreteness: clarity of resolution, directness of reference, an appeal to forms of cognition and recognition. Like nearly any visual image, they obscure, ignore, and withhold as much as they reveal, expose, or indicate. The final shot of *Knife in the Water* signifies a deliberate indeterminacy: after the wife's confession of infidelity, will the husband still drive on, and if so, which road will he take? The opening shot of *Cul-de-Sac* raises inaugural questions of its own: Where is this car coming from? Why is it moving so slowly? How has it come to traverse this vast, roadless space?

Beyond the hermeneutic value of these shots, they point to a figural dimension that is among the most interesting levels of Polanski's work, from the vantage point of film theory. Despite the associative linkage of these shots, the precision and exactitude of Polanski's images do not immediately suggest a concern with figurative imagery in any ordinary sense. On the contrary, these means can readily be seen as part of an effort to control meaning, to hold connotation in check—the opposite of a figural conception of the image that would unleash meaning or multiply significance. Yet Polanski's practice of cinematic figuration remains one of the defining features of his art, and the study of his work yields much that is pertinent to debates about the nature of the figural in film. His images convey a powerful sense of being stranded between matter and symbol. The more concrete they are, the more palpably do they threaten to turn into figment, phantom, mere appearance—bringing to mind Alain Robbe-Grillet's tribute to Kafka's style: "The hallucinatory effect derives from the extraordinary clarity and not from mystery or mist. Nothing is more fantastic ultimately than exactness" (180).[23] Though a kind of figurative imagery runs through nearly all of Polanski's work, it usually has the character of having been crudely materialized, in keeping with the director's overarching concern with the objectification of consciousness in modernity. Deprived of the inwardness of metaphor, Polanski's images become figures made flesh, gross substance retaining vestiges of its significance as symbol but mainly notable for its corporeality as brute matter—slabs of meat, like the rotting rabbit in *Repulsion* or the bloody livers Rosemary gobbles in *Rosemary's Baby;* or pulped faces, like Terry's in *Rosemary's Baby* or Evelyn Mulwray's at the end of *Chinatown.* Figuration in Polanski is linked less to fetishism than to the violence of literal dismemberment: the bodiless heads in *Macbeth* or *The Tenant* never quite become symbols, any more than any other object does in Polanski's features, but neither are they really body parts any longer. "What right has my head," asks Trelkovsky in *The Tenant,* imagining his body being cut apart limb by limb, "to call itself me?" In one sense, the quintessential figure in Polanski is the cut part or the severed member—wrenched or brutalized into a liminal space but still little more than a base object or a bloody clump of flesh.

To understand the nature of the figural in Polanski's work, it is useful to consider the relation of his short films to his features. In the history of cinema since the end of the silent era, the short film has provided a kind of refuge for explorations of outright figuration—think of the films of the surrealists, the classics of the American avant-garde from *Meshes of the Afternoon* (1943) to *Scorpio Rising* (1964), even the early shorts of nascent movements like the French New Wave or the New German Cinema—while the feature has typically sublimated metaphor, metonymy, and other facets of the figural into more literal channels. Major filmmakers like René Clair, Luis Buñuel, François Truffaut, and Jean-Luc Godard, and even lesser ones like Robert Florey or Curtis Harrington, first made short films composed predominantly of figurative imagery of various kinds before going on to make features that were more stably grounded in the rhetoric of narrative, less given to the kinds of formal abstraction that foster figuration most directly.

In each of these cases, however, elements of that abstraction persist in the directors' later work, if only in the recurrence of visual motifs or consistent treatments of theme. In Clair, for instance, a clash between the organic and the mechanical structures the chain of metaphor in *Entr'acte* (1928), and this conflict continues as a thematic strain throughout his work, from *A Nous la Liberté* (1936) to *It Happened Tomorrow*

(1944), drawing upon a consonant fund of imagery that revolves around the fate of the human body in urban space. In Buñuel, the sly, subversive, and enigmatic delineations of priests in *Un Chien Andalou* (1928), to cite only one line of imagery, lay the groundwork for the wayward processions of clergy who inhabit his later films, nearly always appearing as a threat to literal coherence or otherwise bearing a burden of symbolism, representing or speaking for some portentous meaning that remains elusive. The fanciful depictions of children at play in Truffaut's poetic short *Les Mistons* (1957) that return in later features like *The Four Hundred Blows* (1959) and *Small Change* (1976); the vagrant, childlike lyricism of Godard's *All the Boys Are Called Patrick* (1958) that collides productively with a corrosive, callow misanthropy in his films of the 1960s; the portrayal of identity as an arbitrary visual sign in Florey's surrealist short (with Slavko Vorkapich) *A Hollywood Extra* (1928) and in his Hollywood B-movies of the 1940s (*The Face behind the Mask, The Beast with Five Fingers*); or the barely pronounced castration anxieties or other threats to bodily integrity that hover under the piquant veneers of Harrington's shorts of the 1950s (*The Assignation, The Wormwood Star*) and come deliriously to the surface of his camp-horror films of the 1960s and 1970s (*Games, Ruby, What's the Matter with Helen?*)—in each case, the frankly metaphorical depictions of the shorts endure within the more orthodox frameworks of the features, where they simultaneously adapt themselves to a greater literalism and evocatively retain some of their character as abstract figures.

Even more clearly than in most of these examples, Polanski's short films establish a ground of figuration on which much of the rest of his work develops. His career provides an especially significant case because his features differ more markedly from his short films than the mature films of these other directors do from their own earliest works. The difference is not one of temperament, sensibility, or even imagery, each of which is established at the outset of Polanski's career and evolves without appearing to alter fundamentally in the course of his work. Rather, it is a difference in frames of reference; the frameworks of the shorts are those of fable, parable, and allegory, while those of the features emphatically eschew, if not clearly renounce, such forms. For that reason, the continuity, especially in the persistence of the figural, from the larkish allegory of the shorts to the powerfully literalized milieu of the features, provokes a violent juxtaposition of contexts. In Buñuel—the closest to Polanski in style, form, and sensibility among these filmmakers—a level of abstraction is seldom far from the surface, because Buñuel's work, after the initial forays of *Un Chien Andalou*, *L'Age d'Or* (1931), and *Land without Bread* (1932), rarely excludes allegory as a model of understanding. If anything, Buñuel's later features become even more allegorically inclined, so that even the most obdurate figures take their place in a larger structure of meaning, and he returned to the short form late in his career in *Simon of the Desert* (1965), a film with direct affinities to his earliest work—and a reversion of a type that is nearly unthinkable in Polanski's career.[24] This continuity and this disjunction combine in Polanski's work to impart a dimension to visual figures beyond the most common ones of association, enigma, irresolution, and excess—that of the vestigial. Figures in Polanski often seem grotesquely residual, remnants of a vanished order—like stains or scars—allegorical emblems usurped and transplanted into a starkly material realm where the coherent yet abstract moralities of allegory can never obtain.

In Polanski's best-known short film, *Two Men and a Wardrobe* (1959), the two men of the title, reminiscent of the hapless, cosmic vaudevillians of *Waiting for Godot*, emerge from the sea carrying a large paneled bureau and roam through a provincial town. There, amid casual acts of cruelty taking place everywhere around them, they are repeatedly rebuffed—denied access to a streetcar, refused entry to a bistro—because of the cumbersome wardrobe. Finally, after a violent encounter with a gang of young toughs and a brutal, random murder they pass but do not witness, they return to the sea and vanish into the waves, still carrying their burden. A jazzy parable with the overtones of a dark folktale, the film bears its allegory as weightily as the men do their wardrobe, so that nearly every character, action, and object seems infused with an immediate charge of symbolism. Each thing is not only itself—the allegorical framework willfully deprives individuals and objects of their material specificity—but a figure, a signifier of an absent but constant "meaning." Unless such meaning is assigned to the wardrobe, the film remains opaque; once attributed, this latency becomes all too obvious—the wardrobe "is" the characters' alienation, or their condition of exile, or their blindness to everyday violence, or some other abstraction made bulkily manifest. Modernist fables with a mordant skepticism even about their own allegorical forms, Polanski's shorts are in nearly equal measure impishly obscure and dolefully explicit, committed to absurdist allegory so wholeheartedly that it often seems as if they come out the other side again, into full-fledged literalism.

The figures of Polanski's shorts are symbol turning matter, while those of his features are matter turning symbol. A shockingly sudden, discordant image in *Two Men and a Wardrobe* of a dead fish framed against an abstract sky works out the conversion exactly when a subsequent shot reveals that it is an actual fish, literally present in the plot, resting on the upended wardrobe's mirror, after which disclosure the men promptly tear the fish apart for their supper. What, though, of the whole sequence of wardrobes featured prominently in such Polanski features as *Repulsion, Rosemary's Baby,* and *The Tenant?* Functioning literally in the films' plots, each is endowed with an ample substantiality, yet each has a tendency toward a disquieting mutability. In the small but maze-like apartment Carol shares with her sister in *Repulsion,* it is hard to get one's bearings or to keep track of much of anything—the rooms seem to shift location and even change size—but even in that volatile context, the wardrobe is an especially erratic presence. In broad daylight its mirror reflects an intruder who is not really there, while by night Carol gazes at it as she listens to the moans and cries of lovemaking coming from her sister's room, and we share her perspective on the object, as if it were meant to be taken as a dark, hulking embodiment of sex itself. Some time later, it blocks the door through which it appears Carol has just entered the room, yet its obstruction does not impede the rapist who, moments afterward, soundlessly pushes it aside to get to the terrified girl.

In one sense, the meanings of these wardrobes are all too clear. They stand as images of transience, tenancy, and exile. Like the one in *Two Men and a Wardrobe,* this trio of wardrobes is both protective and burdensome. The secretary in the apartment hallway in the first scene of *Rosemary's Baby* is equally solid yet enigmatic—its weight is remarked on as two men shift it away from the closet door it was mysteriously placed to block—while the wardrobe in *The Tenant* is impervious and weirdly mutable: it contains Trelkovsky's identity, which depends more and more on the clothing inside, and reflects it, as he struts and poses before the mirror in drag.

The flatly allegorical image thus propels a series of anamorphoses, to paraphrase Gilles Deleuze, that describe a large, unbounded circuit. As Deleuze remarks in discussing the nature of the cinematic figure, "[T]he virtual image which becomes actual does not do so directly, but becomes actual in a different image, which itself plays the role of virtual image being actualized in a third, and so on to infinity" (56). The transmission of associations that give rise to these figures follows an arc from metaphor to theorem—the movement of film history from its classic to its modern phases, as Deleuze recounts it—the shift from the metaphoric or metonymic combinations of montage to the comprehensive thought reflected in a greater depth of field and temporal comprehensiveness. After the abandonment of figures in modern cinema, according to Deleuze, depth of field "opened up a new direction for the cinema, no longer metaphorically or even metonymically 'figurative,' but more demanding, more constraining, in some sense *theorematic* . . . it now makes the unrolling of the film a theorem rather than an association of images, it makes thought immanent to the image" (173). Far from putting an end to figuration, in Deleuze's model, the movement from montage to depth of field liberates it, giving it new, free berth within the image, where formerly it had been intelligible only *between* images. Against the explicit metaphors of early cinema—in such oft cited juxtapositions as the cut from Kerensky to a strutting peacock in *October* (1927), from factory workers to a herd of sheep in *Modern Times* (1936), from gossiping women to barnyard hens in *Fury* (1936)—Deleuze counters a generalized conceptual field of the modern cinema.

A bridge between the ideas of Deleuze and the practice of Polanski may be found in the writings of Antonin Artaud, who influenced Deleuze's conception of cinematic abstraction and Polanski's interest in the ontology of matter as the death of spirit. Like Polanski, Artaud is, in the words of Susan Sontag, "obsessed with physical matter. . . . Artaud's prose and poetry depict a world clogged with matter (shit, blood, sperm), a defiled world. The demonic powers that rule the world are incarnate in matter, and matter is 'dark'" (Sontag xlvi–xlvii). In his writings on cinema, Artaud looks to material objects as a confirmation of this conviction and a means toward transubstantiation. Writing on "Cinema and Abstraction," Artaud argues that cinema cannot, like abstract painting, dispense with objects, but it can transmute them into a form of abstraction: "Nothing exists except in terms of forms, volumes, light, air—but above all in terms of the sense of a detached and naked emotion that slips in between paved roads or images and reaches a heaven where it bursts into full bloom" (*Selected* 149). Elsewhere, Artaud says that because cinema "works with matter itself," it invents a new kind of abstraction, "[a] certain excitement of objects, forms, and expressions [that] can only be translated into the convulsions and surprises of a reality that seems to destroy itself with an irony in which you can hear a scream from the extremities of the mind" (*Selected* 152).

Polanski's films realize consistently and compellingly a sense of the figural in this sense. In *Knife in the Water*, a film much concerned with visible action, physical presence, and ruthless objectivity—so far from the ethos of allegory—the final shot suggests a dimension of inwardness that has been staunchly negated until that moment. Between the couple in the car—for all the world like the bickering pair of Bergman's *Wild Strawberries* (1957), transplanted from the back seat to the front—there is a final bout of caviling, at once fierce, sour, and strangely affectless. The wife wants the husband to admit that he is scared; the husband mocks her tale of infidelity. The car draws to a stop, and the camera's perspective shifts to a long shot from a low angle, the car poised at the crossing. The extremity of this change in scale indicates—together with the shot's protraction, its emphatically geometrical composition, and the slow, deliberate fade with which it ends—a sudden transport to a different order, where the stalled car becomes an image of a paralyzed marriage, or more generally, of a breakdown in affections or intimacies that has been exhibited throughout with a brisk and clinical neutrality, but to which our ultimate response, previously given no outlet, is now being directly solicited. Part of the point of this portentous final shot, in other words, is to reify an overlay of figurative imagery. We realize that this level of address has been engaged all along, at least as a structuring absence, an undertow, the trace of an elusive subjectivity even after everything has been forcibly externalized, all inner space evacuated.

Although it may seem idiosyncratic, Deleuze's account of cinematic figuration takes its place in a line of thinking that has endured and evolved from the inception of film theory. The earliest claims for film as art in the work of such writers as Vachel Lindsay, Harry Alan Potamkin, and Rudolf Arnheim depended on a conception of the film image as a figurative field, a composite of the pictorial and a kind of cuneiform writing, as in Lindsay's notion of the cinematic hieroglyph. From the start, their work confounded any simple unity of concept and representation within the image. For Arnheim or Potamkin, the plasticity of form in the medium itself endowed film with an intrinsic capacity for abstraction, however objectively concrete its delineations might seem, so that whenever a film broached an actual figure, a visual metaphor or metonymy, it was only realizing explicitly a dimension of the figural that was already present implicitly. Other early writers pointed to the graphic component of the image as the essence of cinematic figuration, most notably Vladimir Nilsen in *The Cinema as a Graphic Art* (1937), a book Polanski may have encountered in the film school at Lodz, as it was widely reissued in 1959. Defining the graphic as an abstract component of the composition that enters via the film image's uses of geometrical form, Nilsen nonetheless makes clear that his own neoformalist emphasis is fully compatible with an aesthetic of socialist realism that he simultaneously—and equivocally—promotes, and his work can easily be seen as an effort to preserve a modernist aesthetic of montage within the holistic, objective image, as against a "passive reproductionalism."

A similar effort appears in the writings of Sergei Eisenstein—who provided an appreciative foreword to Nilsen's book—when he turns, late in his work, from montage as an effect of editing to a growing concern with montage as a figurative force within the image itself. This turn implies a full revaluation of the film shot as a unit of construction, no longer seeing it as uninflected raw material that gains meaning by being placed against other shots in a chain of associations but as a discursive arena in its own right, always animated by the intricate, cross-grained play of text and figure, line and letter. If this shift in Eisenstein's thought also implies a growing commitment to socialist realism, it remains as much a species of transcendental realism as that adumbrated by André Bazin soon after in "The Evolution of the Language of Film" (1950–55)—and, taken together, these dual climacterics of classical film theory form the ground on which Deleuze builds his reflections.

Subsequent theories of the figural in film turned to psychoanalytic concepts, as in work by Christian Metz, Thierry Kuntzel, and Jean-François Lyotard. Here, the figural registers the force of the unconscious at work within the text, retaining an emphasis on the interiority of the image. In Metz and Kuntzel, figuration inheres once again in metaphor and metonymy, now seen to permeate film form itself and to express a kind of generalized, impersonal unconscious—not that of an individual but of a whole culture, or of textuality itself. Metz sees figuration as a fundamental process or effect of film construction, manifested in the displacements of the cut or the dissolve and in the condensations of the mise-en-scène, where a film's greater or lesser awareness of its own fig-ural operations determines its value as either a classic, homeostatic text or a self-reflexive, modernist one. For Kuntzel, film entails a practice of cinematic writing that inscribes a variation of Freudian dreamwork, in which figuration is a constant quantity of the image, enunciated equally in the modernist and the classical text, running the gamut from *M.* (1931) to *The Most Dangerous Game* (1932). Lyotard continues to emphasize the pervasion of the unconscious in the film image, now with an explicitly libidinal component, but like Deleuze, he detaches the energies of the figural from the circumscribed bond of individual figures. In his essay "Acinema," Lyotard argues that figuration permeates film as a function of mechanisms of psychic censoring, the impulse to drive out "bad" images in favor of "good" images, a literal feature of all filmmaking—in the aesthetic composition of the shot, for instance, and the selection or exclusion of specific takes for a final cut—that makes each shot the actualization of a virtual outset, a conceptual incipience that continues to haunt the "finished" film as a kind of noumenal immanence.

As the basis of his conception of the figural in film, Deleuze posits a similar relation between the actuality of a given image and its virtual, conceptual determinants. Not surprisingly, however, considering his wholesale critique of the Freudian model elsewhere, he emphatically discards the unconscious as the binding term of these textual levels. Just as Deleuze, rejecting the linguistic turn of film theory, attempts in his work on cinema to formulate a sign system without signs, so he elaborates a model of figuration without figures, without the hypothetical subjectivity on which most previous models depended.[25] In the modern cinema, Deleuze argues, the "break in the sensory-motor link"—evident in the dissociative editing of Godard, for example, or in the emphases on "dead time" in Antonioni—expresses "more profoundly [the break] in the link between man and world" (173) indicative of the modern age. For Deleuze, this break is what makes subjectivity into a problem, but the split in consciousness is seen less as personal self-alienation, with a whole psychic infrastructure behind it, than as the product of a growing mechanization or objectification of selfhood as a concept. No longer understood as conditional essence from which expression flows organically (as in the masteries of the self-reflexive text, or the recuperative indeterminacies of the talking cure), subjectivity becomes a physical reflex, existing not inside (in the sense that montage was said to create a responsive "inner speech") but between objects in a conceptual field. If the modern cinema consists almost entirely of elements traditionally aligned with subjectivity (affect, cerebration, complex new representations of memory and perceptual time), it is because these are the residua from which a damaged subjectivity must remake itself: "Subjectivity, then, takes a new sense, which is no longer motor or material, but temporal and spiritual: that which 'is added' to matter, not what distends it" (47). Polanski's work concerns and enacts crises of modern subjectivity without any of the redemptive or transcendental rhetoric that often animates Deleuze's writings (or Artaud's, for that matter), and his films square so suggestively with the ideas of *Cinema 2* that Deleuze's total neglect of the director in that book is felt as a clear lack. (The sustained discussion of Artaud in Deleuze's book may be seen as an approximate substitute for the missing analysis of Polanski.) In Polanski's films, we find an acute treatment of the "break in the sensory-motor link" that, instead of throwing the subject back upon a compensating interiority, makes us aware as never before of the rift between inner and outer experience, and the increasing inaccessibility of the former. We witness a transformation of regimes of truth and falsehood, the rise of a "crystalline" image based profoundly in the concrete but tending toward a latent abstraction, a concern with new permutations of the rational and the irrational, an ubiquitous sense of duration as constraint and subjectivity as a mere supplement to a hostile outer world: all key themes of Deleuze's theory of the modern cinema and defining features of Polanski's cinematic art, manifest in the chain of figures that make up his films, by turns elegant and coarse, but always exteriorized and flatly deracinated.

Repulsion provides the fullest example of how figural imagery is rendered in Polanski's work. It is also the clearest illustration of the shift in conception from his short films, because it is specifically about the failure of allegory—the incommensurability of psychology and subjectivity and the inadequacy of psychological explanation to what remains of subjective agency. At the start of the film, it is clear that Carol already inhabits a space of severe abstraction: what we watch in the course of the narrative is not a gradual deterioration of her faculties, not a "mental breakdown," but the slow, material actualization of a long-standing derangement. Her inexorable descent into catatonia is presented as neither cautionary tale nor case study, and because it is unclear whether her condition is to be understood as a horrifying anomaly or as an example of some representative new typology, it could be said that she is stranded between the indicative mode of allegory and the literality of fiction. To the extent that the film functions as a "horror" movie, Carol is both victim and source of the horrors, and this collapse of positions—of subject into object and object into subject—speaks of a dire world of totalized social utility, where all must be visible so that the useless may be identified and banished.

Deracinated figures haunt this world, and Carol's oddity is shown from the beginning to have something to do with her tendency to fixate on these figures—literally, to stare at them. She comes upon a crack in the concrete of the street and crouches beside it, gazing at it inexpressively. Her action suggests that she thinks the crack's shape has meanings, but her affect suggests that she does not expect it to yield them. Similarly, she stares at the reflection of her face in a toaster, at a beam of sun on a chair, at an image of the Eiffel Tower in a postcard, at the folds in a bedsheet. Her disposition throughout is a distracted concentration, her attention turned constantly toward importunate marginalia that nobody else notices, images that seem to contain the sediments of a dispelled significance. Far from being encouraged to see Carol's fixations on these images as misconceived or delusional, the viewer is urgently solicited to share them, to be aware of these figures as both peripheral and even more fraught with meaning than Carol takes them to be. Whether or not Carol is aware of the sameness in form of a crack that later appears in the wall of her apartment to the one she contemplates in the street, we cannot miss it. Later, from a shot of the furrowed bedsheet, Polanski cuts trenchantly to an image of a wrinkled gown at the beauty salon where Carol works. A rare and startling moment of explicit visual metaphor in Polanski's features, the exacting match of these figures points to a

Carol's uncanny stares: Catherine Deneuve
in *Repulsion.*

congruency between home and work as utilitarian social spaces. In the world of this film, work is where one must be seen, so that one's value can be judged, while home is where one thinks one may escape enforced perceptibility, but where one is still under scrutiny because the rent must still be paid.

It is key to the project of Polanski's work to bring into view the unseen so that we understand how the visible may escape real perceptibility. This project depends on our recognition of the role of the cinematic apparatus itself as an instrument of utilitarian objectification, implicated deeply in modernity's impulse to document, to capture reality in a condition of fixed visibility. Carol's loneliness appears as protracted, implosive inactivity that should thereby escape the attentions of an objectifying gaze concerned chiefly with apprehending, revealing, and ranking actions and external-ized agencies. Yet the painstaking itemization of her solitudes occupies the bulk of the film. In fact, Carol has already been judged useless: the first scene of the film shows her being rebuffed for her absence of mind in her workplace, and she is subsequently banished to a small back room where she vacantly pursues her fixation on the peripheral objects whose marginality she shares. Her abstraction is even more visible in public than it is in isolation, but it is still scarcely noticed and certainly not understood. If the repulsion of the title is Carol's, it is what spurs her retreat from the social world of competitive action; if it is that world's, in response to Carol, then it bespeaks only contempt for the unfit.

Because they resist the objectifications of unambiguous meaning, figures in film lie beyond the threshold of utility, and objects in *Repulsion* reveal their figural dimensions before their values densify or after they have expired. The rabbit that rots on a plate on the countertop, and the potatoes that grow new eyes and tangled shoots, become more and more meaningful—evoking growing mental paralysis, perhaps, or arrested fertility—the less they can be thought of as food. A literal emblem of material decay, the crack in the pavement is a portentous instance of matter turning into symbol, while Carol's effort to brush away a beam of sun that has fallen on a chair shows a misrecognition that realizes the defamiliarizing tendency that, in Polanski's films, removes such images from normative contexts of use or value. We are led into a series of parallel misrecognitions in the course of the film: At first we think Carol works in a clinic, a quintessential institution of bureaucratic utility. Only gradually do we realize that it is actually a high-tech spa—an equally distinctive type of modern institution, though implying leisure instead of need, the decorative instead of the curative. And we never can determine which of these terms, hospital or salon, form tenor or vehicle of the overweening metaphor their relation creates.

To watch any film is to stare, but one is rarely as conscious of this fact as one is in viewing *Repulsion*. What accounts for this awareness is precisely the figural dimension of the film, the sense—as against that of more ordinary movies, where things do not mean, but be—in which objects are invested with significance that, however manifest, they yet do not reveal. Carol stares at these objects with a benumbed intensity, befitting the contemplation of what is both radically extrinsic and ineffable, and we stare at her in search of outward proof, evidence, or confirmation—of what, we cannot know, because though all immanence has been leeched to the surface, it still refuses to communicate. Carol's affectless horror throughout the film shows an extreme aversion to this world of radical exteriority, so far progressed, it seems, that the only remaining transaction between inside and outside, between thought and feeling or physical being and sensation, is rape.

The one moment of longing on Carol's part occurs as she gazes through a window at identically robed nuns at play in a neighboring convent, a passing glimpse of another world, removed from everyday utility, where uniformity is all that guards against the threat of reckonings produced by the brutal rendering of differences as merely visible. Carol's fascination with peripheral objects may derive from some awareness of her own marginality, and the attentions she gives them requite the attentions she herself rarely receives, and which she repels when she does. Everybody leaves Carol alone, and yet nobody leaves her alone, and in the end she turns to violence to protect herself against the endless assaults on her own interiority. She does so by seizing on seemingly symbolic objects—the knives and razors that appear everywhere in Polanski's movies as frightening totems—and fiercely returning these weapons to their lot as brute, material things by plunging them into others' flesh.

"Repulsion" cuts both ways—it is at once the act of repulsing and the condition of being repulsed. It is therefore indicative as a state of mind of the modern collapse of subjectivities beyond preservation into an encompassing, utilitarian objectification. The often-drawn comparison to *Psycho* is striking in this regard: in the first half of Hitchcock's film, a woman whose subjectivity is accessible only through the voices of others—in the recriminations heard in voiceover as she drives—pursues a series of unspoken intentions comprehensible only as actions. In other words, because we do not know Marion's intentions, any more than we know Carol's, we are forced to judge them only by their consequences. All too explicably, Marion realizes desire in action, until an arbitrary murder—a brute, material act of great physical consequence—violently severs the remorselessly straight line of this action. Until then, the mise-en-scène bristles with naggingly overexplicit figures that function as direct visual similes: the desert painting against which Marion is framed in the office where she works, for instance, or the mannerist works of art and stuffed birds mounted on the walls of Norman's parlor. After the murder, figures in the film become ever more oblique: the stuffed rabbit with the tattered ear in Norman's room, or the mysterious book Lila opens as she searches the house, or the bronzed likeness of folded hands in Mrs. Bates's chamber, or even the frozen leer of the mother's own mummified face.

Hitchcock's view is a utilitarian one that favors action over introspection—which nearly always entails fixation or obsession. The psychiatrist's final explanation of the plot's action is notable for its lack of thoughtfulness, and it has the purpose only of making the formerly unthinkable newly palpable to objective understanding ("The psychiatrist doesn't lay the groundwork, he merely explains . . ."). This tidy summation liberates us from the swampy, darkish realm of unreadable symbol, restoring the final comprehensibility of figures in the direct superimposition of the mother's skull over Norman's face in the penultimate shot, or the car being lifted from the bog in the ultimate one.

No such explanation is offered in Polanski's work, nor would it be plausible if it were (the structure of *Bitter Moon*, after all, is one long, manic explanation that scarcely even tries to be believable), because the films' main interest is to portray what the utilitarian objectifications of modernity have done to inner lives. If Hitchcock finds that a persistence of introspection is bound to morbidity in the modern world, where mass media, bureaucracy, and the surveillance state all militate against it, he concludes that this loss is ultimately for the best, since any real happiness is only to be found in action, in the abdication of interiority.[26] By contrast, Polanski—whose view of modernity is no less bleak than Hitchcock's—mourns the diminishment of inner life with no hope of its return. Figures in Hitchcock arise from a reservoir of troubled interiority, and they take on redemptive meanings once they achieve an ultimate objectivity, like the figurine of the Virgin Mary in *Juno and the Paycock* (1930) or the crucifix in *The Wrong Man* (1957)—emblems of a private devotion that can properly salvage only after they have been offered for public use or testimony, stripped of their unwholesome inwardness. For Polanski, such excoriation is a fully accomplished and deeply regrettable fact of modern life, and figures in his work have already achieved their status as objects, fixed and glimmering with dim and ever-fading reflections of the human thoughts or feelings that might once have given them meaning.

If *Repulsion* is the clearest indication of how figurative images operate in Polanski's films, *The Tenant* is the most direct expression of the filmmaker's attitude toward such mechanisms. Another story of intense isolation, *The Tenant* is also a parable of generalized surveillance, about a character who accepts as fully just and legitimate the pervasively objectifying structures of modernity, even though they do no more to render him truly visible than they do Carol. Trelkovsky internalizes these structures so completely that his resistance to the sinister impositions of others simultaneously has the effect of demanding these oppressions as deserved punishments. In such a world, the film suggests, defiance amounts to assent, and Trelkovsky ends by performing his own suicide in drag, twice over, for a gallery of hooting spectators. The two key types of figure in *The Tenant*, hieroglyphs and wastage, are linked together and connected to the theme of surveillance by virtue of the indecipherable pictograms inscribed on the walls of the water closet across the courtyard from Trelkovsky's apartment, from which the other tenants openly scrutinize him. But symbols have lost all meaning—the previous tenant's occupation as an Egyptologist is treated as a red herring and an anachronistic joke—while waste matter grotesquely takes on meaning. Whatever Trelkovsky's intent, the clumps of refuse that fall from his sack as he carries out the trash will, he knows, be clearly readable by the other tenants as repellant little emblems of his contempt for his neighbors. But like any good symbol, these material, indexical signs have purposes of their own, for when he returns to retrieve them, they have disappeared. The lumps of excrement another tenant places at the doors of all the building's occupants, except Trelkovsky's, are clearly intended as expressions of contempt for the others, but Trelkovsky understands instantly that her gesture of sparing him will only implicate him. Action overrules intent, and when words fail, shit takes their place, metamorphosed into symbol but still remaining shit. Shit is what is left when the objectification that is everywhere gets internalized once again as meaning, only then there is no inside left for it to go back to—except the intestines.

Figures in Polanski's work frequently condense a relation of inner and outer, surface and depth, into images of recalcitrant surface made to bear the burden of a lost interiority. The faces of the salon's clientele in *Repulsion* look like blank masks, swathed in corrugated towels or bare in their repose, inscrutably awaiting a cosmetic inscription to galvanize them. Identity is not wrought in the spirit but figured on the body—as in the wife's garish painting of her husband's face in *Cul-de-Sac*, or Nancy's blue emblazonry of her own legs in *What?* In *The Tenant*, a sudden, shocking cut to a close-up of Trelkovsky's crusty, adamantine fingernail as he covers it with bright polish is our first irrefutable inkling of his crazed reaction to the conspiracy he imagines against him; he reacts to this theft of his soul by grotesquely transforming the surface of his body. Ghoulishly rhymed with this flinty fingernail are his hard little teeth, one of which is mysteriously wrenched from his mouth by night and stowed in a hole in the wall. The moment recalls Poe's tale "Berenice" (1835), which culminates in the demented narrator's sadistic and fetishistic extraction of the title character's teeth. Pulled from its roots, the tooth stops being a part of the body and becomes a symbol of something: in both cases, the macabre joke is to figure the tooth as the mirror of the dissipated soul, jutting from the body's interior as protrusive bone yet still contained in the mouth, thus occupying a troubled threshold between inside and outside the physical self, which is all that remains of the Cartesian subject—whose motto has been reduced to something on the order of *I chew, therefore I am.*

In this context, the orifices of the body become nothing but holes, and holes recur throughout Polanski's work as untraversable passageways to an unimaginable interior, repellant reminders of an abolished inwardness. Carol's eye and Trelkovsky's mouth are only two such cavities, into which the camera descends as if into a depth so plumbless it is really only another surface. Yet another such crevice appears near the beginning of *What?*—an aperture in the headboard of the bed in which Nancy sleeps on her first night at the villa, a hole that disturbs her so much that she plugs it before she sleeps, only to have the cork mysteriously sucked inside the crack. Just as common as these images of a dormant interiority that continues to consume what comes into its orbit—like a stagnant swamp swallowing dead leaves—are recurrent figures of a lingering or potentially revivifying inwardness that remains inaccessible or threatening. Rosemary becomes more and more an image as her body undergoes the inexorable metamorphoses of its dire pregnancy. Recalling Trelkovsky's coy exclamation as he struts in drag—"I think I'm pregnant!"—it could be said that Rosemary is the apotheosis of the figurative image in Polanski's work, as she is both a bodily presence and a vehicle of meanings taking root "inside" her that she does not suspect. Moreover, figures in Polanski's films are typically "pregnant" in just this way, with a demonic immanence that belies the death of the subject but never redeems it. Among other things, Rosemary exemplifies an ineluctable perversion of the organic, but such persisting figments of inwardness in Polanski's work are often more prosaic commodities of mass production—like the can of pickles Wlady worries so energetically in *The Pianist*. Its inside holds out a promise as cherished as that of a gestating babe—the promise of food—but it proves to be yet another surface that he cannot penetrate.

As a cinema of surfaces, Polanski's films consist of images that are crystalline in many of the usual senses of that word: clear, limpid, lucid, translucent. They may also be called crystalline in the more specialized sense in which Deleuze uses the term. Distinguishing between the organic and the crystalline film image in *Cinema 2*, Deleuze argues that the organic image roughly corresponds with the classical cinema, while the crystal image corresponds roughly with the modern cinema. In Deleuze's model, the former is physical, somatic, material, presenting itself transparently as an actuality, while the latter synthesizes "the actual image and *its* virtual image" (70) into a prismatic composite, translucent instead of transparent.

In the succession Deleuze traces, these images are made up of reflective surfaces that suggest depth by mirroring an image of reality but block access to it by reverting to pure surface. Often, in Deleuze's inventory, these are panes of glass, like those that appear throughout the work of Max Ophuls, or they are literal mirrors like those seen throughout the films of Orson Welles—multipaneled specula like the one that produces multiple Kanes in *Citizen Kane,* or the crystal globe, a kitschy paperweight, that reflects his own past back at him, or the distorting mirrors that shatter at the climax of *The Lady from Shanghai.* The crystal image stands as a sign of the troubled self-reflexivity of the modern cinema, intractable and refractory, refusing to yield the depth it appears to contain.

In Polanski's films, images of water take on some of the figurative weight of the images of mirrors in Welles, or windows and screens in Ophuls, or actual crystals in the films of Polanski's countryman Krysztof Zanussi (another of Deleuze's examples). All crystalline surface and glittering sheen, these images appear as early as Polanski's first short films, often as puddles that throw back reflections instead of allowing glimpses of what, if anything, they contain. In *Knife in the Water, Pirates,* and *Bitter Moon,* the action takes place at sea, and expanses of imperturbable water provide a dense but featureless atmosphere. These environments consist of material blankness, and Polanski's camera emphasizes their glassy, hyaline textures, as something like the formal equivalent of the empty stage in a Beckett play. Placid settings, they would indicate indifference or tranquility if we were prompted to assign them meaning, but they stand in Polanski's work as vast residua of evacuated significance, with no sense that the sea harbors anything at all under its rolling but unruffled surface.

What once was elemental surround is now mere background, these images suggest, so it is little wonder that in *Chinatown,* water turns into utility itself. The name of the bureaucratic department at issue in that film, Water and Power, resonates with great irony in Polanski's work. It seems inevitable that he would have been drawn to a script about the conversion of natural resources into municipal utilities, and the images of water in *Chinatown* differ from those of the films cited above in being not quiescent and inexcitable but roiling and tumultuous—images realized as fierce torrents sweeping through subterranean tunnels, as if the elements were rebelling against being put to such use. All this turmoil does nothing to prevent water from being channeled for hidden purposes, any more than its natural plenitude keeps it from being taken as barter. So ecologically pervasive that it might as well be invisible, water in Polanski's films is everywhere and nowhere, while its hypothetical companion, power, is nowhere and everywhere. Even when we do not see this water, we hear it throughout Polanski's films, always dripping from invisible faucets, with the same uncanny regularity with which its complementary commodity, time, is registered on the soundtracks by the constant ticking of clocks we never glimpse.

Water serves as an especially striking figure in Polanski's work because it is an image of the organic turned crystalline. In elaborating these categories, Deleuze adapts the vocabulary of Wilhelm Worringer's classic study *Abstraction and Empathy* (1908). Worringer argues that dominant styles in art express a culture's relation to the world, with "organic" form communicating a harmonious connection and "crystalline" form illustrating a profoundly severed one. The former promotes an empathy that only replenishes that harmony, according to Worringer, while the latter devolves into an alienating abstraction. For Worringer, contemplation of art always involves self-alienation, but empathy reunites the ego with the work so that, having lost ourselves in contemplation, we may rediscover ourselves in sublimating acts of identification. Abstraction, meanwhile, encloses the ego in the reality of a generalized social alienation. Still, Worringer suggests that abstraction provides an escape from appearances, commodified forms, and received ideas, and it is in this sense that Polanski's vividly concrete depictions subsume abstraction. In his imagery, a shattered world of organic forms is reflected back to us as crystalline figures, haunted by uncanny remnants of matter or symbol, eliciting stunted empathies out of incumbent abstractions. In Polanski's films, when all is said and done, our selves have been lost—the worst has happened—and his art, strangely uncompromising, does not hold out the promise of regaining them but the grim satisfactions of knowing they are already gone.

Notes

1. Bentham did address spheres of private life and motivation in his work on "the springs of action" and "deontology," but he did so in a virulently antimetaphysical vein, concluding that "psychological entities" are essentially "fictitious" (Bentham, *Deontology* 87).

2. Wechsler's profile is among the best examples of this autobiographical impulse, because large sections of the article consist of interviews with Polanski. Thus, the piece illustrates the critic's dogged persistence in this tack and the director's virulent resistance to it.

3. Recent work argues that the Frankfurt School approach minimizes the specificity of twentieth-century totalitarianism's anti-Semitism, among other ideologies, by viewing totalitarianism as a more general by-product of modernity. See especially Diner, *Beyond the Conceivable*, 104–8. Yet, absent the Marxist underpinnings, I argue that this is the line that Polanski's work follows, even to the point of risking the same fault, since—like members of the Frankfurt school—Polanski tends to be interested less in the actual forms of totalitarianism than in how societies presumably free of these impulses reproduce them in spite of themselves. Another key text here, surely one known to Polanski and quite possibly an influence on his work, is Czeslaw Milosz's *The Captive Mind*, which portrays post–World War II Stalinism as a relentless utilitarian nightmare in which inner experience is evacuated and whatever cannot be seen or realized as action is violently devalued or discounted. See Milosz, *Captive Mind*, 54–81, 132–33, and 160–68.

4. Though the word "genrification" refers to the imposition of generic structures on malleable and resistant materials, I use it here in line with its recent adaptations in film studies to connote genre as an ongoing process that never achieves a stable or ideal form, shaped by textual and extratextual influences that move through multiple channels. See especially Altman, *Film/Genre*.

5. Oddly enough, Polanski did consider making a Western based on the fate of the Donner Party. Had this project ever materialized, it would have remained as unimaginable as the Stanley Kubrick Western, *One Eyed Jacks*, that was never to be after Marlon Brando fired Kubrick and completed the film as director himself in 1961.

6. I have pursued further comparisons between these two directors elsewhere. See Morrison, "Old Masters."

7. See Storper, "Transit to Flexible Specialization"; and Jarvie, *Hollywood's Overseas Campaign*.

8. The first parry in this campaign was perhaps the *Time* magazine issue of September 20, 1963, that featured an image from *Knife in the Water* on its cover. (The accompanying article on international cinema was called "A Religion of Film.") Subsequent coverage of film festivals in that magazine, and in the American press generally, tended to argue that they were both too commercial and too esoteric. See Turan, *Sundance to Sarajevo*.

9. See Street, *Transatlantic Crossings*, 223–24; and Segrave, *Foreign Films in America*.

10. These examples are drawn from my own research as well as from Joan Hawkins's useful case study of art horror in a San Francisco art house during

this period. See Hawkins, *Cutting Edge*, 74–79. For further discussion of art cinema and horror, see Budd, Cabinet of Dr. Caligari.

11. Durgnat, *Sexual Alienation in the Cinema*, 204. Lest readers think I am stretching the point by referring to *Cul-de-Sac* as a comedy, I should note that the *Time* review of the film was called "Razor-Edged Slapstick."

12. For further discussion of the theme of humiliation in Polanski's work, see Toles, "This May Hurt a Little."

13. By the time Polanski arrived in Hollywood, this "shoestring" aspect of his earlier work was noted in reviews. John Simon's review of *Rosemary's Baby*, for instance, begins as follows: "When [Polanski] made his first [horror film], *Repulsion*, there were rumors that it was all this gifted director could raise money for." Simon's conclusions are unflattering: "With *Rosemary's Baby*, there are no more mitigating rumors: Polanski likes to make trashy films, and he makes them as routinely as anyone else." See Simon, "Unanswerable Films," 22.

14. Linderman, "Oedipus in Chinatown," 190. Other notable Oedipal readings of the film include Belton, "Language, Oedipus, and *Chinatown*"; and McGinnis, "*Chinatown*."

15. A notable exception is Shetley, "Incest and Capital in *Chinatown*."

16. Shetley attributes this coinage to Mayo, *Los Angeles*.

17. For a discussion of the notion of "trash" aesthetics—albeit one that remains tied to a Euro-American axis—see Sconce, "Trashing the Academy."

18. This line does not occur in Szpilman's memoir, but it bears an uncanny echo to a moment in Cynthia Ozick's well-known miniaturist's rendering of the agonies of the death camps, her short tale "The Shawl" (1980)—an isolated moment of gallows humor amid an impressionist swirl of horror: "Then Stella took the shawl away and made Magda die. Afterward Stella said: 'I was cold'" (518).

19. These notes seem a bit disingenuous. Szpilman's memoir includes materials from the diary of Hosenfeld, a Catholic teacher who loathed Nazism and helped other Jews escape interment as well. The film's repression of these facts leaves the unfortunate implication that Hosenfeld assists Szpilman because of the beauty of his playing—that culture really can be an antidote to politics, as Wladyslaw believes at the film's outset. One especially critical notice of the film paid special attention to this feature, describing Polanski's Szpilman as "Europe's stereotypical Jew: cosmopolitan, artistic, childlike, godless, rootless, utterly unprepared for history, and averse to power. . . . By conflating Jewish identity and European identity, *The Pianist* has the effect of absolving Europe of its guilt" (Oren, "Schindler's Liszt" 28). But in Polanski's film, Hosenfeld emerges as something like the anti-Schindler, helping Wladyslaw not out of conviction but out of cynicism, not out of Schindler-like nobility but world-weary self-interest; once the city is retaken, he knows the hierarchy of power will be reversed. Polanski's treatment is, not surprisingly, more bitter than Szpilman's memoir, but its effect is hardly to absolve anyone of guilt, and our final glimpses

of Wladyslaw resuming his place at the piano have no air of triumph or redemption about them.

20. Perhaps because of this complexity, Polanski's films often confound critics who bring current assumptions in film culture to bear on them, with the result that these commentaries often seem hilariously off-target. In writing about *The Pianist*, for instance, Michael B. Oren writes that the film marks "no departure from Polanski's longtime preoccupation with isolation and cruelty" and that it adds "nothing to the iconography or the understanding of the Holocaust: We have already seen these images of Jews being randomly selected and shot, and more graphically, in *Schindler's List*" (25). The notion that Spielberg's film is the principal—or the only—locus for our having viewed "these images," that once we have "already seen" them there is no reason to see them again, and that the way to measure their power is by gauging how "graphic" they are, speaks for itself. Similarly, the orgy scene in *The Ninth Gate* was taken to task by critics—as was a weirdly parallel scene in Kubrick's *Eyes Wide Shut*—for seeming old-fashioned, not "sexy" enough, as if Polanski and Kubrick had declared themselves competitors in the seemingly endless race to greater celluloid sexual "frankness" (as they had, but not in *these* films!). This is exactly the kind of faux-progressiveness that Polanski, in his late work, moves beyond.

21. See, for instance, Stallybrass, "*Macbeth* and Witchcraft"; and Wills, *Witches and Jesuits.*

22. Pauline Kael's review of *Macbeth* is perhaps the best known example of this claim (Kael, "Current Cinema").

23. My translation.

24. Polanski did contemplate making two short films for Kenneth Tynan's stage production of *O Calcutta* in 1969, but when he learned he would not be able to shoot in widescreen, he abandoned the project.

25. For a discussion of Deleuze's semiotics of film as "a sign system without signs," see Morrison, "Deleuze and Film Semiotics."

26. One writer sees this dimension of Hitchcock's work explicitly in terms of social utility and the thought of Jeremy Bentham. See Bozovic, "Of 'farther uses of the dead to the living.'"

Interviews with Roman Polanski |

In lieu of a single long interview with Polanski, below is a bibliography of key interviews given by the director throughout his career, followed by a sampling of significant comments culled from these materials. Readers should also consult Paul Cronin, ed., *Roman Polanski: Interviews* (Jackson: University Press of Mississippi, 2005).

Burke, Tom. "The Restoration of Roman Polanski." *Rolling Stone,* July 18, 1974, 40–46.
    Behind-the-scenes look at the making of *Chinatown*, with comments by Polanski on the film's conception and on working with his collaborators.

Butler, Ivan. *The Making of Feature Films.* Middlesex, U.K.: Penguin Books, 1971.
    A detailed investigation of general working methods in an interview conducted by the author of the first book in English about Polanski's work.

Carroll, Tomm. "Roman Polanski." *DGA News* 19.6 (December 1994–January 1995): 38–39, 46–47, 62.

On the making of *Death and the Maiden*, Polanski comments on the film's parallels with *Knife in the Water*, on the process of adapting Ariel Dorfman's play, and on the conceptual work of directing films, including discussions of rehearsal, storyboarding, and other technical matters.

Ciment, Michel, Michel Perez, and Roger Tailleur. "Entretien avec Roman Polanski." *Positif* 102 (February 1969): 6–19.

Perhaps the most sophisticated interview of Polanski's career, with emphasis on *Rosemary's Baby*. Polanski discusses the film's place in his career, techniques of realization, the experience of working with the cast, the films of John Cassavetes ("Anyone can take a camera and make a film like he made with *Shadows*"), and the state of contemporary cinema—Polanski singles out *Dr. Strangelove, The Graduate, Bonnie and Clyde,* and *Closely Watched Trains* as recent films he admires. In French; reprinted in English in Cronin, *Roman Polanski,* 31–46.

Costes, Claude. "Entretien avec Raymond Polanski." *Positif* 33 (April 1960): 12–15.

This earliest interview (as indicated by the director's designation as "Raymond") covers Polanski's short films, his experiences in film school, the reception of his films at festivals, and his estimations of contemporary film culture. In French; no English translation available.

De Baecque, Antoine, and Thierry Jousse. "Roman Polanski: Entretien." *Cahiers du cinéma* 445–56 (May 1992): 52–55.

On Polanski's problematic relation to Polish cinema, on working in Hollywood, and on the making of *Bitter Moon.* In French; reprinted in English in Cronin, *Roman Polanski,* 146–53.

Delahay, Michel, and Jean Andre Fieschi. "Landscape of a Mind: Interview with Roman Polanski." *Cahiers du cinéma in English* 3 (1966): 86–91.

    Translated from *Cahiers du cinéma* 175 (February 1966). Covers the director's career through *Cul-de-Sac*, with comments on the relation of his films to Hitchcock's (*Psycho* "is not a film I like to such an extent"), on "fantastic" cinema, and on general working methods.

Engle, Harrison. "Polanski in New York." *Film Comment* 5.1 (Fall 1968): 4–9.

    Comprehensive overview of Polanski's career, with special emphasis on *Rosemary's Baby*. Comments on early career, adapting to Hollywood, and general working methods.

Ford, Renée. "Interpretation" (letter to the editor). *New York Times*, November 17, 1963, 9.

    Polanski's translator at the 1963 New York Film Festival presents his comments in a press conference refuting the notion that *Knife in the Water* contains symbolism.

Gelmis, Joseph. *The Film Director as Superstar.* New York: Doubleday, 1970.

    Comprehensive post-auteurist interview, covering early career and influences, work on all films through *Rosemary's Baby*, projected subsequent projects (including a biography of Paganini and a film about the Donner Party), and the status of the director: "To me, the director is always a superstar."

Glazer, Mitchell. "On the Lam with Roman Polanski." *Rolling Stone*, April 20, 1981, 41–45.

    Profile on the occasion of *Tess*, including comments on contemporary politics from the Polish Solidarity movement to the election of Ronald Reagan in the United States, with some discussion of the 1977 rape case.

Gow, Gordon. "Satisfaction—A Most Unpleasant Feeling." *Films and Filming* 15.7 (April 1969): 15–18.

On the benefits of working in Hollywood, the progression of the Donner Party project, experiences of early childhood, and Polanski's attraction to the macabre.

Greeley, Bill. "A Pole Looks at Capitalistic TV." *Variety,* October 2, 1963, 32.

On the occasion of the New York Film Festival premiere of *Knife in the Water,* Polanski compares American television with Polish media.

Horn, John. "Polanski's Children." *Los Angeles Times,* September 18, 2005, E1.

Interview accompanying the release of *Oliver Twist.* Polanski discusses his adaptation of Dickens's novel as a "children's film."

"*Macbeth* by Daylight." *Time,* January 25, 1971, 45.

On the set of *Macbeth,* Polanski comments on the making of the film and speculates about its reception with the public.

Pizzello, Stephen. "*Death and the Maiden:* Trial by Candlelight." *American Cinematographer* 76.4 (April 1995): 56–70.

Detailed technical interview with the director and his cinematographer on *Death and the Maiden,* Tonino Delli Colli. Comments on Delli Colli's work with Pasolini, Fellini, Welles, and Sergio Leone, approaches to shooting *Death and the Maiden,* its place in the director's career.

"*Playboy* Interview: Candid Conversation with Roman Polanski." *Playboy* 18.12 (December 1971): 93–118, 126.

Perhaps the most comprehensive interview of Polanski's career, this one traces the director's career through *Macbeth,* touching on working methods, choices of projects, and general philosophies: "I have no belief at all in the supernatural of any kind. . . . I am down to earth in my philosophy of life, very rationally and materialistically oriented, with no interest in the occult."

"Polanski at Cannes, May 1968." *Variety,* June 12, 1968, 3.

Source of Polanski's well-known comment that "[p]eople like Truffaut, Lelouch, and Godard are like little kids playing at being revo-
lutionaries."

Polanski, Roman. "The Most Popular Illusionist in the World." *Interview*
(January 1996): 94–97.

Polanski conducts an interview with the magician David Copper-
field for the Andy Warhol–founded magazine *Interview.* Surprisingly
game, adept, and sophisticated in the interview process, the director
also reveals some of his own thoughts on such subjects as the relation
of magic to movies and the eroticism of illusion.

———. *Roman by Polanski.* New York: Morrow, 1984.

Polanski's autobiography is most notable as a public-relations exercise in rehabilitation, drawing largely on the research of his own
recent biographers, with a detailed presentation of the director's
side of the story in the 1977 rape case. Even so, it contains much
useful background information on the conception and production
of all Polanski's films through *Tess.*

"*Rosemary's Baby* Censored in London." *New York Times,* January 14,
1969, 35.

Polanski's corrosive comments on the removal in the United King-
dom of several shots from *Rosemary's Baby:* "The censors' attitude
belongs to the Inquisition."

Schneller, Joanna. "Music of the Heart." *Premiere* (January 2003): 72–75,
86–88.

This discussion of autobiographical impulses in the making of *The
Pianist* elicits Polanski's testiest performance in any interview to date.
After the interviewer's first question, the director remarks that he
remembers why he doesn't like interviews, and he later cuts off the
interview abruptly by saying, "I have to stop now—I've had it."

Sherman, Eric. *Directing the Film: Film Directors and Their Art.* Boston: Little-Brown, 1976.

Includes material from Polanski's 1974 appearance at the American Film Institute. Comments on scriptwriting, directing actors, visuals and camerawork, the editing process, and film as an art.

Thompson, David. "I Make Films for Adults." *Sight and Sound* 5.4 (April 1995): 6–11.

On adapting *Death and the Maiden,* aspects of the director's visual style, the pitfalls of his career in the 1980s, the "trauma" of *Tess,* compromises on *Pirates.*

Thompson, Howard. "The Road to *Repulsion.*" *New York Times,* November 14, 1965, 9.

On the beginnings of Polanski's career and the origins of *Repulsion.*

Thompson, Thomas. "Tragic House on the Hill." *Life,* August 29, 1969, 42–48.

A gloomy and somewhat sensationalistic profile of Polanski as he returns to the site of the Manson murders.

Tynan, Kenneth. "The Polish Imposition." *Esquire* 76.3 (September 1971): 122–25, 180–89.

An account of the filming of *Macbeth* by Polanski's co-author on the script for that film, the noted English critic.

Vaucher, Andrea R. "Roman Oratory." *American Film* 16.4 (April 1991): 38–39, 46–47.

An interview on the occasion of Polanski's appearance in the film *Back in the USSR.* Comments on the current film scene and the state of contemporary morality, on living in Europe versus living in the United States.

Vidal-Hall, Judith. "A Matter of Perception." *Index on Censorship* 24.6 (November–December 1995): 84–90.

On the pressures of censorship throughout the director's career, with emphasis on *Death and the Maiden*.

Warhol, Andy. "Andy Warhol Tapes Roman Polanski." In *Andy Warhol: The Late Work—Photographs/Films/Videos/Books/Interviews*. Ed. John-Hubert Martin. Berlin: Prestel, 2004. 146–60.

Reprinted from Warhol's *Interview* magazine (November 1973), this extraordinary document provides priceless glimpses into the minds of the interviewer and his subject, who emerges as the more journalistically responsible of the two: "You should really ask me some questions when you interview me, because I need something to reply to."

Wechsler, Lawrence. "The Brat's Tale." In *Vermeer in Bosnia: Cultural Comedies and Political Tragedies*. New York: Pantheon, 2004. 83–150.

Reprinted from *The New Yorker* (December 5, 1994), this extensive profile includes an overview of Polanski's career through *Death and the Maiden*, including comments from Polanski on his contempt for psychoanalysis, the motives of the Manson killings, the 1977 rape case, and his nostalgia for the Hollywood studio system, among other topics. The reprinted version also includes Wechsler's 2004 postscript on *The Pianist*.

Weinberg, Gretchen. "Interview with Roman Polanski." *Sight and Sound* 33.1 (Winter 1963–64): 32–33.

Interview on the occasion of *Knife in the Water*. Comments on the "experimental" nature of Polanski's shorts, on the French New Wave, on his ambition to "make a film with just one person," and on the germination of *Cul-de-Sac*.

Excerpts

On the importance of word and image in film and the filmmaker's own relation to language:

"I like to talk, but I don't know how. I have no problem when I talk to my friends, but I feel that for me language is difficult as a means of expression. I had a lot of problems with the writing of my films, although I managed to get over these difficulties through practice. For my first scripts, there were no words, just drawings. When I wrote the script for *Knife in the Water*, there were no drawings, only words. . . . People have said the shots in *Knife in the Water* were well composed—that's because I don't like to talk, I like to show. The picture is the most important part of a film. If it shows nothing, the film makes no sense; if it consists of talking only, there is no need for the picture." (Weinberg 32–33)

On building character in film:
"To me, establishment of character in little things is the most important thing of all in a film. First, though, for *Repulsion,* there had to be the grain of reality. I live in a beautiful, modern, tenth-floor apartment in Paris, and I used to hear this bell, a convent bell, and that's how a bell got into the picture. I thought, hearing it, this was a kind of outside world in contrast to the girl's world of withdrawal." (Thompson, "The Road to *Repulsion*" 9)

On the filmmaker's own cinematic tastes, circa 1965:
"I like all the horror films. They make me laugh like crazy. I like especially *Peeping Tom* and *The Haunting* of Wise. . . . I like all cinema. What I like least is blabla and pseudo-intellectual gimmickry. Let us say that I like action, and that I like particularly Orson Welles, Kurosawa, Fellini, who are my three favorites. To be specific I especially like *Citizen Kane, The Seven Samurai, Throne of Blood, The Hidden Fortress*—extraordinary!—and *8¹/₂.* There is another Japanese film that I like tremendously. I came out from it exhausted, on my hands and knees! It is *Fires on the Plane* of Ichikawa. Among French films, I especially liked *Les Carabiniers*—which is what I prefer of Godard. How could the French critics drop such a film? And, too, *A bout de soufflé, Alphaville, Les Quartre Cents Coups, Jules et Jim, Tirez sur le pianiste.* I also like what Bresson does very much. Not everything but almost. Especially *Pickpocket* and *Jeanne d'Arc.*" (Delahay and Fieschi 41)

On the censorship of Rosemary's Baby *in London:*
"But how is the censor going to protect people against all the things they might find kinky? Some people find shoes stimulating. Do the censors want actors to work in their feet?" (*"Rosemary's Baby* Censored in London" 35)

On moving away from Poland in his work:
"Well, I don't know. I do things which I like. If suddenly you say there is something interesting to do in Alaska I would go and do it. I'm going further and further from Poland. As you know, the earth is round—so who knows, maybe I'll come back from the other side." (Engle 9)

On the protests at Cannes in May 1968:
"Even though I also withdrew from the Cannes jury in support of the French students' revolt, I want to dissociate myself from François Truffaut, Claude Lelouch, and Jean-Luc Godard. I pulled out as a gesture of solidarity with the students, whose actions I wholeheartedly support. Somehow, I just felt indecent sitting on the terrace of the Carlton Hotel sipping a drink, while those newspaper photos of a burning Paris were staring me in the face. I never intended my pulling out to be seen as an anti–Cannes Festival gesture, however." ("Polanski at Cannes" 3)

On Rosemary's Baby *and the problem of closure:*
"What I want is to finish a film without giving the audience the feeling of being satisfied, the trend which Hollywood developed so scientifically and called 'the happy end.' It is a thing which makes a film really mediocre, when a cycle is completed and finished and they live happy forever. I would rather carry packages in the railroad station than do this type of film. However, leaving a film in suspense is an easy way of avoiding a happy end, and there is something in between which is much more difficult but which can be done, and I am thinking of it a lot. . . . In *Rosemary's Baby,* the girl rocks the cradle, but the film is never completed: it will never satisfy. To satisfy is an unpleasant way for me: satisfaction is a most unpleasant feeling." (Gow 18)

On horror:

"What is horror to you may not be horror to me." (Thompson, "Tragic House on the Hill" 46)

On the importance of sound for atmosphere in cinema:

"It's the personality of a film. It's everything. It's the sound, mostly. If you show a landscape, for instance, there will be very little atmosphere in it. But if you show the landscape and hear a fly buzzing, immediately the atmosphere will heighten. Everything in a landscape can affect our emotional state. If you wake up and see the sun on your curtains, you'll feel different than if you're awakened by the sound of rain. In *Rosemary's Baby,* the apartment changed from a gloomy, depressing place to a nice, bright sunny apartment. It goes in an opposite direction than the story of the film is going. . . . I know most of the sound effects I will want as I'm shooting. Later, in editing, others suggest themselves through the images. Ever since I was a child, I realized that good sound transported me into a film and bad sound spoiled my pleasure." (Gelmis 148)

On the director's alleged preoccupation with the macabre:

"All right, I'm not preoccupied with the macabre—I'm rather more interested in the behavior of people under stress, when they are no longer in comfortable, everyday situations where they can afford to respect the conventional rules and morals of society. You can really learn something about a person when he's put into circumstances in which civilized values place his own identity, even his very being, in jeopardy. In a way, *Knife in the Water* was my minute example of this. I took three people and put them in a situation that subjected them to stress, due to their confinement on the yacht and the competition between the two males. In a way, *Cul-de-Sac* was the same situation, where the people could not react the way they were accustomed to. Before the death of my wife, I was working on a film about the Donner Pass group, which got stranded in the Sierra Nevada mountains in 1847. It's an extremely interesting story, because besides being symptomatic of the problems the pioneers faced in the beginning of that country, it shows civilized people reduced to circumstances where they have to decide on the most drastic moral issues, like eating each other, in order to survive. I don't know what I would do in that situation. But I don't think I would eat your flesh. I think I would rather die. Not because I would think there was something morally wrong with eating you after you were dead. I simply don't think I would be willing to swallow your flesh. Would you swallow mine?" ("*Playboy* Interview" 96)

On filming in England and working conditions in British cinema:
   "I think the period of the early sixties in England was a great one for film production, but it didn't last long. Trade unionism is the factor which is killing the British film industry. To take just one example. In *Dance of the Vampires* there is a big ballroom scene, one of the climaxes of the film. We had special effects to prepare, and sixty difficult make-ups. The result was that we couldn't start shooting before noon and were unable to complete the scene within the scheduled time. We had only five days left before the very elaborate set was due to be dismantled—broken up for good. So the producer started negotiating with the studio for overtime. It was very difficult, like having a knife held at one's throat, but eventually an agreement was arrived at. . . . Suddenly two stagehands revived an old argument with the studio about an extra sixpence an hour. These two men decided to strike. . . . This is the sort of thing which is discouraging America from pouring any more money into British production. . . . In addition to this, there's no other country which has only two main cinema circuits—Rank and ABC. The result of this monopoly is that there are many valuable films which no one ever sees. The average filmgoer in a small town is kept in ignorance of what is being produced, and his taste is given no chance of widening and evolving." (Butler 82)

On instinct:
   "But none of us are born with instinct! We're born only with a certain capacity to develop instinct, some to develop their imaginations, others only their muscles! This is not enough realized! That all peoples on this planet through all ages, there were never two born exactly alike, every cell of my organism is different from yours, only certain basic things are genetic, all newborn babies will move its

arm away if you burn it, will suck at the breast if you put one in its mouth, and do things only necessary for survival. Instinct, which is something which tells you by the tone of your wife's voice that she has been fucking other man, that is not born, that is accumulated experience." (Burke 42)

On emotion in cinema:

"You see, I went to film school. I became 'sophisticated.' I had an urge to be intellectual, to be original. Once you establish yourself as a filmmaker, you don't need this anymore. The last thing I need is to attract people to my style or my notoriety. What I need now is to make films that move people. Emotion is essential in art, one way or another. I think that today it is somehow more proper to reach to the literature of the nineteenth century or the first half of our century, literature that deals more with sentiments and feelings than with style. *Tess* was obviously made with this in mind. And *Pirates* as well. What attracts me to that is the adventure—the joy I recall having at the movies as a child, the joy that has dissipated. Certain things are gone. Certain feelings that I remember. . . . You would cry or you would be scared. Now realism or violence or great *technical* things can be demonstrated . . . but *not* the feelings. Somehow the emotion is gone." (Glazer 44)

On politics in the director's work, with reference to Death and the Maiden:

"It depends what you mean by political. In my mind, 'political' relates to a concrete regime, and names, of a country at least, let alone the people. In *Death and the Maiden* I never mention any political leader or a concrete dictatorship that's fallen. I'm talking about an unspecified country in South America. And it's more universal than that, because this sort of situation occurs all around the globe, where former victims are faced with their former oppressors or torturers. They have to live through these kind of encounters and deal with them." (Thompson, "I Make Films for Adults" 8)

On composing with the wide-angle lens:

"The wide-angle lens is used mainly for the depth of field, but I would have to talk a long time about it. I don't know whether it has any sense; maybe it does. Being hung up on visuals, it's very important for me show on the screen what I see in life. I think the way the human being sees life around him, the world around him, would be closely comparable with a picture made by what you would call the wide-angle range of lenses. . . . Now once you are aware of it, when you try to render the three-dimensional world on a picture, you have to compensate for this constancy scaling. Painters do it by applying a false linear perspective. When you take the painting of a master, you see a street, and if you start to put rulers to the lines, you realize that the perspective is not correct. If you do it correct, like that Italian painter, Canaletto, who used the camera obscura, you see the perspective is always too sharp. It just looks wrong, although it is correct from the linear point of view. You have to compensate for it. Now when you have all of this in mind, you realize the most important thing on the screen, for me, is to render the perspective the way I see it, not the way it appears, and not the way it is being deformed by long-distance lenses. . . . So otherwise, when I look at you like this, I see more or less that much. My peripheral vision goes here, but I'm conscious of seeing more than this, so I would put my camera here, and I will look for a lens that will show me that much, and I will come out with a wide-angle lens." (Sherman 217–19)

On film editing:

"There are two reasons for cutting. One is that you can't carry it any further for technical reasons, and the other is that you need another shot. For example, I show a man sitting here and talking with these people. So I see these people, I see him, and suddenly, somehow, he talks here, and I turn and look at him, or he passes a glass of water to someone, so I have to cut. To pan would be nonsensical since it doesn't follow any physiologically known pattern, because when I look from here to you, I am not aware of what is happening. It is like a cut, you see. My eyes somehow disconnect for a moment when they swing over here. To render that, you have to cut.

"But also, when you do a long shot you see you can do more. The acting is easier for actors because they have the run into an important part of the scene sometimes. It's also a question of—in general, a lot of ego on the part of the director. Every director wants to show that he can do it. I got over it; now what I do, I do sometimes a very long shot of a very complicated nature, and then I do a long shot which is the reverse, and then I cut them together. This is a second level. I know I can do it so I do it very long, and then I don't have any regret about cutting it for convenience, for the benefit of the editing." (Sherman 250–51)

On the extremities of American culture:
"I don't understand, why do they freeze the cinemas? What is the attraction to be uncomfortable? I think it's part of American extremities, you know? Everything is to an extreme in this country. It's either too hot or too cold, total prudery or total pornography, you know? I mean, just going from the period when the couple couldn't sleep in the same bed in a movie, to the period of *Devil in Miss Jones* when you see the genitals involving very limited movement. Just a couple of inches back and forth for forty-five minutes. . . . You Americans seem to have serious problems finding any kind of reason. For a while, everything was sprayed with DDT. You couldn't touch produce which would not be just . . . snow white. Now, you can't buy DDT to put on your dog to kill a couple of fleas, you know?" (Warhol 150)

On the ending of Chinatown *and its relation to his wife's murder:*
"No, no, *no.* . . . That ending had absolutely *nothing* to do with my life. It had everything to do with *movies,* with all the movies I saw and adored and couldn't get enough of as a child, in the first years after the war back in Krakow. Why do people always imagine that in order to make a tragic film, you have to have led a tragic life, that only a deeply sad person could perpetrate a deeply sad ending? It's crazy. *Of Mice and Men,* Carol Reed's incredible *Odd Man Out* (have you ever seen it? *Incredible!*), Laurence Olivier's *Hamlet*—I went to see those films again and again, and *those* were the experiences that shaped me. I remember how *shattered* I was by the death of Lenny at the end of *Of Mice and Men,* and yet, walking out of the theater,

even then I realized how a conventionally happy ending would never have given me that same extraordinary combination of pleasure and sorrow together. *That* was the biographical basis for my choices in the ending of *Chinatown,* not any of this other cheap psychological nonsense." (Wechsler 87–88)

On the sequel to Chinatown:
"Well, I would never have been part of [*The Two Jakes*] because I just don't believe in sequels, but I must say that I admired the métier of Jack Nicholson. I think it was a beautifully made picture. Unfortunately, there are serious problems with the story, as we all know. The film is extremely difficult to follow. Furthermore, each time you get hooked on a story and you invest your emotions in some kind of sequence, it's abruptly cut and switched to something new. It's jolting. He loses you every few minutes. But the acting, the camera work, the staging of sequences is quite admirable." (Vaucher 46)

On violence in contemporary film (especially in the work of directors such as Oliver Stone or Quentin Tarantino):
"It's all terribly explicit now, but it's less effective. I fought for reality, and look where it's got to. A little blood goes a long way. I hate all this blood splashing around the screen. It looks phony, unreal, almost a spoof. Because we haven't invested anything in these characters, the only shock is in the violence, not an assault on the emotions. . . . The language of cinema has changed. There's a new grammar, more pace. . . . We wouldn't, after all, expect a novel of the late twentieth century to read like Zola or Dickens, would we now?" (Vidal-Hall 90)

On acting in his own films:
"I usually have an understudy or stand-in for rehearsals who has some kind of acting experience. That allows me to make a set-up. I rehearse first, then he watches me and goes through the same motions. I presume everybody else does it the same way. But acting is always compromised by directing; it's easier to direct while acting than to act while directing. . . . Because when you rehearse and set up the camera and have reliable crews, they will follow your instructions and film it exactly the way you want. So the directing doesn't

suffer. Acting, however, requires certain aspects of human behavior that are variable. When you act, you have to relax and forget about everything around you, and concentrate only on your performance. . . . If you lose the spontaneity because you are thinking about the masses of things the director should be thinking of during the take, then your acting suffers. It is very difficult to take off the director's hat for those few minutes of acting during the take." (Carroll 62)

On the claim that his work is pessimistic:
"I think that's a very superficial analysis of what I do and who I am. The fact that you don't end a film with a forced happy ending doesn't mean that you're not an optimist. If you show tragic events, they have to have a tragic ending. That's the definition of drama; it has to end in tragedy in order to have an impact on the viewer. If you show a bunch of people who do evil, and at the end they're all wonderfully punished, it leads you to believe there's nothing to be done anymore, because someone is taking care of it for you. I prefer to leave the responsibility with the viewer." (Pizzello 63)

On the autobiographical aspects of The Pianist:
"I put certain moments in the picture that I remember well from the Krakow ghetto. As far as emotion is concerned, on the set it was quite seldom. For me, it's work.

"But I must say there were two moments, and they had something to do with the music, probably. The scene when Szpilman is playing for the German officer. Watching the rushes, I could feel the emotion. I also observed it on the set, members of the crew were weeping. It was the middle of the night, bitter cold, very uncomfortable location, all those elements. But they somehow contributed to them feeling fragile. At a moment like that, when this type of scene is being played with conviction that you can actually see on the screen after, it affects people in the crew.

"For me [the most emotional scene] was the one toward the end in the radio station when Szpilman plays piano again. It was the thrill of doing a scene which comes out exactly as you would have expected it." (Schneller 86)

Dwaj ludzie z szafa (Two men and a wardrobe; 1959)
Writer and director: Roman Polanski
In Polish
Cast: Jakob Goldberg, Henryk Kluba
Black and white
14 min.

Gdy spadaja anioly (When angels fall; 1959)
Writer and director: Roman Polanski
In Polish
Cast: Barbara Kwiatkowsi, Roman Polanski, Henryk Kluba, Andrzej
  Kondratiuk
Black and white
21 min.

Le gros et la maigre (The fat and the lean; 1961)
Writer and director: Roman Polanski
In French
Music: Krysztof Komeda
Photography: Jean-Michel Boussaguet
Cast: Andre Katelbach, Roman Polanski
Black and white
15 min.

Ssaki (Mammals; 1962)
Director: Roman Polanski
Writers: Roman Polanski, Andrzej Kondratiuk
In Polish
Music: Krysztof Komeda
Photography: Andrzej Kostenko
Cast: Henryk Kluba, Michal Zolnierkiewicz, Voytek Frykowski
Black and white
10 min.

Knife in the Water (Noz w wodzie; 1962)
Production: ZRF Kamera Film Unit of Film Polski, Warsaw
Producer: Stanislaw Zylewicz
Director: Roman Polanski
Screenplay: Roman Polanski, Jerzy Skolimowski, Jakub Goldberg
Photography: Jerzy Lipman
Editor: Halina Prugar
Sound: Halina Paszkowska
Music: Krysztof Komeda
Cast: Leon Niemczyk (Andrzej), Jolanta Umecka (Krystyna), Zygmunt
   Malannowicz (Hitchhiker)
Black and white
94 min.

La Rivière des Diamants (The river of diamonds), episode in the anthology
   film *Les Plus Belles Escroqueries du Monde* (The beautiful swindlers; 1964)
Production: Ulyssee Productions, Primex Films, Lux Films, Vides
   Cinematografica, Toho Company, Caesar Films, Paris
Producer: Pierre Roustang
Director: Roman Polanski
Screenplay: Roman Polanski, Gerard Brach
Photography: Jerzy Lipman
Editor: Rita von Royen
Music: Kryzstof Komeda
Cast: Nicole Karen (Young Woman), Jan Treulings (Seducer)
Black and white
33 min.

Repulsion (1965)
Production: Compton/Tekli Film Productions, London
Producer: Gene Gutowski
Executive Producers: Michael Klinger, Tony Tenser
Associate Producers: Robert Sterne, Sam Wayneburg
Director: Roman Polanski
Assistant Director: Ted Sturgis
Screenplay: Roman Polanski, Gerard Brach
Photography: Gilbert Taylor
Editor: Alastair McIntyre
Sound: Stephen Dalby
Music: Chico Hamilton
Art Director: Seamus Flannery

Cast: Catherine Deneuve (Carol), Ian Hendry (Michael), John Fraser
(Colin), Yvonne Furneaux (Helen), Patrick Wymark (Landlord), Renee
Huston (Miss Balch), Helen Fraser (Bridget)
Black and white
104 min.

Cul-de-Sac (1966)
Production: Compton/Tekli Film Productions, London
Producer: Gene Gutowski
Executive Producer: Sam Wayneburg
Director: Roman Polanski
Screenplay: Roman Polanski, Gerard Brach
Photography: Douglas Slocombe
Editor: Alastair McIntyre
Sound: Stephen Dalby
Special Effects: Bowie Films
Music: Krysztof Komeda
Art Director: George Lack
Cast: Donald Pleasence (George), Francoise Dorleac (Teresa), Lionel
Stander (Richard), Jack MacGowran (Albert), Iain Quarrier (Christopher),
Jacqueline Bisset (Jacqueline)
Black and white
111 min.

Dance of the Vampires/The Fearless Vampire Killers (1967)
Production: Cadre Films–Filmways, London
Producer: Gene Gutowski
Executive Producer: Martin Ransohoff
Production Manager: David W. Orton
Director: Roman Polanski
Assistant Director: Roy Stevens
Screenplay: Roman Polanski, Gerard Brach
Photography: Douglas Slocombe
Editor: Alastair McIntyre
Music: Krysztof Komeda
Sound: George Stephenson
Art Director: Fred Carter
Production Designer: Wilfred Shingleton
Cast: Jack MacGowran (Professor Abronsius), Roman Polanski (Alfred),
Alfie Bass (Shagal), Jessie Robbins (Rebecca), Sharon Tate (Sarah), Ferdy
Mayne (Count von Krolock), Iain Quarrier (Herbert), Terry Downes
(Koukol)
Color and Panavision
107 min.

Rosemary's Baby (1968)
Production: Paramount/William Castle Enterprises, New York
Producer: William Castle
Associate Producer: Dona Holloway
Director: Roman Polanski
Assistant Director: Daniel J. McCauley
Screenplay: Roman Polanski, based on the novel by Ira Levin
Photography: William Fraker
Editors: Sam O'Steen, Robert Wyman
Art Director: Joel Schiller
Production Designer: Richard Sylbert
Music: Krysztof Komeda
Sound: Harold Lewis
Cast: Mia Farrow (Rosemary), John Cassavetes (Guy), Ruth Gordon
   (Minnie), Sidney Blackmer (Roman), Maurice Evans (Hutch), Ralph
   Bellamy (Dr. Sapirstein), Angela Dorian (Terry), Charles Grodin (Dr. Hill),
   Patsy Kelly (Laura Louise)
Color
137 min.

Macbeth (1971)
Production: Playboy Productions/Caliban Films, London
Producer: Andrew Braunsberg
Associate Producer: Timothy Burrill
Executive Producer: Hugh M. Hefner
Director: Roman Polanski
Second Unit Director: Hercules Bellville
Screenplay: Roman Polanski, Kenneth Tynan, based on the play by William
   Shakespeare
Photography: Gil Taylor
Editor: Alastair MacIntyre
Art Director: Fred Carter
Music: Third Ear Band
Cast: Jon Finch (Macbeth), Francesca Annis (Lady Macbeth), Martin Shaw
   (Banquo), Nicholas Selby (Duncan), John Stride (Ross), Stephan Chase
   (Malcolm), Paul Shelley (Donalbain), Terence Bayler (Macduff), Diane
   Fletcher (Lady Macduff), Andrew Laurence (Lennox), Keith Chegwin
   (Fleance), Maisie MacFarquhar (Blind Witch), Vic Abbot (Cawdor)
Color
140 min.

What? (Che?; 1973)
Production: C. C. Champion, Rome/Les Films Concordia, Paris/Dieter
    Geissler Produktion, Munich
Producer: Carlo Ponti
Director: Roman Polanski
Screenplay: Roman Polanski, Gerard Brach
Photography: Marcello Gatti, Giuseppi Ruzzolini
Editor: Alastair McIntyre
Art Director: Franco Fumagalli
Music: Claudio Gizzi
Sound: Piero Fondi
Cast: Sydne Rome (Nancy), Marcello Mastroianni (Alex), Hugh Griffith
    (Noblart), Romolo Valli (Giovanni), Guido Alberti (Priest), Gianfranco
    Piacentini (Tony), Roger Middleton (Jimmy), Roman Polanski (Mosquito)
Color
112 min.

Chinatown (1974)
Production: Long Road Productions, Paramount-Penthouse Presentation,
    New York
Producer: Robert Evans
Associate Producer: C. O. Erickson
Director: Roman Polanski
Screenplay: Robert Towne
Photography: John A. Alonzo
Editor: Sam O'Steen
Production Designer: Richard Sylbert
Art Director: Ruby Levitt
Music: Jerry Goldsmith
Sound: Robert Cornett
Cast: Jack Nicholson (Jake Gittes), Faye Dunaway (Evelyn Mulwray), John
    Huston (Noah Cross), Darrel Zwerling (Hollis Mulwray), Perry Lopez
    (Lieutenant Escobar), John Hillerman (Yelburton), Diane Ladd (Ida
    Sessions), Roy Jenson (Mulvihill), Roman Polanski (Punk), Dick Bakalyan
    (Loach), James Hong (Evelyn's Butler), Belinda Palmer (Katherine
    Mulwray), Curly (Burt Young)
Color and Panavision
130 min.

The Tenant (Le locataire; 1976)
Production: Marianne Productions, Paris
Producer: Andrew Braunsberg
Associate Producer: Alain Sarde

Executive Producer: Hercules Bellville
Director: Roman Polanski
Screenplay: Roman Polanski, Gerard Brach, based on the novel by Roland
    Topor
Photography: Sven Nykvist
Editor: Francoise Bonnot
Production Designers: Pierre Guffroy, Eric Simon
Art Directors: Calude Moesching, Albert Rajau
Music: Phillippe Sarde
Cast: Roman Polanski (Telkovsky), Isabelle Adjani (Stella), Shelley Winters
    (Concierge), Melvyn Douglas (Monsieur Zy), Jo Van Fleet (Madame Dioz),
    Bernard Fresson (Scope), Lila Kedrova (Madame Gaderian)
Color and Panavision
125 min.

Tess (1980)
Production: Renn Productions, Paris/Burrill Productions, London
Producer: Claude Berri
Co-producer: Timothy Burrill
Associate Producer: Jean-Pierre Rassam
Executive Producer: Pierre Grunstein
Director: Roman Polanski
Screenplay: Roman Polanski, Gerard Brach, John Brownjohn, based on the
    novel by Thomas Hardy
Photography: Geoffrey Unsworth, Ghislain Cloquet
Editors: Alastair McIntyre, Tom Priestly
Production Designer: Pierre Guffroy
Art Director: Jack Stephens
Music: Phillippe Sarde
Cast: Nastassja Kinski (Tess), Peter Firth (Angel Clare), Leigh Lawson (Alec
    D'Urberville), John Collin (John Durbeyfield), Rosemary Martin (Mrs.
    Durbeyfield), David Markham (Reverend Clare), Arielle Dombasle (Mercy
    Chant)
Color and Panavision
190 min.

Pirates (1986)
Production: Carthago Films, in association with Accent-Cominco, Paris
Producer: Tarak ben Amar
Co-executive Producers: Mark Lombardo, Umberto Sambucco
Directors: Roman Polanski, Gerard Brach, John Brownjohn
Photography: Witold Sobochinski
Editors: Herve de Luze, William Reynolds

Music: Phillippe Sarde
Cast: Walter Matthau (Captain Red), Cris Campion (Frog), Damien Thomas
(Don Alfonso), Charlotte Lewis (Dolores), Olu Jacobs (Richmond), David
Kelley (Surgeon), Roy Kinnear (Dutch), Emilio Fernandez (Angelino),
Wladislaw Komar (Jesus), Luc Gamati (Gonzalez), Robert Durning
(Commander of Marines), Tony Peck (Spanish Officer)
Color and Panavision
117 min.

Frantic (1987)
Production: Warner Brothers/Mount Company Production, New York
Producers: Thom Mount, Tim Hampton
Director: Roman Polanski
Screenplay: Roman Polanski, Gerard Brach
Photography: Witold Sobochinski
Editor: Sam O'Steen
Music: Ennio Morricone
Cast: Harrison Ford (Dr. Richard Walker), Betty Buckley (Sondra Walker),
Emmanuelle Seigner (Michelle), Dominique Virion (Desk Clerk), Yves
Reignier (Inspector), John Mahoney (Williams), Jimmie Ray Weeks
(Shaap), Yorgo Voyagis (Kidnapper), David Huddleston (Peter), Raouf Ben
Amour (Dr. Metlaoui)
Color
120 min.

Bitter Moon (1992)
Production: Films Alain Sarde/Pathe
Producer and Executive Producer: Robert Benmussa
Co-producer: Alain Sarde
Director: Roman Polanski
Screenplay: Roman Polanski, Gerard Brach, John Brownjohn, Jeff Gross
Photography: Tonino Delli Colli
Editor: Hervé de Luze
Production Designers: Willy Holt, Gerard Virard
Art Director: Philippe Turlure
Music: Vangelis
Cast: Hugh Grant (Nigel), Peter Coyote (Oscar), Emmanuelle Seigner
(Mimi), Kristin Scott Thomas (Fiona), Victor Banerjee (Mr. Sikh)
Color
139 min.

Death and the Maiden (1994)
Production: Fine Line/Mount Film Company
Producers: Josh Kramer, Thom Mount
Co-producers: Ariel Dorfman, Bonnie Timmerman
Associate Producer: Gladys Nederlander
Executive Producers: Jane Barclay, Sharon Harel
Director: Roman Polanski
Screenplay: Ariel Dorfman, Rafael Yglesias, based on Dorfman's play
Photography: Tonino Delli Colli
Editor: Hervé de Luze
Production Designer: Pierre Guffroy
Art Director: Claude Moesching
Costumes: Milena Canonero
Color
103 min.

The Ninth Gate (La neuviemen porte; 1999)
Production: Studio Canal/Orly Films/Via Digial
Producer: Roman Polanski
Co-producers: Mark Allen, Antonio Cardenal, Inaki Nunez, Alain Vannier
Associate Producer: Adam Kempton
Executive Producers: Michel Cheyko, Wolfgang Glattes
Director: Roman Polanski
Assistant Director: David Campi Lemaire
Screenplay: Roman Polanski, Enrique Urbizu, John Brownjohn, based on the
    novel *Il Club Dumas* by Arturo Perez Reverte
Photography: Darius Khondji
Editor: Hervé de Luze
Production Designer: Dean Tavalouris
Art Director: Gerard Viard
Costumes: Anthony Powell
Music: Wojciech Kilar
Cast: Johnny Depp (Dean Corso), Lena Olin (Liana Telfer), Frank Langella
    (Boris Balkan), James Russo (Bernie), Jack Taylor (Victor Fargas), Barbara
    Jefford (Baroness Kessler), Emmanuelle Seigner (The Girl)
Color
133 min.

The Pianist (Der pianist; 2002)
Production: Canal Plus (in partnership with several production companies
    across Europe)
Producer: Robert Benmussa
Executive Producer: Timothy Burrill

Co-producer: Gene Gutowski
Director: Roman Polanski
Screenplay: Roman Polanski, Ronald Harwood, based on the book by
  Wladyslaw Szpilman
Photography: Pawel Edelman
Editor: Hervé de Luze
Production Designer: Allan Starski
Art Decorator: Gabriele Wolff
Costumes: Ann B. Sheppard
Music: Wojciech Kilar
Cast: Adrien Brody (Wladyslaw Szpilman), Thomas Kretschmann
  (Hosenfeld), Ed Stoppard (Henryk), Emilia Fox (Dorota), Frank Finlay
  (Father), Julia Rayner (Regina), Jessica Kate Meyer (Halina), Maureen
  Lipman (Mother)
Color
150 min.

Oliver Twist (2005)
Production: Sony Pictures, Runteam II Ltd., Medusa Productions
Producers: Robert Benmussa, Roman Polanski, Alain Sarde
Executive Producers: Timothy Burrill, Petr Moravec
Director: Roman Polanski
Screenplay: Roman Polanski, Ronald Harwood, based on the novel by
  Charles Dickens
Photography: Pawel Edelman
Editor: Hervé de Luze
Art Decorator: Jindrich Koci
Costumes: Anna B. Sheppard
Music: Rachel Portman
Cast: Barney Clark (Oliver Twist), Jeremy Swift (Mr. Bumble), Michael
  Heath (Mr. Sowerberry), Gillian Hanna (Mrs. Sowerberry), Chris Overton
  (Noah Claypole), Harry Eden (Artful Dodger), Ben Kingsley (Fagin),
  Edward Hardwicke (Mr. Brownlow), Jamie Foreman (Bill Sykes), Leanne
  Rowe (Nancy), Elvis Polanski (Boy with hoop)
Color
130 min.

Adorno, Theodor W. *Minima Moralia: Reflections from Damaged Life.* Trans. Edmund Jephcott. London: Verso, 1984.
———. *The Stars Down to Earth, and Other Essays on the Irrational in Culture.* Ed. Stephen Crook. New York: Routledge, 1994.
———, and Max Horkheimer. *Dialectic of Englightenment: Philosophical Fragments.* Trans. Edmund Jephcott. Stanford, Calif.: Stanford University Press, 2002.
Altman, Rick. *Film/Genre.* London: British Film Institute, 1999.
Amis, Martin. "Roman Polanski." In *Visiting Mrs. Nabokov and Other Excursions.* New York: Harmony Books, 1993. 229–54.
Andersen, Thom. "Red Hollywood." In *Literature and the Visual Arts in Contemporary Society.* Ed. Suzanne Ferguson and Barbara Groseclose. Columbus: Ohio State University Press, 1985. 141–96.
Arendt, Hannah. *The Origins of Totalitarianism.* New York: Harcourt Brace, 1951.
Arnheim, Rudolf. *Film as Art.* Berkeley: University of California Press, 1957.
Artaud, Antonin. *Selected Writings.* Ed. Susan Sontag. Trans. Helen Weaver. New York: Farrar, Straus, and Giroux, 1976.
———. *The Theater and Its Double.* Trans. Mary Caroline Richards. New York: Grove Press, 1958.
Astruc, Alexandre. "The Birth of the New Avant-Garde: La camera-stylo." In *The New Wave.* Ed. Peter Graham. New York: Doubleday, 1968. 17–24.
Auerbach, Erich. *Mimesis: The Representation of Reality in Western Literature.* New York: Doubleday, 1957.
Bataille, Georges. *L'Erotisme.* Paris: Editions de Minuit, 1957.
———. *Inner Experience.* Trans. Leslie Anne Boldt. Albany: State University of New York Press, 1988.
Bazin, André. *What Is Cinema?* Trans. Hugh Gray. Berkeley: University of California Press, 1967.
Bellour, Raymond. *The Analysis of Film.* Ed. Constance Penley. Bloomington: Indiana University Press, 2000.

Belmans, Jacques. *Roman Polanski.* Paris: Editions Seghers, 1971.

Belton, John. "Language, Oedipus, and *Chinatown.*" *Modern Language Notes* 106.5 (1991): 933–50.

Bentham, Jeremy. *Deontology, A Table of the Springs of Action, and the Article on Utilitarianism.* Ed. Amnon Goldworth. Oxford: Clarendon Press, 1983.

———. *Panopticon, or the Inspection House.* Dublin: Thomas Byrne, 1791.

Bisplinghoff, Gretchen, and Virginia Wright Wexman. *Roman Polanski: A Guide to References and Resources.* Boston: G. K. Hall, 1979.

Bordwell, David. "The Art Cinema as a Mode of Film Practice." *Film Criticism* 4.1 (Fall 1979): 56–64.

Bozovic, Miran. "Of 'farther uses of the dead to the living': Hitchcock and Bentham." In *Hitchcock: Past and Future.* Ed. Richard Allen and Sam Ishii-Gonzales. London: Routledge, 2004. 243–56.

Brooks, Peter. *The Melodramatic Imagination.* New Haven: Yale University Press, 1985.

Budd, Mike. The Cabinet of Dr. Caligari: *Texts, Contexts, Histories.* New Brunswick, N.J.: Rutgers University Press, 1990.

Butler, Ivan. *The Cinema of Roman Polanski.* New York: A. S. Barnes, 1970.

———. *Horror in the Cinema.* New York: A. S. Barnes, 1970.

Cameron, Ian. Introduction to *Second Wave.* Ed. Ian Cameron. London: Studio Vista, 1970. 5–6.

Chappetta, Robert. "*Rosemary's Baby.*" *Film Quarterly* 22.3 (Spring 1969): 35–38.

Coates, Paul. *The Red and The White: The Cinema of People's Poland.* London: Wallflower Press, 2005.

———. *The Story of the Lost Reflection: The Alienation of the Image in Western and Polish Cinema.* London: Verso, 1985.

Cottom, Daniel. *Why Education Is Useless.* Philadelphia: University of Pennsylvania Press, 2003.

Cronin, Paul, ed. *Roman Polanski: Interviews.* Jackson: University Press of Mississippi, 2005.

Darwin, Charles. *The Descent of Man, and Selection in Relation to Sex.* New York: Appleton, 1927.

De Grazia, Edward, and Roger K. Newman. *Banned Films: Movies, Censors, and the First Amendment.* New York: Bowker, 1982.

Deleuze, Gilles. *Cinema 2: The Time-Image.* Trans. Hugh Tomlinson and Robert Galeta. Minneapolis: University of Minnesota Press, 1989.

Dickens, Charles. *Oliver Twist.* New York: Random House, 1982.

Dimendberg, Edward. *Film Noir and the Spaces of Modernity.* Cambridge, Mass.: Harvard University Press, 2004.

Diner, Dan. *Beyond the Conceivable: Studies in Germany, Nazism, and the Holocaust.* Berkeley: University of California Press, 2000.

Durgnat, Raymond. *Sexual Alienation in the Cinema*. London: Studio Vista, 1972.

Eagle, Herbert. "Exile and Emigration in the Films of Roman Polanski." In *Living in Translation: Polish Writers in America*. Ed. Halina Stephan. New York: Rodopi, 2003. 289–312.

———. "Polanski." In *Five Filmmakers: Tarkovsky, Forman, Polanski, Szabo, Makavejev*. Ed. Daniel J. Goulding. Bloomington: Indiana University Press, 1994. 92–155.

Eisenstein, Sergei. *Film Form: Essays in Film Theory*. Ed. and Trans. Jay Leyda. New York: Harcourt Brace Jovanovich, 1949.

Ellison, John T. "Religion." *Time*, April 8, 1966, 18–22.

Evans, Robert. *The Kid Stays in the Picture*. New York: Hyperion, 1994.

Farber, Manny. *Negative Space*. New York: Praeger, 1971.

Ferguson, Frances. *Pornography, the Theory: What Utilitarianism Did to Action*. Chicago: University of Chicago Press, 2004.

Fischer, Lucy. *Cinematernity: Film, Motherhood, Genre*. Princeton, N.J.: Princeton University Press, 1996.

Foucault, Michel. *Discipline and Punish: The Birth of the Prison*. Trans. Alan Sheridan. New York: Pantheon, 1977.

Freud, Sigmund. "Humor." In *The Standard Edition of the Complete Works of Sigmund Freud*. Vol. 21. Trans. James Strachey. London: Hogarth Press, 1953. 159–66.

Frye, Northrop. *The Anatomy of Criticism*. Princeton, N.J.: Princeton University Press, 1957.

Fuksiewiecz, Jacek. *Polish Cinema*. Warsaw: Interpress Publishers, 1973.

Girard, René. *Deceit and Desire in the Novel: Self and Other in Literary Structure*. Trans. Yvonne Freccero. Baltimore: Johns Hopkins University Press, 1965.

Goulding, Daniel J., ed. *Post–New Wave Cinema in the Soviet Union and Eastern Europe*. Bloomington: Indiana University Press, 1989.

Halevy, Elie. *The Growth of Philosophic Radicalism*. London: Faber, 1952.

Hardy, Thomas. *Tess of the D'Urbervilles*. Ed. John Paul Riquelme. New York: Bedford Books, 1998.

Harper, D. W. "Wilhelm Worringer: A Locked Home." Unpublished manuscript in the author's private collection, 2005.

Hawkins, Joan. *Cutting Edge: Art Horror and the Horrific Avant-Garde*. Minneapolis: University of Minnesota Press, 2000.

Heffernan, Kevin. *Ghouls, Gimmicks, and Gold: Horror Films and the American Movie Business, 1953–1968*. Durham, N.C.: Duke University Press, 2004.

Hoffman, Piotr. *Violence in Modern Philosophy*. Chicago: University of Chicago Press, 1989.

Jarvie, Ian C. *Hollywood's Overseas Campaign*. Cambridge: Cambridge University Press, 1992.

Kael, Pauline. "The Current Cinema" (Review of *Macbeth*). *The New Yorker,* February 5, 1972, 76–80.

Kauffmann, Stanley. *Figures of Light.* New York: Harper and Row, 1971.

Kott, Jan. *Shakespeare, Our Contemporary.* Trans. Boleslaw Taborksi. New York: Doubleday, 1964.

Kuntzel, Thierry. "The Film Work." Trans. Lawrence Crawford, Kimball Lockhart, and Claudia Tysdal. *Enclitic* 5.1 (Spring 1978): 38–61.

———. "The Film Work, 2." Trans. Nancy Huston. *Camera Obscura* 5 (Spring 1980): 6–69.

Leach, James. "Notes on Polanski's Cinema of Cruelty." *Wide Angle* 2.1 (1978): 32–39.

Leaming, Barbara. *Polanski, a Biography: The Filmmaker as Voyeur.* New York: Simon and Schuster, 1981.

Linderman, Deborah. "Oedipus in Chinatown." *Enclitic* 5–6 (1981–82): 190.

Lindsay, Vachel. *The Art of the Moving Picture.* New York: Macmillan, 1922.

Lyotard, Jean-François. "Acinema." In *The Lyotard Reader.* Ed. Andrew Benjamin. Trans. Paisley Livingston. Oxford: Blackwell, 1989. 169–80.

Marciniak, Katarzyna. "Cinematic Exile: Performing the Foreign Body on Screen in Roman Polanski's *The Tenant*." *Camera Obscura* 15.1 (2000): 1–43.

Mayo, Morrow. *Los Angeles.* New York: Knopf, 1933.

McGinnis, Wayne D. "*Chinatown:* Roman Polanski's Contemporary Oedipus Story." *Literature/Film Quarterly* 3.3 (1975): 249–52.

Mendik, Xavier, and Steven Jay Schneider. *Underground USA: Filmmaking beyond the Hollywood Canon.* London: Wallflower Press, 2002.

Metz, Christian. *The Imaginary Signifier: Psychoanalysis and the Cinema.* Trans. Celia Britton, Annwyl Williams, Ben Brewster, and Alfred Guzzetti. Bloomington: Indiana University Press, 1982.

Miller, J. Hillis. *The Disappearance of God.* Cambridge, Mass.: Harvard University Press, 1963.

Milosz, Czeslaw. *The Captive Mind.* Trans. Jane Zielonko. New York: Knopf, 1953.

Mitford, Jessica. *The American Way of Birth.* New York: Dutton, 1992.

Morrison, James. "Deleuze and Film Semiotics." *Semiotica* 88.3–4 (1992): 269–90.

———. "The Old Masters: Kubrick, Polanski, and the Late Style of Modern Cinema." *Raritan* 22.2 (Fall 2001): 29–47.

Naremore, James. *The Magic World of Orson Welles.* 2d ed. Dallas: Southern Methodist University Press, 1989.

———. *More than Night: Film Noir in Its Contexts.* Berkeley: University of California Press, 1998.

Ndalianus, Angela. *Neo-Baroque Aesthetics and Contemporary Entertainment.* Cambridge: Massachusetts Institute of Technology Press, 2004.

Nilsen, Vladimir. *The Cinema as a Graphic Art.* New York: Hill and Wang, 1959.

Oren, Michael B. "Schindler's Liszt." *New Republic,* March 17, 2003, 28.

Ozick, Cynthia. "The Shawl." In *The Scribner Anthology of Contemporary Short Fiction.* Ed. Michael Martone and Lex Williford. New York: Simon and Schuster, 1999. 516–20.

Paul, William. *Laughing Screaming: Modern Hollywood Horror and Comedy.* New York: Columbia University Press, 1994.

Perez, Michel. "*Rosemary's Baby.*" In *Positif: 50 Years.* Ed. Lawrence Kardish. New York: Museum of Modern Art, 2003. 101–5.

Polanski, Roman. *Roman by Polanski.* New York: Morrow, 1984.

Poole, Ross. *Morality and Modernity.* London: Routledge, 1991.

Potamkin, Harry Alan. "Style and Medium in the Motion Pictures." In *Film Theory and Criticism.* 5th ed. Ed. Leo Braudy and Marshall Cohen. New York: Oxford University Press, 1999. 289–302.

"Razor-Edged Slapstick" (Review of *Knife in the Water*). *Time,* November 18, 1966, 122–23.

Rickels, Laurence A. *The Vampire Lectures.* Minneapolis: University of Minnesota Press, 1999.

Robbe-Grillet, Alain. *Pour un Nouveau Roman.* Paris: Gallimard, 1963.

Rodowick, D. N. *Reading the Figural, or Philosophy after the New Media.* Durham, N.C.: Duke University Press, 2001.

Scarry, Elaine. *Resisting Representation.* New York: Oxford University Press, 1994.

Schur, Thomas. "Rethinking Melodrama: From Figuration to the Figural." Unpublished manuscript in the author's private collection, 2004.

Sconce, Jeffrey. "Trashing the Academy: Taste, Excess, and an Emerging Politics of Cinematic Style." *Screen* 36.4 (Winter 1995): 371–93.

Segrave, Kerry. *Foreign Films in America.* Jefferson, N.C.: MacFarland, 2004.

Shetley, Vernon. "Incest and Capital in *Chinatown.*" *Modern Language Notes* 114.5 (1999): 1092–1109.

Simon, John. "Unanswerable Films, Answerable Letters." *The New Leader,* July 8, 1968, 22–23.

Singer, Ben. *Melodrama and Modernity.* New York: Columbia University Press, 2001.

Sontag, Susan. "Artaud." Introduction to *Selected Writings,* by Antonin Artaud. Ed. Susan Sontag. Trans. Helen Weaver. New York: Farrar, Straus, and Giroux, 1976. xvii–lix.

Stallybrass, Peter. "*Macbeth* and Witchcraft." In *Focus on* Macbeth. Ed. John Russell Brown. London: Routledge, 1982. 189–209.

Storper, Michael. "The Transit to Flexible Specialization in the U.S. Film Industry: External Economies, the Division of Labor, and the Crossing of International Divides." *Cambridge Journal of Economics* 13 (June 1989): 273–305.

Strachownya, Graznya. *Roman Polanski i Jego Filmy* (Roman Polanski and his films). Warsaw: Wydawnictwo Naukowe PWN, 1994.

Street, Sarah. *Transatlantic Crossings: British Feature Films in the USA.* New York: Continuum, 2002.

Szpilman, Wladyslaw. *The Pianist.* Trans. Anthea Bell. New York: Picador, 1999.

Toles, George. "This May Hurt a Little: The Art of Humiliation in Film." *Film Quarterly* 48.4 (Summer 1995): 2–14.

Topor, Roland. *The Tenant.* Trans. Francis K. Price. New York: Doubleday, 1966.

Truffaut, François. "A Certain Tendency of the French Cinema." In *Movies and Methods.* Vol. 1. Ed. Bill Nichols. Berkeley: University of California Press, 1976. 224–36.

———. *Correspondence, 1945–1984.* Ed. Gilles Jacob and Claude de Givray. Trans. Gilbert Adair. New York: Farrar, Straus, and Giroux, 1990.

Turan, Kenneth. *Sundance to Sarajevo: Film Festivals and the World They Made.* Berkeley: University of California Press, 2002.

Tuska, Jon. "Roman Polanski." In *Encounters with Filmmakers: Eight Career Studies.* Westport, Conn.: Greenwood Press, 1991. 239–76.

Tyler, Parker. *Underground Film: A Critical History.* New York: Grove, 1969.

Vahanian, Gabriel. *The Death of God: The Culture of Our Post-Christian Era.* New York: Braziller, 1961.

Warshow, Robert. *The Immediate Experience.* New York: Doubleday, 1962.

Watt, Ian. *The Rise of the Novel.* Berkeley: University of California Press, 1957.

Wechsler, Lawrence. "The Brat's Tale: Roman Polanski." In *Vermeer in Bosnia.* New York: Pantheon, 2004. 83–150.

Welles, Orson, and Peter Bogdanovich. *This Is Orson Welles.* Ed. Jonathan Rosenbaum. New York: Harper Collins, 1992.

Wexman, Virginia Wright. *Roman Polanski.* Boston: Twayne, 1985.

Williams, Linda. "Film Madness: The Uncanny Return of the Repressed in Polanski's *The Tenant.*" *Cinema Journal* 20.2 (Spring 1981): 63–73.

Wills, Gary. *Witches and Jesuits: Shakespeare's* Macbeth. New York: Oxford University Press, 1995.

Worringer, Wilhelm. *Abstraction and Empathy: A Contribution to the Psychology of Style.* Trans. Michael Bullock. London: Routledge and Kegan Paul, 1953.

Index

JAMES MORRISON is an associate professor of film and literature at Claremont McKenna College. He is the author of *Passport to Hollywood: Hollywood Films, European Directors*, among other books, and coauthor (with Thomas Schur) of *The Films of Terrence Malick*.

Books in the series Contemporary Film Directors

The University of Illinois Press
is a founding member of the
Association of American University Presses.

Composed in 10/13 New Caledonia
with Helvetica Neue Extended display
by Jim Proefrock
at the University of Illinois Press
Designed by Paula Newcomb
Manufactured by Thomson-Shore, Inc.

University of Illinois Press
1325 South Oak Street
Champaign, IL 61820-6903
www.press.uillinois.edu